WORDSWORTH AND COLERIDGE

Lyrical Ballads

WORDSWORTH AND COLERIDGE

Lyrical Ballads

Critical Perspectives

PATRICK CAMPBELL

palgrave
macmillan

Published by
PALGRAVE MACMILLAN
Houndmills, Basingstoke, Hampshire RG21 6XS and
175 Fifth Avenue, New York, N. Y. 10010
Companies and representatives throughout the world

PALGRAVE MACMILLAN is the global academic imprint of the Palgrave
Macmillan division of St. Martin's Press, LLC and of Palgrave Macmillan Ltd.
Macmillan® is a registered trademark in the United States, United Kingdom
and other countries. Palgrave is a registered trademark in the European
Union and other countries.

ISBN-13: 978– 0–333–52258–5 hardback
ISBN-10: 0–333–52258–3   hardback
ISBN-13: 978–0–333–52259–2 paperback
ISBN-10: 0–333–52259–1   paperback

This book is printed on paper suitable for recycling and
made from fully managed and sustained forest sources.

A catalogue record for this book is available from the British Library.

Printed and bound in Great Britain by
Antony Rowe Ltd, Chippenham and Eastbourne

To My Mother and Father

Contents

List of Abbreviations

B&J   *Wordsworth and Coleridge, 'Lyrical Ballads'*, ed. R. L. Brett and A. R. Jones (London: Routledge and Kegan Paul, 1963, reissued as a University Paperback 1968). This edition uses the text of the 1798 edition and includes the 1800 poems and Preface. Line references to the 1798 poems and page references to the 1800 Preface relate to this edition.

BL   S. T. Coleridge, *Biographia Literaria* (1817), ed. J. Shawcross, 2 vols (Oxford: Clarendon Press, 1907).

CC   Alun R. Jones and William Tydeman (eds), *Coleridge: 'The Ancient Mariner' and Other Poems, a Casebook* (London: Macmillan, 1973).

CCH   J. R. de J. Jackson (ed.), *Coleridge: The Critical Heritage* (London: Routledge and Kegan Paul, 1970).

CL   *Collected Letters of Samuel Taylor Coleridge*, ed. E. L. Griggs, 6 vols (Oxford: Clarendon Press, 1966–71).

EL   *Letters of William and Dorothy Wordsworth. The Early Years, 1787–1805*, ed. E. de Selincourt, 2nd edn, rev. Chester L. Shaver (Oxford: Clarendon Press, 1967).

FN   Notes dictated to Isabella Fenwick by William Wordsworth in 1843 and published in *PW*.

LL   *Letters of William and Dorothy Wordsworth. The Later Years, 1821–1853*, ed. E. de Selincourt, 3 vols (Oxford: Clarendon Press, 1939).

PrW   *The Prose Works of William Wordsworth*, ed. W. J. B. Owen and Jane Worthington Smyser, 3 vols (Oxford: Clarendon Press, 1974).

PW   *The Poetical Works of William Wordsworth*, ed. E. de Selincourt and Helen Darbishire, 2nd edn (Oxford: Clarendon Press, 1952–9).

WC   Alun R. Jones and William Tydeman (eds), *Wordsworth: 'Lyrical Ballads', a Casebook* (London: Macmillan, 1972).

Introduction

Northrop Frye, arguably the most distinguished of contemporary critics, recently announced his sense of exhilaration at the number of approaches now used in the study of literary documents and undreamt of a century ago. While these critical initiatives have sometimes bypassed the genre of poetry, *Lyrical Ballads* has hardly suffered from neglect. Indeed, the chorus of critics is still far from unanimous about the volume's merit and meaning – continuing testimony to its perennially elusive appeal.

There is nothing novel about such responses. *Lyrical Ballads* was widely discussed upon its publication in 1798, and the appearance of the Preface two years later merely fanned the flames of controversy. That these initial reactions *were* mixed should surprise no one. For a start, the reviewers were unaware that there were two authors with different objectives. And Wordsworth was at pains to stress that he was reconnoitring new terrain: the Advertisement talks of 'experiments' and the reader's inevitable 'strangeness and aukwardness' when confronting the unfamiliar. For his part Coleridge would later recall their wish to 'give the charm of novelty to things of every day' (*BL*, ch. 14). Yet the degree of real innovation, indeed the very meaning of that word 'experiments', has been debated ever since. Though there are few dissenters to the view that *Lyrical Ballads* occupies a pivotal place in English literary history, many critics now set it apart from other verse outpourings of the day more on grounds of formal excellence or intensity than on the basis of its innovative content – or even its language.

Such a sober assessment is countered by commentators who see in the volume and its prose glosses a reflection of cultural and

political crisis, an energised reaction to moribund and hackneyed traditions. For these analysts, novelty resides everywhere
in the enterprise: in the poets' stated aims, in the versification,
diction, genres and themes of the poems themselves, even in the
attention-seeking title. Twentieth-century parallels would have
to be sought in Yeats's revolutionary desire to embrace the
'enterprise' of 'walking naked' in *Responsibilities*, or Eliot's
conscious rejection of Georgian diction and values in *Prufrock –
1917*.

At all events the volume's roller-coaster ride through literary
history is testimony to the caprice of critical fashion. Oddly,
while the growing chorus of approval for *Lyrical Ballads* provided ammunition for the argument that both poets had shot
their creative bolts by 1810, the individual ballads often failed to
register with the poetry-reading public. In Palgrave's *Golden
Treasury*, a cultural barometer of Victorian taste, only two of
forty-one poems by Wordsworth were from the 1798 edition. Nor
have authorial judgements always stood the test of time. 'Goody
Blake and Harry Gill' was a Wordsworth pet poem; he would
have been insulted by its appearance in a modern anthology of
'Sick Verse' (1963). On the other hand, 'The Ancient Mariner'
almost failed to make the second edition because of Wordsworthian doubts.

What characterises the recent critical debate is its scholarly
and scrupulous character. The poems and their prose super-
structure may be 'problematic' or 'paradoxical', but that is all
the more reason for close and attentive analysis. And, if both the
volume as a whole and its constituent parts reveal inconsistency
and diversity as well as unity, then it is incumbent upon the
critic to attend to this textual complexity.

Regrettably, such an *embarras de richesse* has meant some
curtailment of scope. It soon became clear to me that, in a study
of this length, meaningful comparison with the second edition of
1800 was an impossible pipe-dream, as was exhaustive coverage
of the criticism of every single ballad. And how much space
could be devoted to Coleridge? After all, his contribution – a
mere four poems out of twenty-three – was statistically slight. At
the same time it was impossible to ignore the status of 'The
Ancient Mariner', a celebrated poem that critics usually cosset
in splendid isolation, conveniently forgetting not only its lead-off
role in the collection but also any links it may have with the

ballads that follow. Wordsworth's 'Tintern Abbey' occupies a place in the pantheon almost as monolithic. So I felt justified in devoting separate sections to both poems, despite the inevitable dangers of overlap with the sections on critical methodologies. The same 'star treatment' was accorded to 'The Idiot Boy' and 'The Thorn', owing to the recent critical preoccupation with these ballads.

Most of the critical categories discussed chose themselves. The inclusion of opinion from magazines of the day – still frequently misrepresented – reflects a desire both to begin at the beginning, to highlight the shift in critical perspective over two centuries, and to uncover those quasi-Augustan pronouncements about poetry that provoked Wordsworth's rejoinder in the Preface. The survey of Victorian commentary provides a continuing history of taste and a lead-in to recent criticism – the staple of this book. In examining the background to *Lyrical Ballads* – biographical, political, philosophical and literary – I have focused on the key issues rather than attempt a comprehensive survey of context. Other books admirably fulfil this need.

One of the distinctive features of *Lyrical Ballads* is its surrounding penumbra of explanatory and justificatory comment. That these authorial statements have a role in the debate is undeniable, even if critics have tended to approach the Preface (like 'The Ancient Mariner') as an autonomous text. Part of that 'first great step in clarifying the role of criticism that could unify the mental elements in the creative process' (Frye, 1986, p. 32), these *ex cathedra* explanations also merit inclusion because of the discussion they continue to generate.

Equally one could hardly ignore the claims of formalist, psychoanalytical or political analysts. While the very presence of authorial intention has proved a disincentive to 'New Critical' purists seeking to exclude extra-textual matters, much mid-twentieth-century commentary does reflect such formalist concerns as coherence, ironic modes, narrative procedures and genre. And, while psychoanalytic approaches, whether Freudian or Jungian, now seem almost venerable, 'The Ancient Mariner' has consistently fallen victim to psychological-symbol hunters, both because Coleridge the man is a far more rewarding subject than Wordsworth the man and because the poem, uniquely symbolic or revealingly personal, has attracted critics in droves. They have been also drawn – if less lemming-like – to the victimised women of Wordsworth's ballads – apparent spectres of a conscience unable to repress a sense of personal guilt.

The perennial difficulty of categorising critics – and literature usually resists pigeonholing, though we like to think that such classifications aid understanding – is most apparent in the section on left-wing criticism. While traditional Marxists have foregrounded the socio-political background to the enterprise, a newer school of 'theorists' has addressed the 'problematic' nature of individual poems, their subversion and erasure of meanings which the writer apparently does not want to stress. 'Tintern Abbey' has proved particularly susceptible to such revisionist readings, as do those of other maverick critics who defy easy classification. But, though the tentacles of post-structuralism have fastened onto *Lyrical Ballads*, feminist criticism has barely touched it. There are women writers aplenty on Wordsworth and Coleridge – Mary Jacobus and Heather Glen have recently written major studies of the volume, for example – but there is no full-scale feminist critique of *Lyrical Ballads*. There is little, for example, on the portraiture of female victims of a patriarchal society, on the vampiric woman of 'The Ancient Mariner' or on the crucial role of Dorothy. Jan Montefiore (1987, pp. 10–11) objects to the exclusivity of 'a man speaking to men' but praises the emphasis on personal and transcendent experience, an emphasis which 'theorists' – who regard transcendence as a hegemonic con-trick – find particularly irksome. It is a pity that she has not written on *Lyrical Ballads*.

I should add that, in selecting critics for inclusion, I have not always been seduced by excellence – though I hope that it has usually been a significant criterion. The most distinctive, even the most influential, speakers in this debate are not always the most perceptive or thorough: just as the ballads drew attention to themselves by their very iconoclasm, so too do these maverick critics – witness some of the wilder psychological readings of 'The Ancient Mariner' or the materialist hermeneutics applied to 'Tintern Abbey'. Again, illuminating comments on individual poems are often embedded in larger works or general studies and need, perforce, to be prised out. However, the search for specificity has not prevented me from including provocative observations not geared directly to *Lyrical Ballads* but by their very acuity worth any risk involved in drawing a connection.

In airing my own views, I have tried to plug some of the gaps left by the survey's inevitable partiality. To this end I have adopted the stance of self-styled pluralist critic in my examination of the less-vaunted poems from the 1798 edition. In the process, and taking my cue from 'problematists', I have sought to show that their apparent simplicity and wholeness is often deceptive, that even the less rewarding 'experiments' pose disconcerting questions or reveal unsuspected inner tensions. Yet as part of a grand design they also reveal affinities that go beyond the idea of formal companion pieces or even the statements of Advertisement and Preface. To explore this notion of unity in diversity, I have concluded the study by considering 'The Ancient Mariner' in its context of opening poem and have sought to show how this least compatible of bedfellows in fact prefigures the rest of the volume in significant ways.

1

Lyrical Ballads:
The Current of Opinion

Contemporaneous criticism: the magazines

'Up to 1820 the name of Wordsworth was trampled under foot', thundered De Quincey. While that is the over-emotional reaction of a friend, it is none the less true that *Lyrical Ballads*, aimed at the solar plexus of reader complacency, initially attracted some erratic counters. Cottle feared that such blows would destroy the entire enterprise: 'the severity of most of the reviews' was 'so great that its progress to oblivion, notwithstanding the merits which I was quite sure they possessed, seemed ordained to be as rapid as it was certain' (quoted in Smith, 1932, p. 29). These reactions say more about the prevailing state of periodical journalism and literary taste than about the actual poetry, but that in no way diminishes their significance both as cultural indicators and as first shots across the bows of an unfamiliar intruder. Nor should we forget that Wordsworth, in common with the other poets of the Romantic period, was 'more strongly affected by this periodical criticism than have been any other important group of writers in the English-speaking world at any time'. The reminder comes from the Foreword to Donald Reiman's *The Romantics Reviewed*, a definitive nine-volume compilation containing facsimiles of all known contemporaneous reviews (1972, I, p. xxvii).

Reiman's collection is unlikely to be found outside major libraries. Less exhaustive but still illuminating are the following collections, which may prove easier to track down: M. P. Hodgart, and R. T. H. Redpath's *Romantic Perspectives* (1964);

Graham McMaster's *William Wordsworth* (1972), which ranges
over nearly two centuries of criticism; J. L. Hayden's *Romantic
Bards and British Reviewers* (1978), which oddly includes only
two early critiques; and J. de Jackson's volume on reactions to
Coleridge's poetry in the Critical Heritage series (1970: *CCH*).

To read the early criticism is to realise that the basic facts
about the reception of *Lyrical Ballads* are frequently over-
simplified or even misrepresented. Within a year or so of
publication, the 1798 edition cropped up in no fewer than *nine*
reviews, all in different periodicals. While the great age of the
literary periodical was yet to come – it coincided with the rise of
the *Edinburgh* (1802) and the *Quarterly* (1809) – there were
already in 1798 at least sixty different journals catering to the
needs of a rapidly expanding reading public. Hodgart and
Redpath (1964) quote the bookseller Lackington's estimate that
in 1803 'four times as many books were being sold then as had
been twenty years before'. Such a 'spate of literary products' was
what the age demanded; it was 'part and parcel of the rapidly
expanding economy following on the industrial and agricultural
revolutions' (p. 18).

Opinions were what these *arriviste* readers wanted and what
they got. Poems were good, bad or a bit of both; every reviewer
saw his role as a critic in the Greek sense of the term, as a judge
rather than as an enlightened interpreter. Assertions, often
politically grounded, rarely sought corroboration in the text;
some poems were not even identified in reviews. The approach
was unashamedly belle-lettrist and subjective: irony and
humour were the heavy-handed weapons; painterly and literary
analogies provided a gauge of artistic worth and a reminder of
the reviver's erudition. Not that the views on poetry were
straightforwardly Augustan anyway. Though recent analysts
have often made this assumption, it was the work of minor, now
forgotten poetasters such as Erasmus Darwin that was currently
attracting most readers. His name features more than once in
reviews of *Lyrical Ballads*.

One of the earliest responses, perhaps the first, was Southey's
article in the *Critical Review* of October 1798. Friend and fellow
poet, Southey was none the less writing for a Tory journal. Such
divided loyalties probably explain both his acknowledgement of
an exceptional talent and his objections to banality of subject
matter. Using a fashionable analogy from fine art, he censures

'The Idiot Boy' for failing to emulate the exalted subject matter of Raphael, and finds in Flemish painting an equivalence for 'the worthlessness of its design and the excellence of its execution'. But at least its stylistic virtues raise it above 'the other ballads of this kind', which Southey finds equally 'bald in story, and . . . not so highly embellished in narration'. 'The Ancient Mariner' is dismissed as lacking in unity and, in a possible conflation of the ballads of Bürger, Flemish art and the legend of the Flying Dutchman, branded as 'a Dutch attempt at German sublimity'. He concludes by way of reference to the Advertisement that 'the experiment has failed, not because the language of conversation is little adapted to "the purposes of poetic pleasure", but because it has been tried upon uninteresting subjects' (Reiman, 1972, I, 308–10).

Faced with a series of 'experiments', Southey responded as most critics would have done – equivocally. That he was a friend but also pandering to a conservative readership doubtless created additional tensions. Yet this 'mixed' critique in fact became the model for subsequent reviewers, as did Southey's praise of 'The Idiot Boy' and his ill-judged dismissal of 'The Ancient Mariner'. Two months later, the anonymous critic of the short-lived *Analytical Review* predictably echoed Southey's remarks in complaining of an 'extravagance' that was reminiscent of a 'mad German Poet' and a regretted absence of 'the simplicity of our ancient ballad writers' (Reiman, 1972, I, 8). Meanwhile the *Monthly Mirror*, 'more a journal of "wit" than of "fashion"' (Reiman, 1972, II, 685), had published an unmemorable notice which, while preoccupied with applause for Darwin, did remark 'sentiments of feeling and sensibility, expressed without affectation, and in the language of nature'. The review went on to inveigh against the 'depraved taste for sonnets' (a current vogue *not* reflected in *Lyrical Ballads*) and to quote 'Lines Left . . . in a Yew-tree', a meditation presumably more to the reviewer's taste.

One expects more of the *Monthly Magazine*, if only because it was the staunchly liberal journal in which the poets originally intended their efforts to appear – to help defray the costs of a projected walking-tour. But in truth the review (January 1799) fails to rise above hack journalism; its comment that 'some of his pieces are stiff, but others are stiff and laboured' better fits the reviewer's own efforts. Treated alongside Mr Cottle's *Malvern*

Hills (who remembers that now?), the volume attracts a small notice at the end of a long review in which 'The Ancient Mariner' is again singled out for opprobrium.

1799 spawned four other periodical reviews. The *New Annual Register* simply summarises current opinion without even bothering to name poems ('with others we have been less satisfied'). The January issue of the short-lived *New London Review* toes the Southey line that 'our poet seems to want nothing but more fortunate topics', attacks the 'inartificial and anti-poetical manner' of 'Goody Blake and Harry Gill', predictably applauds the poeticisms of 'The Female Vagrant' (an early and more modish contribution) and censures – guess what? – the inconsistencies of 'The Ancient Mariner'. In a clinching theatrical flourish of the kind beloved by these reviewers, the note of moral censure is repeated: 'If ever he disgusts by the meagreness and poverty of his composition, it is precisely where, aiming at simplicity, he copies the rudest effusions of our vulgar ballads' (Reiman, 1972, II, 793).

The intensity of the reviewers' reaction to such inappropriate subject matter is entirely predictable. As D. W. Harding has remarked about mainstream late-eighteenth-century writing,

> the relevance of the lower classes, except perhaps as objects of compassion, had been denied or ignored; they were regarded negatively, as lacking cultivation, and any positive values that their way of life might express were disregarded in a period when the cultivated were preoccupied with order and elegance.   (1976, p. 44)

The note of an uncompromising puritanism is also sounded by Dr Burney in the June 1799 issue of the *Monthly Review*. But he at least initiates a systematic survey of individual poems that reveals, in Redpath's view, 'intelligent and sensitive contact' (1964, p. 53) and, in Reiman's, a willingness to miss 'the point of almost every poem' (1972, II, 713). So much for the consistency of *modern* critics! Burney's artistic predilections for 'lofty subjects' and 'polished measures' are forthrightly expressed: can 'doggrel' verses, he inquires, equal 'the sublime numbers of a Milton?' (p. 713). But his blow-by-blow analysis of ballads that he deigns to call poetry at least offers nuggets of information, gestures in the direction of interpretation. That he quotes *three* of the least experimental poems is predictable; that he quotes then *in full* suggests that he is doing the authors a conscious service in providing a wider audience for their efforts. And his sniping comments on these all-too-gloomy 'rustic delineations of low life' reveal the workings of a lively and opinionated mind that at least feels for the victims if not for the poet. Why, he demands, did the author suffer 'this poor peasant to part with the last of the flock'? And why is 'Old Man Travelling' an indictment of a war we can no more avoid (the Napoleonic campaign) than Hercules the shirt of Nessus? In commenting that the son in hospital 'might have died by disease', Burney clearly sets his stall against the anti-war sentiments of the poem's conclusion (p. 716).

The October number of the *British Critic* produced a strikingly new critical emphasis. Assuming, like his earlier brethren, that the poems 'seem to proceed from the same mind' (Reiman, 1972, I, 128), the reviewer hinted, inaccurately, at Coleridge's sole authorship. Significantly though, he (Francis Wrangham?) praised that very simplicity that Southey and company had found so irksome, attacked Erasmus Darwin ('meretricious frippery of the *Darwinian* taste') and very properly included the Advertisement's authorial justification of the enterprise. His proposal that 'The Ancient Mariner's antiquated words ... might with advantage be entirely removed without any detriment to the effect of the poem' (p. 128), conceivably prompted Wordsworth, already having grave misgivings about his friend's ballad, to edit out some archaisms and orthographical devices in the second edition.

This modest *volte-face* in taste, albeit still couched in the rounded periods of Augustan prose, deserves an extended quotation:

We fully agree with the author, that the true notion of poetry must be sought among the poets, rather than the critics; and we will add, that, unless a critic is a poet also, he will generally make but indifferent work in judging of the effusions of Genius. In the collection of poems subjoined to this introduction, we do not often find expressions that we esteem too familiar, or deficient in dignity; on the contrary, we think that in general the author has succeeded in attaining that judicious degree of simplicity, which accommodates itself with ease even to the sublime. It is not pomp of words, but by energy of

thought, that sublimity is most successfully achieved; and we
infinitely prefer the simplicity even of the most unadorned
tale in this volume, to all the meretricious frippery of the
Darwinian taste.

Such a revisionary assessment failed to stem Jeffrey's vitupera-
tive onslaught in the *Edinburgh Review* (October 1802), the
opening fusillade in a sustained attack upon the 'Lake Poets'. In
a foreseeable political outburst against levelling poetry, and its
'perverted taste for simplicity', Jeffrey pokes fun at a poet who
'commemorates with so much effect, the chattering of Harry
Gill's teeth, tells the tale of the one-eyed huntsman . . . and
beautifully warns his studious friend of the risk he ran of
"growing double" '. His pragmatic aesthetic is that poetry
should exalt the mind: 'its standards . . . in common with
religion . . . were fixed long ago' and cannot be called in
question; he is appalled that 'for all sorts of vice in the lower
orders of society' the poets have 'the same virtuous horror and
the same tender compassion' (Reiman, 1972, I, 418). One is
tempted to ask, 'What vice?' – the shooting of a bird, the
gleaning of dead sticks from a neighbour's hedge? It is patently
not the *vices* that Jeffrey objects to, but the sympathetic stress on
poverty and suffering, the belief that the 'ordinary' (twice used
disparagingly) can generate intense emotions in poetry.

I have mentioned this critical thunderbolt for what are, I
hope, interesting reasons. True, it is not *exactly* contemporaneous: it came too late to influence either edition of the poems.
But its confident scorn, though working against the softening of
attitude towards *Lyrical Ballads* now becoming evident in the
monthlies, seems to have erroneously persuaded modern commentators that Jeffrey's was *the* prevailing response. Better
written certainly, it was hardly typical. Not that I subscribe to
McMaster's assertion that Wordsworth's audience – one 'fed by
the eighteenth century; one to which neither Wordsworth's
sentiment nor his humour was unacceptable' (1972, p. 24) –
took easily to his material. The evidence of these reviews is
inconclusive. What *is* true is that, whether dissenting or estab-
lishment, Whig or Tory, these critics and their readers were still
fixated in a neoclassical tradition which applauded reason and
common sense. Poetry, a more rarefied commodity than prose,
should exalt *and* instruct. Badly written poetry would not only

fail to communicate; it might corrupt the dialect of the tribe. Since literature was, like all the arts, in essence, mimetic, it had to remain within the boundaries of the probable. Hence audience confusion in the face of a wildly disparate collection of poems asking to be considered as 'experiments'. One of the reasons why 'The Idiot Boy' was so often singled out for mention was that its *subject* fell outside the acceptable parameters for poetry. It has become a modern critical cliché that this poem was, after 'Goody Blake' 'the most highly esteemed' (McMaster, 1972, p. 24), but in truth the reviewers were happiest on familiar terrain where poetic diction ruled – conversation pieces such as Coleridge's 'The Nightingale', the short, meditative poems, and above all 'Tintern Abbey'.

That the reviewers barely mentioned these poems was sure proof of their acceptability. 'Tintern Abbey' provoked not a single adverse word. But the positive benefits of the reviews, in acquainting a much wider and more varied audience with *Lyrical Ballads*, are obvious. In this guise, the poems infiltrated many more households than did whole volumes of verse. These reviews quote six poems *in full* and there are substantial 'extracts' from 'The Idiot Boy', 'The Ancient Mariner' (twice), 'The Female Vagrant' and 'Tintern Abbey'. After such exposure, the stage was set for a more informed and less partisan treatment. James Montgomery's retrospective look at *Lyrical Ballads* in the *Eclectic Review* of January 1808 provided just that: a sensitive revaluation of the volume's fidelity to the Preface and its theories. Again stressing the merits of 'Tintern Abbey', the reviewer pointed out that 'for such tales as "The Last of the Flock" ... "the real language of men" may be employed with pleasing effect', but when the poet wants to 'present *ordinary* things in an unusual way', by casting over them "a certain colouring of imagination", he resorts to 'splended, figurative and amplifying language' (Reiman, 1972, I, 335). Such an assessment of the volume has proved remarkably enduring.

Victorian and later criticism: some trends

The debate about *Lyrical Ballads*, which generated both the lively and diverse critiques of the magazines and the Preface of 1800, spluttered intermittently during the ensuing decades.

McMaster comments acutely that for many Victorians, incl
ing J. S. Mill, Wordsworth became 'essentially normative,
longer the wild eccentric' of some of the initial reviews, and
'anodyne . . . a form of spiritual convalescence for the inhum
ity of Victorian materialism' (1972, p. 170). That the volu
was coming to be seen as central evidence in the case of yoı
Wordsworth the poet therapist, was already evident in
nostalgic tone of the *Critical Review* of August 1807, which, wl
recalling the delights of 'Tintern Abbey' and 'a few more pieι
from the first edition, declared that the poet *'has had* the poʻ
to draw "iron tears" from our stony hearts' (emphasis adde
Hazlitt's percipient essay, no doubt mindful of Wordswori
own statements, marked another turning-point, though sou
ing one note that only now has become recurrent: namely,
volume's 'unaccountable mixture of seeming simplicity and ı
abstruseness':

> It is one of the innovations of the time. It partakes of, anι
> carried along with, the revolutionary movements of our a
> the political changes of the day were the model on which
> formed and conducted his poetical experiments. His Muse
> cannot be denied, and without this we cannot explain
> character at all) is a levelling one. It proceeds on a principlι
> equality, and strives to reduce all things to the same standa
> It is distinguished by a proud humility. It relies upon its c
> resources, and disdains external show and relief. It takes
> commonest events and objects, as a test to prove that natur
> always interesting from its inherent truth and beauty, with
> any of the ornaments of dress or pomp of circumstances to
> it off. Hence the unaccountable mixture of seeming simpliι
> and real abstruseness in the *Lyrical Ballads*. Fools h
> laughed at, wise men scarcely understand, them. He takε
> subject or a story merely as pegs or loops to hang thought ɛ
> feeling on; the incidents are trifling, in proportion to
> contempt for imposing appearances; the reflections are ρ
> found, according to the gravity and aspiring pretensions of
> mind.   (1825, p. 132)

In the very year of publication, Lamb had found the bless
of the water-snakes deeply cathartic ('stung me into high pl
sure through suffering' (letter to Southey, 8 November 17ς

but twenty years passed before two reviews offered a powerful
vindication of 'The Ancient Mariner'. In 1818 the *Monthly
Magazine* (no. 46) pronounced it 'the finest superstitious ballad
in literature', passing on, in the process, the familiar charge of
incoherence ('only fit for the inmates of Bedlam') to 'Christabel'
(*CCH*, p. 435). More dramatically, in October 1819 Lockhart of
Blackwood's Edinburgh Magazine, both indulging 'the fallacy of
expressive form' and conveying his own sense of kinship with the
poet through a critical language of unalloyed transcendence,
declared it 'the wildest of all the creations of genius . . . the very
music of its words is like the melancholy mysterious breath of
something sung to the sleeping ear'. Lockhart admitted to
'incoherence', but it was that 'of some mighty vision', lovely and
terrible by turns (*CCH*, p. 439). And not only did the critic
glimpse a mystery; he also offered an extended reading of the
poem's message: 'Pain, sorrow, remorse, these are not enough;
the wound must be healed by a heart-felt sacrifice to the same
spirit of universal love which had been bruised in its infliction'
(p. 443). He concludes,

> One feels that to him another world – we do not mean a
> supernatural, but a more exquisitely and deeply natural world
> – has been revealed, and that the repose of his spirit can only
> be in the contemplation of things that are not to pass away.
> The sad and solemn indifference of his mood is communicated
> to his hearer, and we feel that even after reading what he had
> heard, it were better to 'turn from the bridegroom's door'.
>
> (*CCH*, p. 445)

Such views have become commonplaces of modern criticism and
have anticipated at last three independent approaches to interpretation: the poem as moral fable ('sacrifice to universal Love'),
as enigma ('the prince of superstitious poets') and as melody and
music ('master of the language of poetry') (*CCH*, p. 436ff.).
Leigh Hunt in the *Examiner* (21 October 1821) lent his voice to
the moral seekers by abstracting from the poem a lesson for
'those who see nothing in the world but their own unfeeling
common-places, and are afterwards visited with a dreary sense
of their insufficiency' (*CCH*, p. 479). Such a debate was inevitably fuelled by the poet's own response to the celebrated
strictures of Mrs Barbauld, a fellow poet who felt that the ballad

'was improbable, and had no moral' (*Table Talk*, 31 May 1830, quoted in *CC*, p. 30). In replying that 'the obtrusion of the moral sentiment so openly on the reader' constituted its chief fault, Coleridge provided ammunition for recent critics who have arraigned a conclusion reeking of apostasy, a superfluous sop to conventional Christianity. Predictably no such opinions surfaced in Victorian England. Nelson Coleridge's *Quarterly Review* critique (August 1834) confirmed the poem's rehabilitation, making for it a claim, now a cliché, that it is 'one of the most perfect pieces of imaginative poetry . . . in the literature of all Europe', its only flaw 'the miraculous destruction of the vessel', which brings the 'preternatural into too close contact with the actual framework of the poem' (*CC*, p. 83).

Thus by the year of Victoria's accession, a period usually associated with the ebb-tide of English Romanticism, *Lyrical Ballads* had, both as a whole and in parts, achieved the kind of critical status scarcely anticipated by its creators. None the less *criticism* of the volume had a long way to go. It was still overwhelmingly evaluative or didactic, often couched in the expressive terms that many critics today find distractingly evasive, and it was still offering little in the way of close textual analysis. Nor, too close to events, did such early criticism regard *Lyrical Ballads* as a central document in the Romantic movement. Disturbingly different, yes; even unique; but hardly 'embodying in symbolic form the whole mythological structure of romanticism in individual and general terms' (*CC*, p. 16). Indeed, Wordsworth's contributions failed to cut much ice with the doyen of Victorian anthologists, F. T. Palgrave. *Two* ballads out of forty-one poems by Wordsworth in *The Golden Treasury* is a pretty poor return.

But certain *données* had been offered up. Though later nineteenth-century criticism is generally undistinguished, it at least asserts either the publication's overall significance or the value of some individual components. Swinburne followed Lockhart in seeing 'The Ancient Mariner' as possessing 'more of breadth and space, more of material force and motion, than anything else of the poet's' (*CC*, p. 89). But the poem was becoming increasingly detached from its original context; not only Swinburne, but also Victorian belle-lettrists such as Pater and Watson, evaluated it against *Coleridge's* other masterpieces 'Christabel' and 'Kubla Khan'.

On the other hand, Wordsworth's ballads were increasingly seen both as part of a grand design and as a product of that creative decade when almost all his best work was produced. The nineteenth century was in fact responsible for polarising opinion about Wordsworth, a polarisation which Abrams believed was initiated by the poet himself in two very different theoretical statements: the Preface of 1800, from which he emerges as the simple affirmative poet of primal feelings, essential humanity and vital joy; and the 'Essay Supplementary to the Preface' of 1815, which confronts the reader with a complex poet of paradox, ambiguity and transcendence. These alternative routes to the poetry were followed respectively by Matthew Arnold (1879) and A. C. Bradley (1909). Taking his cue from the 1800 Preface and thereby hinting at his own dissatisfaction both with the ratiocinative poetry of Victorian England and Wordsworth's later output, Arnold bore testimony to the poetry's expression of a 'joy offered to us in nature, the joy offered to us in the simple, primary affections and duties' (*WC*, p. 71). In 'this iron time', Wordsworth reawakened our capacity to feel, to loose 'our heart in tears' and to respond to 'the freshness of the early world' ('Memorial Verses' [1850], ll. 43–57).

Such a view was infectious. As Humphry House (1955) remarks in 'Wordsworth's Fame', even Keble's hymns sometimes 'point towards that [Wordsworthian] view of Nature as providing an automatic sort of psychotherapy' (p. 39) that finds expression elsewhere in Tennyson's 'The Two Voices'. More interesting still, House also observes that Wordsworth's use of 'human beings as *ethical symbols* had a particular appeal in the age dominated by the conflict between philanthropy and doctrinaire utilitarianism' (p. 42, emphasis added). Though his quoted example is the Leech Gatherer, one finds of course equally compelling paradigms of human fortitude in the aged and destitute figures of *Lyrical Ballads*.

Thirty years after Arnold, Bradley set out explicitly to supplement what he regarded as Arnold's valid but all-too-partial view. He offered a reading which has ultimately proved more enduring and which has permeated interpretations not only of the 'sublime' poetry but of the 'simple' ballads as well. Arguing that 'the road into Wordsworth's mind must be through his strangeness and his paradoxes, and not round them', Bradley saw him as quintessentially the poet of solitude and sublimity rather than the Arnoldian sympathiser with 'small and humble things' (1909, 1965 edn, p. 101). Valorising the Wordsworth of yew-trees rather than the Wordsworth of daffodils, he looked to a poet of vatic utterance that made him above all a mystic and visionary; 'He apprehended all things, natural or human, as the expression of something which, while manifested in them, immeasurably transcends them.' This transcendental reading of the poetry, coupled, it must be said, with a growing distaste for that dark 1798 world where suffering and misery are inevitable concomitants, and a changing taste for 'wild' landscape that accorded better with the 'Lake' poetry, led to a waning of critical enthusiasm for *Lyrical Ballads* and a resurgence of interest in the 'sublime' Wordsworth. One manifestation of this process is the failure of both the 1900 and 1972 editions of *The Oxford Book of English Verse* to include even one Wordsworth poem from *Lyrical Ballads*. Such a polarisation is also reflected in mid-twentieth-century appreciations that have privileged either Arnold's or Bradley's road to the poet, diverse approaches that have 'yielded two Wordsworths':

> One Wordsworth is simple, elemental, forthright, the other is complex, paradoxical, problematic, one is an affirmative poet of life, love and joy, the other is an equivocal or self-divided poet whose affirmations are implicitly qualified (if not annulled) by a pervasive sense of mortality and an ever-incipient despair of life; one is the great poet of natural man ... the other is a visionary or mystic who is ultimately hostile to temporal man and the world of sense ....
>
> (Abrams, 1972, p. 4; 1984, p. 149)

While Abrams' entire summary is worth reading, we should bear in mind other side-effects. Bradley's notion of the philosopher poet, for example, has stimulated a whole sequence of learned disquisitions on philosophical indebtedness. What it does not explain is the movement away from preponderantly judicial 'belle-lettrist' criticism towards the kind of carefully researched and documented scholarship that characterises recent responses to *Lyrical Ballads*. That trend reflects something much wider: the enhanced status of literature as a subject for serious research in our institutions of higher education.

To return to Abrams' point, it is easy to spot the 'two voices', even within the pages of this slender study. In general, those critics who have accorded high praise to the volume in terms of its originality and simplicity have taken the Arnoldian prescription. Thus Helen Darbishire talks of Wordsworth's capacity to portray 'simple men and women who are moved by the great emotions' and sees *Lyrical Ballads* as the product of a personal rite of passage, 'a sort of arctic expedition, into a region where life was reduced to its elements . . . his aim to penetrate the heart of man and the inner life of nature' (1950, p. 61). Not surprisingly, her vote goes to the elemental ballads. Bateson, homing in on this 'Wordsworth problem *par excellence*' (1956, p. 3) none the less regards the 'two voices', like Hazlitt, as potentially complementary – the pathos and social realism of the ballad combined with the subjective and sublime element can produce great poetry. Unfortunately this potential for cross-fertilisation does not fecundate *Lyrical Ballads*.

Such Arnoldian perspectives which emphasis the Preface's notion of 'a man speaking to men' are naturally alien to the letter of 'New Criticism' – which discounts the *intentions* of the artificer. Nevertheless, analyses of individual poems in terms of structure, tone or the deployment of ironic masks owe much to 'formalist' perspectives. If the unique symbolic potentialities of 'The Ancient Mariner' have stimulated the most celebrated essays (e.g. Warren, 1946; Burke, 1941), the 'simple' ballads have been increasingly seen, particularly in the United States, as deceptively complex structures, yielding rewarding secrets to discerning textual analysts. The blending of the 'two voices' in *Lyrical Ballads*, a sound to which Bateson was apparently deaf, is now finding an attentive audience.

Moreover, these disciples of the 'problematic' Wordsworth, while unearthing elaborate strategies in *Lyrical Ballads*, have also sensed a dialectic between consciousness and non-consciousness: ambiguities in the surface meaning that might afford clues to deep and unspoken preoccupations of the poet. Such a struggle on the part of the poet's consciousness (imagination) to escape the shackles of 'not itself' (nature) was, on Abrams' view, 'a revived form of Bradley's neo-Hegelian approach to that poet' (1984, p. 151).

De Man's 'Intentional Structure of the Romantic Image' (1960), in focusing on this conflict, has provided the probable stimulus for a number of displacement theorists (see Ch. 4,

section on 'Tintern Abbey'), though one might justifiably conclude that paradoxical or problematic readings of the ballads
derive ultimately from Bradley or even Hazlitt. In the same way,
the longstanding debate about their originality has only really
gathered momentum since Mayo's 1954 essay called in question
the ballads' right to be considered genuinely innovative and
experimental. That is another major controversy that cannot be
kept out of the pages of this book.

2
Criticism in Context, 1797–8

The social and political background

1798 was a year of violent political ferment, local as well as national. The Marxist critic E. P. Thompson reveals an England not only 'engaged in a war of national defence' but 'suppressing Irish rebellion with a ferocity which outdistances the French terror'. Wordsworth and Coleridge were all too aware of its local manifestations – the creation of a new volunteer corps to defend the Somerset coast, which meant that 'even the lanes around Stowey and Alfoxden resounded with tramping feet' (1969, p. 167). That radicals were now under suspicion may explain the dearth of explicit political comment in *Lyrical Ballads*. The pacifist sentiments of 'The Female Vagrant' (1791–2) find only a muted echo in 'Old Man Travelling' (1798) and disappear entirely from the other Alfoxden contributions. Yet Browning's later slur, that the 'lost leader' turned Tory 'just for a handful of silver', is a long way from the facts of 1798. Critics are agreed that what the friends *were* turning their backs on were Jacobinism, Godwinian necessity, narrow sectarianism of any kind. In a self-consciously phrased letter of 10 March, Coleridge confessed, 'I have snapped my squeaking baby-trumpet of Sedition and the fragments lie scattered in the lumber-room of Penitence. I wish to be a good man and a Christian, but I am no Whig, no Reformist, no Republican' (*CL,* I, 238). Where politics do enter poetry is in the strident anti-Gallic rhetoric (a 'blind' and 'adulterous' country) of 'France, an Ode' (1798).

Here Coleridge also voices his growing conviction that liberty cannot 'possibly be either gratified or realised under any form of human government' but belongs to all individuals imbued with 'the love and adoration of God in Nature' ('Argument' to poem). Written during the same period (February–April 1798) and published in a quarto pamphlet later in the year with 'Frost at Midnight' and 'Fears in Solitude', all three poems register in Nicholas Roe's words 'disturbing currents in Coleridge's political, personal, and creative life, even in this most fruitfully productive springtime' (1988, p. 263). 'Frost at Midnight', wholly personal in its frame of reference, makes no mention of political events – for example, the French attack on Switzerland. But 'Fears in Solitude' is informed by Coleridge's 'unregenerate awareness of political failure and isolation', his sense that a jingoistic government and a people 'clamorous for war and bloodshed' together add up to impending disaster for the nation.

> Throughout the poem Coleridge's awareness of a radical collapse of hope in France and Britain finds no compensating alternative that might resemble Wordsworth's great statements of belief in 'Tintern Abbey', or, indeed his own conclusion to 'France: An Ode'.   (Roe, 1988, p. 265)

These poems were written at the very time when *Lyrical Ballads* was taking shape. Yet most commentators have bypassed them when assessing the impact of political events on the Coleridge of 1798.

R. J. White (1938), for example, regards the biblical allusions in the prose as firmer evidence of Coleridge's growing revulsion from the inhuman excesses of a revolution gone wrong. Carl Woodring's *Politics in the Poetry of Coleridge* (1961) cites sixteen analysts of Coleridge's political thought (including Coleridge!) but concludes that they generally draw on his poems 'only for decoration' (p. 36). Like Keats, the creative Coleridge seems allergic to politics. Since his political poems are in Woodring's opinion palpably inferior, perhaps we should be thankful that such partisan efforts are absent from *Lyrical Ballads*. But that is not to discount them as evidence of a key Coleridgean perspective during those crucial months.

Thompson in fact sees 1798 as the year when the 'Jacobite' poets began their 'capitulation to the traditional paternalistic culture' that was to prove 'inimical to the source of their art' (1969, p. 175). But Roe takes issue with such a 'reductive paradigm' in which radical commitment is succeeded by 'withdrawal' or 'apostasy', maintaining that the radical years were integral to each poet's later creative life, and especially Wordsworth's. In seeing 'Tintern Abbey' as illustrative of this process (the poem charts two experiences separated by *five* years), Roe joins forces with a number of recent commentators (Levinson, McGann, Simpson) who have attempted to return the poem to the political moment of its composition. The poem's subtitled date, 'July 13, 1798' is thus doubly significant: the eighth anniversary of the day Wordsworth reached French shores, the ninth of the eve of Bastille Day. While it means that the poem *is* inexorably linked to Wordsworth's own 'awareness of revolutionary failure' and to Coleridge's despair, it does propose 'blessed' compensations of a less political kind (Roe, 1988, p. 272).

Not that critics have ever doubted *Wordsworth's* social or political awareness. The prophetic outburst in the Preface against the effects of a mechanistic urban life-style now breeding an unhealthy 'craving for extra-ordinary incident' (B&J, p. 249) left its mark on contemporaries such as Hazlitt who believed anyway that the political changes of the day had inspired in *Lyrical Ballads* 'levelling' poetry based on 'a principle of equality' (1825, 1954 edn, p. 132).

Yet, according to some recent commentators, there are worrying distortions in the Wordsworth picture. True, he rightly presaged a ghastly future in which the steady brutalisation of labour went hand-in-hand with exploitation by demagogues and opportunists; true, the ballads depict a world in which the poor and underprivileged are victimised. But for Simpson Wordsworth does 'play up the pastoral motif' in these poems (1979, p. 62); they depict a rural landscape that *actually* had more cattle than sheep, a world where Wordsworth's 'mellowed feudality' (*PrW*, III, 175) ignored the all-too-real presence of rapacious and enclosing landlords (who, incidentally, disappear from the verse after the 'mansion proud' and 'proferred gold' of the *much earlier* 'Female Vagrant'). Indeed 'The Last of the Flock' appears to justify acquisitiveness.

Such critical views, which anticipate the later, conservative image of the poet, find fuller expression in Kenneth Maclean's pioneering *Agrarian Age* (1950). Skirting the much reconnoitred area of the poet's reaction to the 'Satanic Mills' of an emergent industrialism, he traces the sense of loss in *Lyrical Ballads* to the socio-economic changes wrought by the *agrarian* revolution. In local terms, this meant the decline of small proprietors, the 'statesmen' of the poetry and the emergence of a Lake Country chock-a-block with tourists and fair-weather migrants, 'Rich Manchester merchants and Liverpool attorneys ... putting up big summer homes that marred the entire side of a mountain' (Maclean, 1950, p. 91). Maclean locates this deterioration in a factory system that ruined cottage industry, hastened the eclipse of the hand-loom and prompted sons to move to industrial centres in the quest for work. While the shift from water power to steam power saved a threatened landscape, ironically it made victims of its inhabitants. There is none the less, Maclean argues, an element of parochialism and even elitism in the poet's belief that these evils are solely 'industrial and bourgeois'. The improving and enclosing landed class 'were fully as responsible as the "cits" for the unfortunate condition of rural life' (p. 95), a fact which Wordsworth chooses to ignore. Maclean reminds us that the 'statesmen' of poems such as 'The Last of the Flock' were frequently not freeholders but 'copyholders' compelled to serve their landlords on 'boondays' and pay fines when lord or tenant died. Wordsworth was 'silently satisfied ... that a touch of feudalism should remain in society, that independence should not be complete and entire' (p. 101). While the Simpson–Maclean charge may be justified, we should remind ourselves that 'The Female Vagrant' offers a longer view. The pity is that the rapacious landlord of that poem is displaced in the ballads of 1798. In these the revolutionary stance is more-or-less abandoned.

Biographical considerations: collaboration or conflict?

Lyricad Ballads was, of course, the outcome of a joint undertaking. Scholars are agreed about the basic events in the burgeoning friendship: the first meeting of the two poets in September 1795; Coleridge's enthusiastic response to 'Salisbury Plain' in March/April of 1797; Coleridge's visit to Racedown in June 1797; Wordsworth's domestic move to Nether Stowey in order to be near his friend in July, and his longer stay at Alfoxden during the spring of 1798 when the bulk of the ballads were written and earlier poems vetted for possible inclusion. We know too that Wordsworth and Dorothy spent part of the summer conveniently close to Bristol, the better to see *Lyrical Ballads* through the press; that 'Tintern Abbey' was written in July following a visit to the Wye valley that retraced the steps of an earlier journey; and that a sharpening awareness of the poem's merits prompted its inclusion as the final contribution – both sequentially and chronologically – to the volume. Nor is the business of authorship in dispute: Coleridge's four poems included 'The Ancient Mariner' in accordance with his brief to concentrate on 'persons and characters supernatural, or at least romantic' (*BL*, ch. 14).

But, ever since the revelation of a joint commitment, critics have argued the toss as to who was the prime mover in the enterprise, the really fecundating presence. Such a polarisation, as Mark Reed observes, can be dangerous inasmuch as it may 'encourage a committed student consciously or unconsciously to take sides for or against one of the poets' (*CC*, p. 119). Thus Walter Pater's late-Victorian pronouncement that Coleridge's friendship with Wordsworth was 'the chief "developing" circumstance of his poetic life' (*CC*, p. 100) has been countered by I. A. Richards' assertion that Coleridge was Wordsworth's 'creator' and responsible for 'finding the style which Wordsworth was to advocate' in the Preface *as well as* uttering half of his thoughts and 'designing Wordsworth's major poems for him' (Coburn, 1967, p. 15).

The predictable process of critical qualification has followed in the wake of these sweeping claims. Indeed, four articles written within a few years of each other question the very idea of co-operation. Griggs (1951, repr. 1963) sees Wordsworth's egotism and self-reliance as a stumbling-block to mutual reciprocity. Coleridge could and did offer warm encouragement born of idolatry, and Wordsworth clearly benefited (p. 56). On the other hand, Griggs maintains, Wordsworth's condescension towards 'The Ancient Mariner' 'probably reacted more unfavorably upon Coleridge's creative power than has hitherto been suspected', perhaps even precipitating his extraordinary announcement two years later, 'I abandon Poetry altogether – I leave the higher and deeper kind, to Wordsworth' (*CL*, I, 337; quoted in Griggs, 1963, p. 59).

Buchan's 'The Influence of Wordsworth on Coleridge, 1795–1800' (1963) further explores Griggs's thesis of incompatible temperaments. Echoing the conventional wisdom in highlighting

the Alfoxden idyll as a 'seedtime', characterised by an ameliora-
tion of Wordsworth's sense of remorse and a growing sense of
nature's healing agency after the traumas of a revolution and an
affair gone wrong, he suggests that the poet was able to utilise
'the trivial, commonplace events of the Alfoxden neighbourhood,
such as an old huntsman's gratitude or the rumour of a dead
child buried under a thorn tree' and expand them into general
truths about humanity (quoted in *CC*, p. 152). Coleridge, on the
other hand, was temperamentally unable, once in the grip of
reverie, to exploit these narrative materials ('incidents of common life') but instead produced 'highly explosive symbols aris-
ing from deep in his mind'. Lured into a world of fantasy, he
found there 'stirring into vivid imaginative life a Virgil's Hades
of ghostly shapes'. Temperamentally poles apart, the friends had
now 'reached the point of seeing the world outside and the world
within very differently, and they would never agree on the
relationship between them' (p. 151).

This notion of a creative symbiosis, systematically and cor-
dially fostered during those thirteen months and initiated by
Coleridge's leap over the gate to greet his friends in June 1797,
was already under fire from Stephen Parrish (1958), the first to
take seriously Coleridge's retrospective avowal that 'a radical
Difference' of opinion about 'the language appropriate to poetry'
existed between them (letter to Sotheby, 13 July 1802, *CL*,
p. 812). For Parrish the key word, re-emphasised in subsequent
discussions, is 'ventriloquism', Coleridge's pejorative epithet
for Wordsworth's self-confessed ability to project himself into his
creations, for short spells of time 'perhaps, to let himself slip into
an entire delusion, and even confound and identify his own
feelings with theirs' (1802 Preface, quoted in Parrish, 1973,
p. 139). It was this clash of *views* and not the inherent differences
stressed by Buchan that led Wordsworth to complain that the
'principal person' of 'The Ancient Mariner' had 'no distinct
character', and to take a quite different approach in his own
'supernatural experiment', 'The Thorn'. Here Wordsworth
made the terrible events of curse and murder not supernatural or
even real, but only the products of the superstitious imagination.
For Parrish this is solid evidence of a widening gulf in the
friends' thinking. When Coleridge later committed his views to
paper, he, for his part, asserted that 'The Thorn' was, like the
curate's egg, both good and bad: good where 'the poet's own

imagination' was involved and where passages were 'spoken in his own character; bad in those sections 'exclusively appropriate to the supposed narrator' (*BL*, ch. 17) – Wordsworth's 'dramatic propriety' versus Coleridge's 'poetic propriety' (Parrish, 1973, p. 140). But, since Wordsworth soon abandoned his experiments with dramatic monologues, we can assume that his partner's views had left their mark.

Reed's 'Wordsworth, Coleridge and the "Plan" of the *Lyrical Ballads*' (1965) is the most scholarly attempt to piece together events during the volume's gestation. Like Parrish and Buchan before him, he senses a widening divergence of aims. But what has obfuscated this division, according to Reed, is the *retrospective* attempt by both poets to 'adjust and clarify' (*CC*, p. 123) their own views concerning the circumstances of composition and the nature of their early relationship. For Reed the entire plan was very much Wordsworth's, a project 'appropriated to himself as early as 30 April, 1798' (p. 117) and acknowledged in Dorothy's reference to 'William's poems'. Consequently his own pieces naturally dovetailed into the scheme, whereas Coleridge typically 'accepted without hesitation a secondary role in the historic venture, too quickly ignoring distinct differences in aim and attitude between himself and his admired companion' (p. 118). Like Griggs, Reed accounts Wordsworth's callousness more disturbing than the 'generous weakness' of Coleridge (p. 119), and accuses Wordsworth of an all-too-grudging recognition of his debt to the intellect of his collaborator. Even allowing for Coleridge's 'nearly infantile dependence on Wordsworth's strength of personality', the latter's myopia and insensitivity remain unforgivable.

Norman Fruman doubts that Wordsworth owed any 'debt' to Coleridge at all. Vividly subtitled 'The Damaged Archangel', his massive work (1972) questions many received opinions about Coleridge and not least the suggestion that he influenced the Wordsworth of *Lyrical Ballads*. The cast of their minds was ever completely different. Wordsworth distrusted 'the synthesizer of other men's ideas', privileging instead 'radical originality'. Moreover, the 'primary concerns' of the 1800 Preface 'are not those which can be found in any of Coleridge's writings before he met Wordsworth' (p. 288). 'The introduction of ordinary folk into literature, *without patronization*, is one of the most original of Wordsworth's achievements. There is no hint of or even sym-

pathy with this aim in any of Coleridge's writings.' Indeed
Fruman goes further than Reed in asserting that not only was
Coleridge's role in the enterprise pretty slight, but that 'nothing
has gone further to obscure the actual historical situation into
which *Lyrical Ballads* was born than the subsequent writings of
Coleridge on the subject' (p. 289).

We are a long way from Brett's conviction that Coleridge's
'psychological self-awareness', coupled with his belief that 'all
things are parts of a living whole', was 'the secret of the healing
power Coleridge brought to Wordsworth' in 1798 [1971, p. 177).
Indeed, the traditional picture of complementary minds gently
attuned – Coleridge's dream-like fancies anchored by Wordsworth's deep-rooted contact with the natural and the everyday –
is clearly one which has undergone substantial revision in recent
years.

The philosophical context

In *Table Talk* Coleridge declared that 'No man was ever yet a
great poet without being at the same time a profound philosopher (1832, 1917 edn, p. 130). A self-styled metaphysician, he
often spoke of his own plans for a *magnum opus* while conceding
that Wordsworth possessed the genius of a great philosophical
poet and that 'since Milton no man has manifested himself equal
to him' (*CL*, p. 582). There was nothing new about such exalting
of the thinker–poet, but the authors of *Lyrical Ballads*, both in
their creative and expository statements, gave the debate a fresh
impetus.

Although he confessed to a preference for Coleridge the
thinker–*talker*, Hazlitt cajoled the reader round an assault-
course of philosophers assimilated or rejected by the poet. Yet
hopes that their presence would add weight to the verse proved
illusory; he had to concede that Coleridge's one poem of
authentic 'genius' generated its power from 'wild, irregular,
over-whelming imagination' rather than profundity of message.
On the other hand the strength of Wordsworth's early poetry *did*
derive from a simple didacticism, its delivery of 'household
truths' (1825, repr. 1954, p. 131). This touching belief in the
consolatory message of the homely *Lyrical Ballads* became a
commonplace of Victorian criticism, in which Wordsworth

emerged as 'the only poet who will bear reading in time of distress' (Stephen, 1879, p. 218). But, while acknowledging that this ethic was 'distinctive and capable of systematic exposition', Stephen only hinted at specific debts. That task would become a preoccupation of later scholarship. Other commentators questioned the value of *any* extractable philosophy. For Arnold (1879), always seeking in poetry an answer to the question 'How to Live?', the *Lyrical Ballads* were the reality, the philosophy an illusion that needed to be dismissed out of hand before readers of Wordsworth could do him justice. Bateson epitomises modern adherents of the Arnoldian line, declaring that Wordsworth was 'not primarily a thinker but a feeler' whose ideas have only a 'marginal relevance' to the elucidation of the poetry (1956, p. 40).

None the less the sober seekers of influence have not gone away, undeterred by the psycho-pathological pronouncements that what count are 'the half-conscious half-animal terrors and ecstasies, and *not* the discoveries of the intellect' (Bateson, 1956, p. 40), or by the argument that Coleridge's philosophical dabblings were a monumental irrelevance in distracting him from the inspirational business of writing poetry. For Shawcross it is mere prejudice, easily rebutted, that his 'speculative writings' are 'dearly purchased at the expense of more poetry of the type of . . . "The Ancient Mariner"', a prejudice 'not confirmed by the facts of his life' (*BL*, 1907 edn, p. iv). How, one wonders, would Shawcross have reacted to Fruman's irreverent thesis in *Coleridge, the Damaged Archangel* (the phrase is Charles Lamb's) that there is no interaction in Coleridge's poetry between personal and received ideas since he *has no* ideas of his own, that he lacks any originality as a philosopher and that his unacknowledged kleptomania was not an occasional aberration but habitual and ingrained.

Not that the debt-collectors agree among themselves about the key influences. As Rader says, 'the chasms which separate their interpretations are broad and deep' (1967, p. 2). Rejecting Bradley's tendentious assumption that philosophy represents a world-view incompatible with poetry, most Wordsworthians pick out one or two pivotal influences. Thus his early biographer Legouis sees in the Wordsworth of *Lyrical Ballads* a son of Rousseau; Beatty finds evidence of a reaction against Rousseau and more especially Godwin in favour of Hartley and associa-

tionism. Maybe the authors (J. C. Maxwell and S. C. Gill) of
'Wordsworth' in the Oxford *Bibliographical Guide* are right in
pronouncing, rather despairingly, that the truth about his
philosophical debts 'can never be decided with the finality that
individual scholars would like' (1971, p. 170).

However, Arthur Beatty's *William Wordsworth: His Doctrine
and Art* (1922, 2nd edn 1927) remains a seminal work in the
field, not only because it is the first closely argued attempt to
forge links between the poetry and Hartley, but because it argues
the demise of 'Necessarianism' – the belief that men are made
what they are by circumstances – during the creation of *Lyrical
Ballads*. Dissenting from the Arnoldian position, which refuses to
'grant any value to his philosophy or system of thought', Beatty
believes that Wordsworth studied life not only at first hand 'but
also its reflection in books' (1927, p. 20). The key *reflector* for
Beatty is David Hartley's *Observations on Man, his Frame, his
Duty, and His Expectations* (1749): the key *reference* is the
allusion in the Preface to the ways in which our feelings and
ideas are *associated* in a state of excitement' (B&J, p. 247;
emphasis added). Beatty summarises Hartley's basic position
thus:

> Like all systems of philosophy founded on that of Locke, all
> innate ideas are banished; and all mental states are derived
> from sensation. These sensations are the primary, ultimate
> and irresolvable facts of our mental life and are the result of
> our direct contact with external things: and they, through the
> powers of association, are transformed into the complexes of
> those forms of mental life which succeed those that partake of
> the simplicity and directness of sensation. According to Hart-
> ley, association is the law of the mind, as gravitation is the law
> of the physical world. He is the original exponent of the law of
> association . . . and we have abundant evidence that Word-
> sworth gave this law his full credence.   (1927, p. 109)

Placing *Lyrical Ballads* in the philosophical context of a waning
Godwin and a waxing Hartley, Beatty shows how associationist
ideas both permeate these poems and assist our interpretation of
them. But, anxious not to overstate his case, he concedes the
patchwork nature of the volume, that some poems – not all early
– do deal with humanitarian issues close to Godwin's heart (e.g.

'The Thorn', 'The Convict', 'Lines Left . . . in a Yew-tree'). On the other hand, some poems deliberately fly in the face of a Godwinian ethic that derided such human emotions as pity, filial devotion and family feeling. 'The Idiot Boy' and 'The Mad Mother' are thus founded on maternal passion, 'Simon Lee' on gratitude; 'The Complaint of the Forsaken Indian Woman' is 'a picture of the soul in the face of death', and its counterpart, 'We Are Seven', 'a picture of the child's inability to understand what death is'. More positively and crucially Beatty discovers in Hartley's tripartite hierarchy of mental complexes linked by associative processes ('sensations', 'sensible' ideas, complex ideas), a ready-made formula that Wordsworth could and would relate to his own life. Thus 'childhood' is the age of sensation, 'youth' that of simple, 'sensible' ideas, 'maturity' that of intellectual concepts. Stated in these terms 'the foundation of his greatest poems and of his most characteristic theories and teaching was complete' (Beatty, 1927, p. 116).

Beatty's book has proved remarkably durable. While privileging the Hartley nexus (Beatty reminds us of Coleridge's enthusiasm and the christening of his first-born 'David Hartley', after the great master of Christian philosophy), it also evaluates other potential influences – Erasmus Darwin's theory of personification is rightly dismissed as inimical to *Lyrical Ballads* – and initiates the interpretation of 'Tintern Abbey' as an autobiographical 'growth of mind' which anticipates *The Prelude* and thus chimes with Hartleian notions of mental development. In short, it argues a convincing theoretical basis for *Lyrical Ballads*.

Stallnecht, on the other hand, emphasises no single philosophic debt and regards Hartley's imprint on the volume as 'transcendentalized' by the two poets (1958, p. 33). From Boehme, via Coleridge, comes the pantheistic theory of imagination so characteristic of Wordsworth (p. 43). Here he is at odds not only with Beatty but with the latest editors of *Lyrical Ballads* (1963), who trace 'a renewed dependence upon Hartleian psychology' to the 1800 Preface and with it the beginnings of an artistic schism between the friends (B&J, p. xxxvii). More significantly, Stallnecht reveals two apparently conflicting traditions in Wordsworth's 1798 thought: 'on the one hand the political theory of the French Revolution, on the other the faith of the mystical idealist'. These ideas prove briefly reconcilable before 'the mystic overcomes the rationalist' (1958, p. 67); both 'tend towards egalitarianism; support freedom of conscience and of worship', one through political independence, the other through liberty of the individual spirit (p. 66). The relevance to *Lyrical Ballads* of such dualistic thinking is obvious – though Stallnecht refrains, tantalisingly, from making precise connections. But he is unable to resist a stab at 'The Ancient Mariner', equating the shooting of the albatross with 'reason's conquest of feeling' (p. 151) and confounding the Mariner–Coleridge connection by arguing that it is *Wordsworth's* indulgence in analytical reasoning which destroys any capacity for communion between man and nature. The Mariner–Wordsworth's reintegration requires the benevolent intervention of the Hermit (Coleridge?) with his offer of a more enlightened religion. Such an interpretation anticipates that of Warren Stevenson (1983).

If Stallnecht is, like Beatty, better at detecting than interpreting, Piper's *The Active Universe* (1962) also fails, on its own admission, to allow literary critical intelligence enough play. When he does turn to *Lyrical Ballads*, he finds in 'Lines Left . . . in a Yew-tree' evidence of the 'close interweaving of the two poets at this time', a poetic embodiment *both* of the crucial Wordsworthian prescription of direct communication with nature through the free exercise of the imagination and what Piper concludes is the Coleridgean notion (derived from Hartley) of the three ages of man, about to become a cornerstone of Wordsworth's poetic faith. In 'The Ancient Mariner' of March 1798 the Wordsworthian perspective dominates: the scientific knowledge that we associate with Coleridge in earlier poems is still there, but the poem derives its psychological unity from 'its full realisation of the vital experience which the doctrine of the living universe offered the poet' (Piper, 1962, p. 88).

Rader's *Wordsworth: A Philosophical Approach* (1967) takes issue with Piper over the ascendancy of Wordsworth's thinking in 1798. Not that this inflection was new. As early as 1889, Walter Pater had maintained that 'Coleridge's philosophical speculations do really turn on the ideas which underlay Wordsworth's poetic practice' (*CC*, p. 100). But, for Rader, Coleridge's philosophical position was 'an indispensable key to the interpretation of Wordsworth's ideas'. Disagreeing also with Beatty (the Hartley spell was 'not of long duration and was combined with quite different allegiances' – Rader, 1967, p. 11), he sides with Stallnecht in seeing Coleridge, with Wordsworth *in tow*, now moving in the direction of philosophical idealism. Hartley is now 'transcendentalized by Coleridge, and at once modified and exalted by Wordsworth's own mystical experience'.

What appeals about Rader's work is its common-sensical insistence that Wordsworth's direct experience of life was by far the most important source of his ideas, that second to this was 'the living presence of Coleridge' even if his ideas were 'an almost impenetrable thicket of philosophical allusions' (1967, p. 10). Books and philosophies – 'these barren leaves' of 'The Tables Turned' – came a poor third. Such a view stresses the anti-rationalist cast of Wordsworth's mind, a view already explored by A. N. Whitehead in *Science and the Modern World* (1926). What impelled the early Wordsworth, in his opinion, was a moral repulsion to science's obsession with abstractions. But James Averill's *Wordsworth and the Poetry of Human Suffering* (1980) challenges Whitehead (and Beatty) by arguing that the 'clear and solid evidence' of mathematics and science (*The Prelude*, X. 904) was precisely what the poet *did* turn to in the spring of 1798, a change of direction manifested not in the birth of the great philosophical poem but in the 'little cells, oratories, and sepulchral recesses' of *Lyrical Ballads* (Averill, 1980, p. 158). Following Sheats in bringing Darwin into the argument, Averill notices that Beatty, 'the major disseminator of the Hartleian view . . . mentions . . . *Zoonomia* not at all' (p. 154n.), despite Wordsworth's own acknowledgement in the Advertisement. For Averill, the various ballads portraying people *in extremis* owe a substantial debt to the key chapter in *Zoönomia* (1796) entitled 'Diseases of Increased Volition'. And Darwin's conviction that scientific study might not only prove 'an inexhaustible source of pleasurable novelty' (Averill, 1980, p. 158) but also alleviate distress and even mitigate the effects of insanity would have given Wordsworth a compelling reason to read on. Fifty years later readers would be making the same claims for *Lyrical Ballads*!

E. D. Hirsch's *Wordsworth and Schelling* (1960) offers a very different kind of argument. His thesis is a development of Bradley's *aperçu* that Wordsworth's poetry is 'an imaginative expression of the same mind which, in his day, produced in Germany great philosophies' (1909, 1965 edn, p. 129). Granted that Wordsworth and Schelling did not know each other's work, the chronological closeness of *Lyrical Ballads* and Schelling's

Ideen is, maintains Hirsch, symptomatic of 'an astonishing spiritual closeness'. While it may not *prove* the existence of a 'homogeneous Zeitgeist' (1960, p. 2) it does lend credence to the view that Romanticism (as opposed to Lovejoy's 'Romanticisms') is a meaningful historical term. Granted such cultural conditions, great minds *do* think alike.

Literary influences

No single article has done more to undermine the time-hallowed assumptions of full-blooded experimentation in *Lyrical Ballads* than Robert Mayo's 'The Contemporaneity of the *Lyrical Ballads*' (1954). Uncompromising in forging firm links with the magazine poetry of the day, it provided an antidote to generations of critics (Elsie Smith, Oliver Elton, and so on) who had insisted on the image of 'revolutionary' poems in which the very excesses were new. Even for Wordsworthians such as Helen Darbishire who were happy to acknowledge the influence of the traditional ballads, meaning of course the kind of poems collected in Percy's *Reliques*, such 'magazinish' elements were alien to the spirit of the volume. Wordsworth himself paid his dues to Percy in the 'Essay, Supplementary to the Preface' (1815): 'I do not think there is an able writer in verse of the present day who would not be proud to acknowledge his obligations to the Reliques; I know that it is so with my friends; and, for myself, I am happy in this occasion to make a public avowal of my own (*PrW*, III, 78).

Wordsworth's comments probably reflect a calculated desire to convey an impression both of serious innovation *and* of respectable literary antecedence, for elsewhere he complains of the 'trash which infests the magazines' (letter to W. Mathews, 8 June 1794: *EL*, p. 126), a judgement reinforced by Coleridge's condemnation of his own efforts as 'miserably magazinish' (*PW*, I, 141). Perhaps these pronouncements also explain early critical reluctance to seek connections between 'magazinish' material and the ballads and to privilege the links with Percy. But Mayo's conclusions have proved hard to dislodge, solidly based as they are on an exhaustive comparative analysis of magazine verse of the decade. He duly recognises Wordsworth's abhorrence of the 'inane phraseology' of fashionable poetasters, but insists that he 'belonged to their generation', read their offerings, 'addressed himself to their audience' and shared their interest in making money (*WC*, p. 80). Even the want of unity which Legouis and others have found in *Lyrical Ballads* is a reflection of the heterogeneity of the literary fashion, of that 'confused and eddying flood of popular poetry' (*WC*, p. 81) flowing through the five major magazines of the day. For Mayo, *Lyrical Ballads* faithfully mirrors the preoccupations of fashionable verse – nature, the simple life, humanitarianism, sentimental morality; 'for nearly every character, portrait or figure there is some seasoned counterpart in contemporary poetry' (*WC*, p. 87). Desertion and separation culminating in child murder ('The Thorn') or death ('The Complaint of the Forsaken Indian Woman'), prostitution, loneliness and poverty ('The Female Vagrant'), madness ('The Mad Mother') and personal loss ('Old Man Travelling') belong to the stock-in-trade of poems that Mayo plucks as evidence from the magazines. 'The Last of the Flock' recalls 'The Dead Beggar' of Charlotte Smith, victim of a reluctant parish charity, 'The Female Vagrant' 'mendicant' poems such as T. Lacey's 'The Beggar Girl'. Both 'The Convict' and Coleridge's 'The Dungeon' echo contemporary pieces trumpeting the need for penal reform, and 'Tintern Abbey' is part of an extant tradition of topographical poetry. Even the maverick 'Ancient Mariner' is 'not completely unrelated to the anguished and homeless old sailors of the poetry departments' (*WC*, p. 93). What for Mayo sets *Lyrical Ballads* apart from this plethora of versifying is its sheer excellence, its 'intense fulfillment of an already stale convention' (p. 84). Viewed casually the poems might 'merge with familiar features of the landscape; read carefully they would give suddenly a tremendous impression of clarity, freshness, and depth' (p. 111).

Mayo has his detractors. Some critics have seen fit to ignore his conclusions (twelve years later Margaret Drabble was still espousing the cause of *Lyrical Ballads* as 'a revolution in poetry', 'completely new' and 'different in language, in intention and in subject matter' – 1966, p. 21), but most subsequent commentators have discreetly modified rather than abandoned Mayo's arguments. Not so historicists who have asserted that his evaluative conclusion (quoted above) is unacceptably subjective and impressionistic in a way that undermines the careful, historically based scholarship that informs the rest of the article. And

Jordan's *Why the Lyrical Ballads?* (1976), an even more painstaking analysis of contemporaneous minor verse, arrives at very different conclusions. The volume is not, in his estimation, either derivative or conventional. Indeed, its studied avoidance of *topical* themes (war, slavery, patriotism) and the faddish 'genres' of satire, sonnet and elegy is part of a deliberate search for that honesty and freshness that elevates these poems above their rivals.

Parrish's guarded reaction is more typical. While agreeing with Mayo that the originality of *Lyrical Ballads* resides more in excellence than in innovation, he feels, like Darbishire, that we ignore the role of the traditional ballad at our peril. Direct and moving renditions of tragic tales and 'lyrical' in their metrical impulse, Wordsworth *did* find them irresistible.

Judith Page's 'Style and Intention in Wordsworth's *Lyrical Ballads*' (1983) starts from a similar if more guarded position: the ballad is Wordsworth's point of departure for his literary enterprise because it is not a traditional literary mode. By returning to folk origins, Wordsworth begins his project to renovate English poetry with a form that predates the 'influence of French neo-classicism on English taste'. But she is quick to make the qualification – like many before her – that to replicate 'the naive consciousness – or unselfconsciousness – of the folk' is not Wordsworth's aim; he is 'a literary artist who values originality and not an antiquarian who wants to imitate the folk ballad' (1983, p. 293). Indeed, to anyone familiar with the formal characteristics of the traditional ballad genre – Page lists 'impersonal narration, formulaic diction, compression of events, stanzaic symmetry, parallelism, and repetition' (p. 294) – Wordsworth discounts the first entirely and largely ignores the second in the endeavour to 'subordinate external action to feeling' (p. 296).

In the matter of literary provenance Parrish was one of the first of many to argue the pull of Bürger's German ballads – for him more evident in 'The Ancient Mariner' than in the rustic pieces. His 'Leaping and Lingering: Coleridge's Lyrical Ballads' offers reinforcement of this view:

> He was attracted to Bürger's poems as early as 1796, and we can tell what he liked in Bürger from the Bürgeresque features he incorporated in 'The Ancient Mariner'. These included not

only the magical haunting air of miracle and terror that
supernatural events evoke, as in the 'ghostile crew', but what
the *Monthly Magazine* (which published Taylor's translation
in 1796) called in its March issue the 'hurrying vigour' of
Bürger's 'impetuous diction' as in such lines as these:

> To and fro they are hurried about;
> And to and fro, and in and out
> The stars dance on between.
>   (1985, pp. 109–10)

It was to alert its reader to this contagion that the *Critical Review*
of October 1798 fired its opening salvo: the poem was merely 'a
Dutch attempt at German sublimity' (B&J, p. 320).

Wordsworth's admiration for 'German sublimity' was beginning to pall by 1798. 'Incidents' were 'among the lowest
allurements of poetry'. Bürger provoked 'a hurry of pleasure' but
no 'recollection of delicate or minute feelings', and no delineation of character beyond that of Bürger himself (letter to
Coleridge, *EL*, p. 234). Parrish, one of those who emphasise
Percy's influence on Wordsworth, none the less finds reverberations of Bürger's 'impetuous diction' in 'The Idiot Boy', where
the verbal patterns of 'Lenore' are echoed, and 'the macabre,
terrifying midnight ride of Bürger's ghostly lovers' is parodied in
the 'half comic, blundering ride of Wordsworth's idiot' (*WC*,
p. 133). More significantly, 'Des Pfarrers Tochter von
Taubenheim' ('The Lass of Fair Wone' in Taylor's translation)
profoundly metamorphosed though it be from sensational ballad
to psychological study by the addition of an involved narrator
and by Wordsworth's refusal to descend to explicit infanticide
and 'mould'ring flesh', has left its mark on 'The Thorn'.

Such specific conclusions about influence conceal the main
burden of Parrish's earlier (1959) study. His abiding conviction
that the 'experiments' were 'primarily and distinctively experiments in *dramatic technique*' (*CWC*, p. 154) has much exercised
subsequent commentators. That single-minded assertion has
initiated a whole series of examinations (by Danby, Hartman,
Jacobus, Ryskamp and Sheats, among others) of those dramatic
tensions between reader, narrator, poet and character that
apparently reside in these poems.

Parrish is, however, on thin ice when exploring their 'lyrical' potentialities, a point taken up by Ryskamp (1965). Dredging up a definition of 'ballad' from the *Encyclopaedia Britannica* of 1797, he argues that its primary meaning of 'song' would have rendered the title *Lyrical Ballads* tautological, and justified its ultimate rejection by Wordsworth. Like Mayo, Ryskamp regards the ballads of the collection as 'closer to the halfpenny ballads being hawked about the street than to the lyrical adaptations of Percy' (1965, p. 360); in fact they are the *least* lyrical pieces in the volume. Nor are they pictorial, like Cowper's poetry. Eschewing an Augustan tradition in which artistic comparisons and painterly effects were common motifs both in poetry and its criticism, Wordsworth seeks dramatic tension and *psychological* subtlety via a process of self-revelation which is often unconscious ('We Are Seven' or 'Anecdote for Fathers'). Such a Parrish-like conclusion is convincing enough; less secure is Ryskamp's thesis that the virtues of originality are chiefly encountered in non-balladic pieces such as the expostulatory poems or 'Lines Left . . . in a Yew-tree'.

Ryskamp's reference to 'halfpenny ballads' aligns him with a school of thought that sees the influence of the broadside on *Lyrical Ballads*. Usually preoccupied with murders and other sensational news items, the broadside is also mentioned by Carl Woodring as one of four categories of ballad drawn on by the poet. But Linda Venis, basing her findings on sixty-seven chapbook poems of the decade 1790–1800, resists the 'claimed connection' between street verse and the *Lyrical Ballads*. Only two of these contemporary broadsides deal directly with the lives of humble people. Furthermore their 'stale diction', hyperbole and personification are quite at odds with Wordsworth's 'cultural primitivism'. Venis concludes, as have many before her, that Wordsworth's real models were 'humble men and women', themselves the repository of profound thoughts and feelings (1984, p. 625).

The very thoroughness of recent full-length studies of the 1798 edition entails an unswerving commitment to this vexed issue of literary influence. In a chapter entitled 'Magazine Poetry and the Poetry of Passion', Jacobus (1976) concedes that Mayo has accurately demonstrated the ballads' links with the genres and themes of magazine verse. But she sees the fundamental difference between them not simply as one of quality (Mayo) or dramatic strategy (Parrish) or even psychological subtlety (Ryskamp), but as defined by Wordsworth's insistence that there must be a real engagement of authorial feeling, even to the point of a near-Keatsian empathy with the *dramatic personae* of the poems. Such as identification sets *Lyrical Ballads* apart from mere magazine stuff which, by employing 'a literary idiom at odds with the distress it portrays' (Jacobus, 1976, p. 184), rejects such an intimate kinship between poet/reader and character. What *could* also be argued is that Wordsworth's *early* ballads (for instance 'The Female Vagrant') have not yet come to terms with this incompatibility of form and content.

In his essay 'Wordsworth Revisited', Hartman (1987) takes a similar line. If the volume was 'a stumbling block for its generation', it was not on account of a humble subject matter that did not differ markedly from the predominantly Christian sentiments of the magazines. Both 'reflected the taste of a growing class of 'bourgeois readers' (p. 7). But the poet's deliberately low-key, even flat, approach was in conscious reaction to magazine verses where 'the manner helped to raise the matter'. Wordsworth disdained 'this yeasty virtue of style', prepared to disregard 'that ironclad law of literary and social decorum' which limited the [neoclassical] poets' role to "what [oft] was thought, but ne'er so well express'd" ' (p. 8). While agreeing about Wordsworth's conscious rejection of stylistic felicities, Marilyn Butler (1981) believes that such a stance in fact mirrors current artistic practice. Moreover, the poet's address to a wide public and not a narrow coterie *is* further proof of neoclassical tendencies.

It would be wrong to regard the critical debate about literary influence as polarising over the issue of originality versus eclecticism or, more specifically, the *Reliques* versus the magazines. In the genre of the folk ballad there was, in any case, much blurring of distinctions. Many ballad imitations or reworkings by poets were, as Butler points out, adulterated by an essentially modern sensibility, by those very excesses of ornamentation that Wordsworth criticised in the work of Percy or Bürger. And Jacobus, though arguing persuasively for additional debts to the exotic and primitive pastisches of Ossian, Collins and the dialect ballads of Burns, perceives in the central themes of *Lyrical Ballads* (nature, the self, the imagination) emanations from three eighteenth-century literary sources: Thomson, Cowper and Akenside. In a tightly argued and allusive chapter, Jacobus shows both Coleridge and Wordsworth enriching these existing traditions, adding self-revelation to Cowper's introspection, 'meditative passion' to Thomson's vision, and 'the transforming power' of imagination to Akenside's intellectuality and 'passive receptivity' (1976, pp. 57–8). The central impulse of *Lyrical Ballads* is embodied in this refurbishment of existing models, in 'the attempt to provide a more significant *literary* experience than his readers were used to finding in the overworked themes and genres of their time' (p. 208). By comparing a poem from *Town and Country Magazine* (1794) and Wordsworth's 'Lines Written in Early Spring', Glen arrives at similar conclusions. Whereas the popular verses are neatly conclusive and portray a natural world readily 'assimilable to human attitudes and feelings' (1983, p. 40), Wordsworth's speaker is separated from the scene he describes; the tone is one of unease and inconclusiveness. If, for Jacobus, Wordsworth's reworkings of existing models result in a greater richness and complexity of experience, for Glen they generate those very feelings of 'strangeness and aukwardness' that the poet predicted in the Advertisement. Either way – and Humphry House similarly detects in the high seriousness of 'The Nightingale' a distillation of Cowper's poetic manner (1953, p. 71) – the ballads easily outdistance their models, either literary or popular, native or German.

3

Lyrical Ballads: Recent Interpretative Stances

Formalist approaches: 'The Bridle of Pegasus'

Formalists might be forgiven for ignoring Romantic poetry. After all, for two centuries it has been dismissed by its detractors as adolescent, form*less* or escapist. Yet a critical concern with formal control – I. A. Richards' 'Bridle of Pegasus' (Richards, 1935, ch. 9) – is a useful starting-point for analysts of *Lyrical Ballads*. We may not subscribe to Wallace Stevens' view (1951) that 'the style of a poem and the poem itself are one', but it is harder to dissent from Allen Tate's belief that 'the formal qualities of a poem are the focus of the specifically critical judgement because they partake of an objectivity' that content lacks (1941, p. 110).

That unalloyed formalist criticism of the volume *is* in short supply reflects less on Romantic poetry in general – after all 'New Criticism' *has* converged on the lyric – than on the nature of *Lyrical Ballads* and on the ticklish business of ignoring context. For the critic bent on examining the formal devices of a single poem to the exclusion of 'environment' or intertextuality, it is distracting, to say the least, to be reminded at every turn that *Lyrical Ballads* is a collection and subject to outside influences, while the expository pronouncements of both poets make it very difficult to exclude 'intention' from the debate.

With the 'confessional' poems, the problem is exacerbated. Rader, on the horns of this dilemma, concedes that, while it may be dangerous to put the poet into the poem, the bulk of Wordsworth's output is 'more or less autobiographical' (1967,

p. 4). Such a grudging admission, though barely applicable to the 'ballads', at least avoids the convolutions of Beardsley's strained distinction between poet and speaker: 'It is not Wordsworth, in the poem, but a speaker who may or may not be similar to him, musing near Tintern Abbey; it is entirely irrelevant to the understanding of the poem – though relevant to a causal explanation of its having been written – that Wordsworth himself visited the spot' (1958, pp. 240–1). Such formal niceties echo his and Wimsatt's pronouncements in 'The Intentional Fallacy' about an autonomous text 'detached from the author at birth' which 'goes about the world beyond his power to intend about it or control it'.

That these formalist positions should come under attack is scarcely to be wondered at. De Man, for example, has questioned the formalist obsession with structural unity, suggesting that, far from discovering therein the coherence of the natural world, 'New Critics' have usually uncovered multifaceted meanings that involve a slide from text-based unity to an interpretative harmony *imposed* by the critic (the so-called 'hermeneutic circle'). Yet such approaches do provide a sober antidote to the excesses of contextual or transcendental criticism. And, knowingly or not, they reflect the Coleridgean idea of 'organic form', whereby an artefact reveals a unity analogous to that of natural phenomena. Undeniably, most probing discussions of individual ballads owe some debt to formalist procedures, which emphasise not just coherence but also ambiguity (Empson), paradox (Brooks) or irony, as part of a controlling belief in the verbal icon. 'New Criticism' can take *some* credit for the plethora of recent and systematic text-based discussions of the ballads.

Colin Clarke's *Romantic Paradox* (1962) offers a typical modification of the absolutes of 'New Criticism'. Reluctant to be drawn into the debate over the 'intentional fallacy' (confusion of the poem and its origins), his reading of 'Tintern Abbey' rejects Wimsatt's primary metaphors of 'evanescence and intangibility' for a fabric woven round the metaphor of penetration (p. 51), a process whereby the literal landscape becomes part of the inner life of the observer. The climactic metamorphosis of natural world to person occurs in the lines 'Knowing that Nature never did betray / The heart that loved her' (ll.122–3). Qualified Wimsatt then, but still formalist in its insistence on the poem's metaphoric coherence, Clarke's account also typically stresses its tensions, its 'pervasive plurality of meaning' (p. 52). Indeed his conclusion touches its forelock to two 'New Critical' catch-phrases: 'The primary *paradox* of sense-awareness is so cunningly elaborated in "Tintern Abbey" that it would be difficult to find a better instance of what Mr Wimsatt has called *"romantic wit"* ' (p. 53; emphasis added).

Long before De Man, critics were aware of the dangers of the 'hermeneutic circle'. Talking of 'The Ancient Mariner', D. W. Harding spoke robustly of the need to attend to 'what precisely the poem says' without wringing meaning from 'one fragment of the poem without regard to the control exercised over it by the rest' (Coburn, 1967, p. 64). By implication Harding was allying himself with a chorus of detractors who have seen in Robert Penn Warren's essay 'A Poem of Pure Imagination: An Experiment in Reading' (1946), a too-slavish insistence on the structural *coherence* of Coleridge's poem. Yet Warren's critique remains both a pivotal statement of 'New Critical' principles and a yardstick by which all subsequent interpretations tend to be judged. That Crane, Bostetter, House and Beer – among many others – take exception to some of his findings is at least evidence of the essay's centrality in the debate. Such disapproval was directed not at Warren's key interpretation of the poem as a celebration of the 'one life', but at the 'rigid' discussion of its symbolic patterning. Humphry House thus objected less to the relative coherence of the moon–bird–mist–wind cluster than to Warren's attempts to force other aspects of the poem into congruence with it. His conclusion takes issue with the 'New Critical' belief that the poem possesses a determinate, if complex, meaning:

Mr Warren has permanently enriched our understanding of the poem by insisting on its statement of the 'context of values' in which the crime and punishment and reconciliation occur; his symbolist 'equations' serve to point out elements which may be involved in this context; but the decision to 'adopt Coleridge's later terminology' in stating the equivalents symbolised has ... the effect of making the poem seem more technical and diagrammatic than Mr Warren first found it, or than Coleridge could ever have admitted it to be.

(House, 1953, p. 113)

Elder Olson's objections were more radical. A paid-up 'Chicago School' member in conscious opposition to the narrowness of 'New Criticism' and anxious to move beyond symbols, systems and texts to 'aspects of reality' which works illuminate, or to a consideration of their 'moral, political and social effects', he objected not only to an interpretation which he regarded as 'really uncontrolled analogy' but to the very *idea* of a precise, informing symbolism in the poem, since 'Coleridge's discussion of the origins of the *Lyrical Ballads* . . . offers no hint of symbolism in this sense' (1948, repr. 1952, p. 142).

Lionel Stevenson (1949) similarly dismissed thoughts of metaphoric precision. None the less, in distancing the poet from his protagonist, he appears to subscribe to that principle of American formalist criticism adumbrated in Beardsley's discussion of 'Tintern Abbey'. Coleridge, he argued, was objectively portraying a mind quite unlike his own. The poem was nothing less than the dramatic monologue of a 'primitive seaman' hallucinating a surreal sequence of events to explain the solitary torments of exposure and thirst. In equating the distorted symbolism with the escalating delirium of the victim, Stevenson has more in common with the magazine reviewers of 1798–9 than with Penn Warren and his symmetrical analysis!

The protracted debate over the meaning of 'The Ancient Mariner' is considered in Chapter 4 (the poem is rarely discussed as part of *Lyrical Ballads* anyway). But formalist approaches have been adopted and adapted in regard to other poems, particularly the so-called 'ballads' 'Simon Lee', 'Goody Blake and Harry Gill', 'The Idiot Boy' and 'The Thorn'. J. F. Danby's much-anthologised chapter on these poems in *The Simple Wordsworth* (1960) quickly reveals his then-innovative preoccupation with Wordsworth's irony, a tone of voice reflecting the shifting interplay between speaker and character, reader and poet: 'The mixed mode of the dramatic-narrative poem allows for a range of voices, and each voice for an ironic shift in point of view. It is unfortunate that Wordsworth's irony has not been much remarked' (p. 37).

But Danby's critical perspective, though enormously influential, resists easy definition. The emphasis on irony, on the structural devices of poetic mask, bespeak formalist preoccupations, but his insistence on Wordsworth as arch-manipulator and intentional artificer breathes a less rarefied air than the

'New Critic' with his icon-like view of the poem as an autonomous structure of meanings, to be judged without recourse to
the artist's professed aims. Indeed, Danby's preference for plural
readings that stay plural ('the co-presence of alternatives, the
refusal to impose on the reader a predigested life-view') anticipates 'problematic' interpretations of these poems, while his
insistence that 'the reader should enter, himself, a full partner in
the final judgement on the facts set before him' marks a move in
the direction of reader-response theory (p. 38).

Paul Sheats' later essay (1973a) extends the notion of reader
involvement. He romantically visualises Wordsworth, maestro-
like, conducting 'the emotions of his reader like a symphony' and
shows how this process is orchestrated in 'Simon Lee' (Abrams,
1975, p. 134). Like Danby, Sheats believes that the abhorrence
or plain indifference we experience in confronting Simon's
swollen ankles is faithfully exploited by the poem. Aware of our
negative reaction, the poet becomes a 'redeemer bent on the
reader's salvation'. As a consequence of this plea to our better
natures, the narrator's final, charitable gesture – I struck, and
with a single blow / The tangled root I sever'd (ll. 93–4) – is an
act with which we gladly identify. In this receptive frame of
mind, we can embrace the final 'paradox' (Danby's word too)
that, though Simon is decaying physically, his emotional capacities
remain undiminished. Averill takes this idea of a 'community of
knowledge between narrator and reader from which the poetic
object is excluded' a stage further. In inviting the reader to
'partake in the poetic making', the poem asks what are the
proper subjects for poetry and blurs distinctions between the
poem and the world outside it, between 'the tale and the
not-tale'. We end up aware not just of Simon Lee but of what it
means to *read* 'Simon Lee' (1980, p. 165). Like Danby, Sheats
and Averill have revealed the poet's power to effect our literary
and psychic re-education through a sequential analysis of tone
and structure. But categorisers should beware. In maintaining
that the meaning of these ballads is not self-formulated and that
the reader, aided and abetted by the poet, must act on the text to
produce meaning, these critics reveal emphases as elusive as the
poems they discuss.

This contemporary critical preoccupation with irony in *Lyrical
Ballads* is something that pre-Danby Wordsworthians would
have found misplaced. As Richard Gravil succinctly remarks in

an *aperçu* that recalls Averill and Sheats, 'irony's purpose is not the communication of content, but to make the mind aware of its own processes'. On the whole the nineteenth century went for 'content'. Gravil (1982) shows that it is now perfectly possible to devote a convincing essay to the subject of irony. Indeed he acknowledges an indebtedness to Danby, Mayo, Owen and Jacobus and the revelation of 'genial coincidences' with interpretations by Parrish and Sheats. There are, Gravil considers, three kinds of poem: anecdotes, 'studies of human suffering' and what he dubs 'anti-ballads' ('Simon Lee', 'The Idiot Boy', 'The Thorn'). In the first group, poems such as 'We Are Seven' and 'Anecdote for Fathers' operate ironic procedures on two levels. Thus the irony *reverses* the didacticism of the 'do-good' *poet* so that it is 'the presumptuous adult at whom the moral finger is wagged'. But on another level the *speaker* haltingly acquires a capacity for ironic self-awareness ('oh dearest, dearest boy! my heart / For better lore would seldom yearn'). This second process, however, is not completed in 'We Are Seven', where the persona ends up 'as unenlightened as he began' (1982, p. 45).

Goody Blake invites initial censure from the reader – after all Harry Gill cuts a respectable figure as a local farmer, while Goody is a 'highly improvident old woman' whose way of life recalls the foolish virgins. But ironic reversal follows. In the conclusion this chastisement of improvidence in the name of bourgeois virtues is seen for what it is; Harry's chilly fate invites us to 'think' on the *real* moral of this cautionary tale (p. 48).

Belonging to the category of 'anti-ballad', 'Simon Lee' is shot through with ironies. 'Generic confidence' (in its ballad insistence on unfolding a good yarn) gives way to 'bewilderment as we wonder what kind of a poem this is intended to be'. 'Destabilisation' is then succeeded by parody – of the 'bogus mediaevalism' and the contrived sentimentality of the opening lines. But such ploys quickly vanish in a deliberately bathetic structure that recalls the ballad burlesque in 'The Idiot Boy'. But further ironies reside in both poems: that such simple themes and events can invoke something more powerful and less bogus than mere Gothic sensationalism – the unvarnished presentation of 'salutary experience' (p. 51). As Gravil concludes,

The strategy . . . is ironic. And the objective is to scrutinise the duplicities of the imagination. . . . The deepest irony is that

which probes the ironist's own illusions, and in *Lyrical Ballads*
Wordsworth goes beyond his critique of the sensational and
the sentimental, to discipline the egotistical sublime.

(1982, p. 56)

The issue of 'genre'

'Genre' criticism, that branch of literary studies which seeks
characteristics of an artistic form in individual works, is currently
out of favour, if we are to believe the American historicist Siskin.
He sees 'genre' studies as a tyrannical discipline that 'imposes an
historical narrative on single forms, treating each one as an
independent organic unity evolving naturally towards greater
sophistication'. The result is 'a Romantic development tale such
as *the* Novel's rise or *the* lyric's flowering' (1988, p. 10). To
believe this 'tale' is to accept that *Lyrical Ballads* charts the
progress of both 'lyric' and 'ballad' towards that greater sophistication identified by Siskin. Thus the ballads incorporate more
lyric features as a consequence of the lyric's rise 'within the
generic hierarchy'; their lyricisation reflects a 'newly dominant
form'.

Whether one accepts Siskin's denunciation of such a stance or
not, the uneasy marriage of lyric and ballad in the title has
proved contentious ever since the volume's first appearance. The
British Critic's sense of bafflement nearly two centuries ago ('The
title of the poems is, in some degree, objectionable; for what
ballads are not lyrical?') finds a number of recent reverberations,
not least in John Jordan's preoccupation with 'one of the
interesting and probably finally unanswerable questions of
literary history' (1976, p. 172). Mayo is more dismissive. 'Not a
significant innovation in 1798' nor matching the contents of the
collection, *Lyrical Ballads* is probably a title 'casually chosen'
and deliberately 'nondescript – uniting poems of diverse subjects
and kinds' (*WC*, p. 101). For him, what does differentiate the
lyrical ballad from its antecedents is its abandonment of that
staple of the folk ballad, the quatrain, in favour of a more
sustained stanzaic unit. Parrish, so often at odds with Mayo,
similarly develops the idea of 'lyrical' as related to rapidity of
rhythm, quoting both Wordsworth's wish to employ the 'assist-
ance of Lyrical and rapid metre' (1800 note to 'The Thorn', *PW*,

II, 512) and his conviction that the medium of verse contributes to the peculiar power of 'Goody Blake'. 'Goody Blake' works as a poem because 'the important truth illustrated by the tale was communicated to people' who would not have heard or responded to it ' "had it not been narrated as a Ballad, and in a more impressive metre than is usual in Ballads" ' (*WC*, p. 139, quoting *PW*, II, 401n.).

Parrish's belief that the heightened drama created by the speaker's involvement inevitably generates lyrical impulsion appears to draw on an earlier interpretation articulated by, among others, Campbell and Mueschke, who see the title as 'a kind of public pronouncement that [Wordsworth] was to use the ballad not so much for purposes of pure narrative as the vehicle of personal emotion which he had learned to objectify and sublimate' (1933, pp. 23–6). Such a view, now a critical commonplace, has been reiterated by Parrish in his recent article:

> a 'lyrical' ballad was lyrical in two respects – its passion ('all poetry is passion', Wordsworth declared) arose, as in any lyric, from the mind of the speaker or the dramatic narrator of a ballad tale, and it was heightened by the employment of 'lyrical' or rapid metre so as to convey this passion to readers unaccustomed to responding to the common language of men in common life.   (1985, p. 106)

That such a title was not only a warning but also a challenge to Wordsworth's readers has been convincingly argued by Bateson and more recently by Jordan and Hamilton. For Bateson 'a lyrical ballad was a deliberate hybrid-like tragi-comedy'. What Wordsworth sought was not the tragic tale of a stock ballad but something less predictable and more subtle – a concentration on 'the emotions embodied in the story' (1956, p. 137).

Emphasising polarisations of a different kind in the title, Jordan (1976) devotes a whole chapter to the question 'What is a "Lyrical Ballad"?' 'Finely crafted songs of popular feeling', they tread, in his estimation, a tight-rope of tension – on the one hand *lyrics* with 'elaborate metrical devices', on the other 'emanations of truth and reality' whose unforced diction and syntax renders them 'less artificial' and presumably more *ballad-like* (p. 80). This kind of thinking is endorsed by Hamilton, who sees in the portmanteau title evidence of the poet's awareness of the inadequacy of each genre taken in isolation. He detects, moreover, a conscious wish to upset audience complacency about their mutually exclusive nature. Wordsworth's *combination* of lyric and ballad is deliberately problematic; the fusion is evidence of his distrust of the conventional boundaries of poetic genres, which he 'blurs' and combines to 'multiply perspectives from which the subject is observed' (1986, p. 45).

The evidence of the poems themselves tends to buttress such a view. Jordan has noticed that Wordsworth, unlike the poetasters of the magazines, was 'uncommonly chary of any genre descriptions in the 1798 edition' (1976, p. 144), further evidence for him of the poet's search for an earthy originality and honèsty. Wordsworth not only refuses the modish tag of 'tale' for such narratives as 'Simon Lee'; he resorts to fashionable labels only in one 'complaint' ('The Forsaken Indian Woman') and one 'sketch' ('Old Man Travelling') – and that despite the 'genre'-consciousness of the contemporary collections. Yet I remain unconvinced that we should attach much importance to Jordan's argument. After all, there *are* perfunctory attempts at categorisation in the 'Advertisement'. 'Goody Blake and Harry Gill' is mentioned as a 'tale' based on 'a well-authenticated fact'; 'The Thorn' is classed as a fictional narrative, 'The Ancient Mariner' as ballad pastiche and 'Expostulation and Reply' and 'The Tables Turned' as conversation pieces. Thus it becomes possible to place the 'experiments' on a continuum between fact and fancy. Starting from Wordsworth's own tripartite division of the poems into 'absolute inventions', 'facts based on personal observation' and 'facts' recalled by friends, 'The Thorn' is a *fiction* ('not supposed to be spoken in the author's own person'), 'Goody Blake' a *fact* based on hearsay ('founded on a well-authenticated fact') and 'Expostulation and Reply' a *fact* grounded in the author's own experience.

Some commentators have attempted to pigeonhole the items in the collection more precisely: in searching for formal analogues, they have often uncovered evidence of eclecticism at the same time. In this connection the generic term 'ballad' has proved an elusive quarry. Most analysts are agreed that the word best fits the direct, narrative pieces in the volume and was intended so to do; there is less unanimity about whether these 'ballads' privilege *story* and its organising mechanism of plot, or dramatic monologue, where the emphasis is on character and psychological exposure.

Yet another of the paradoxes that critics must confront is the fact that only five of the poems use the ballad quatrain, and four of these are precisely those subjective and expository pieces that have nothing in common with genuine ballads ('not ballads at all, but lyrics in which Wordsworth reveals his feelings and his faith' – Moorman, 1957, p. 369). Jones and Tydeman conclude that, if one discounts Coleridge's contributions, only three poems ('Goody Blake and Harry Gill', 'The Thorn', 'The Idiot Boy') actually fulfil the requirements of the genre, though, in terms of narrative thrust or anecdotal character, four others ('The Female Vagrant', 'We Are Seven', 'Simon Lee', 'The Last of the Flock') approximate to ballads (*WC*, p. 15). On the principle that song is integral to ballad, some commentators would extend the list to include 'The Mad Mother' and 'The Complaint of a Forsaken Indian Woman', but Mary Moorman for one is loth to accept this (1957, p. 369).

One of the problems is that the word 'ballad' covers a multitude of sins. Jordan believes that for Wordsworth's and Coleridge's contemporaries it was redolent both of 'a flavour of primitive antiquity and a suggestion of a basis in fact' (1976, p. 183). In that case, the only poem in *Lyrical Ballads* that could have passed muster as authentic on the first count is 'The Ancient Mariner', the only one with 'a flavour of . . . antiquity'. The model for this definition is obviously the anonymous ballads, both 'authentic' and reworked, in Percy's *Reliques*, but we have also to reckon with broadside ballads, ballad pastiches written by poets and hacks, and ballads (such as those by Bürger) outside the native tradition. Any or all of these might figure in the magazines or anthologies of the day. However, what indubitably attracted Wordsworth to the ballad was its elemental quality, its 'most functional type of metre and diction, the mere skeleton of poetic language'. As Jones and Tydeman have recognised, Wordsworth felt the need 'after the extreme artificiality of the late eighteenth-century mode' of 'An Evening Walk' and 'Descriptive Sketches', to 'rebuild his whole poetic procedures from the most basic materials in order to express a radically altered attitude of thought and feeling' (*WC*, p. 16). While Coleridge recognised in the ballad a potential for music, magic and symbolism, Wordsworth was drawn to its common language, its dramatic situations and its roots in simple life.

Modern scholars have further added to our knowledge of *Lyrical Ballads* by linking the minor genres of the volume to current poetic practice. Hartman (1964), discovering connections not only with traditional but even classical forms, divides the volume into complaints (taking a less literal line than Jordan) and plain-song lyrics such as 'It is the First Mild Day of March'. 'Lines Written At a Small Distance from my House' derives from the Horatian epistolary poem; the 'Yew-tree' poem has direct links with Greek inscription and epitaph; 'Lines Written in Early Spring' recalls the ancient thanksgiving poem which makes or creates a date in the 'living calendar'. His conclusion (p. 151) is that antiquity – buttressed by current vogues (the use of well-known tales or traditions) – contributes to every poem. No other critic discerns so clear a classical imprint on the sub-genres of the volume, though a newer generation of commentators – Butler and Abrams for example – has discovered neoclassical elements in both Preface and Advertisement.

Mayo proposes more conventional categories of ballad, complaint, fragment (tale), sketch and anecdote, predictably finding comparable examples in the magazines to support his thesis 'that the volume represents', *inter alia*, the 'culmination of a long and complicated process of development' (*WC*, p. 107). The two kinds of ballad, 'objective' and 'subjective', narrative and lyrical, bedfellows both in the *Reliques* and in the magazines, find generic equivalents in 'Goody Blake' or 'The Idiot Boy' (narrative) and 'Lines Written in Early Spring' (lyrical). The complaint ('a lyrical poem which directly expresses grief . . . or resentment', a plaintive tale told in the first person) is the genre of 'The Mad Mother' and 'The Female Vagrant' as well as 'The Forsaken Indian Woman' (p. 102). Fragments, traditionally incomplete as the title implies, find a subtler parallel in 'The Foster Mother's Tale' with its unanswered questions (who, for example, is the 'strange man' who has left Maria 'troubled with wilder fancies' [ll. 12–13]?). 'Old Man Travelling', modestly described by the author as 'A Sketch', has the visual qualities – figure in a landscape – that 'artistic' readers would be expected to appreciate, and 'We Are Seven' and an 'Anecdote for Fathers' are illustrative of moral truths (the intuitive wisdom of the child) that audiences would anticipate, at least in the 'anecdote' (*WC*,

p. 105). That they are also studies in child psychology is something that they could hardly have expected.

Parrish's cataloguing of forms is likewise geared to his own argument. Since he equates the unique virtues of the ballads with their *dramatic* intensity, his categorisation is grounded in their narrative and presentational strategies. He reminds us that five are spoken by a dramatic character (for example the Ancient Mariner, or the sea captain of 'The Thorn') and three in a colloquial authorial voice (as in 'Simon Lee'), while four are dialogues involving the poet/speaker (the so-called 'expostulatory' pieces). By this token 'Tintern Abbey' must be a dramatic dialogue between self and soul. In his discussion of 'The Ancient Mariner', Lionel Stevenson has elaborated on one aspect of Parrish's thesis, seeing Coleridge's 'invention' as satisfying all the conditions of the dramatic monologue subsequently refined by Browning, an experiment which could well be 'added to the list of poetical innovations which Coleridge created in his half-intuitive way' (1949, p. 41). And, in detecting affinities with 'mock-epic', Danby sees 'The Idiot Boy' as 'a Wordsworthian comedy' in which the familiar features of the Augustan genre are given an individual resonance by the poet's off-beat treatment (1960, p. 52).

'Tintern Abbey' has, as in other respects, provoked a private debate of its own about generic provenance. Critics concur in seeing its ready acceptance as a reflection of reader recognition of a respectable Augustan genre, defined by Dr Johnson as poetical description of landscape plus 'historical retrospection or incidental meditation' (1783, 1905 edn, I, 77). Thus Mayo locates it firmly in the extant mode of topographical verse, a 'lyrical meditation' inspired by the *genius loci* of the poem's setting. Abrams agrees, but in valorising the poem's literary uniqueness (his category for it is 'the *greater* Romantic lyric' – emphasis added) he has come under fire from the historicist brigade. Willing to accept that 'Tintern Abbey' is formally descended from Augustan poems that, like it, have a title specifying a geographical location and contain 'a description of that scene with the thoughts that the scene suggested', Abrams none the less believes that the loco-descriptive poem was a mere springboard for the superior meditations of Wordsworth (1984, p. 84). But Siskin takes exception to the view that the poet's expressiveness naturally transcends the limits of conventional form, refusing to see in this lyricised but fragmented ode part of an irresistible development towards even greater excellence in one genre. It was 'formally an experimental dead end for Wordsworth' (1988, p. 29).

Psychoanalytical perspectives

'Freudian literary criticism is a bit like the Holy Roman Empire: not holy, not Roman, not an Empire; not Freudian, not literary, not criticism'. Harold Bloom's dismissal of this critical mode (Salusinszky, 1987, p. 55) has not deterred its advocates from getting to work on *Lyrical Ballads*, where they have exhumed the 'sub-text' of Wordsworth's repressions, or dissected the text of 'The Ancient Mariner', that 'happy stamping-ground for psychological symbol-hunters, whether of Freudian or Jungian persuasions' (Prickett, 1975, p. 27). Curiously, 'confessional' poems such as 'Tintern Abbey', where the element of spiritual autobiography narrows the gap between speaker and poet, have proved less rewarding to the psychoanalyst, despite recent talk of 'displacement' strategies.

Though it is currently fashionable to underplay the connection, there none the less exists a body of biographical criticism which locates in the fated women of the volume evidence of Wordsworth's remorse at his rejection of Annette Vallon. Unable to confront these feelings directly (one recalls Shelley's opinion of him as 'a solemn and unsexual man'), he hides behind the formal procedures of art. Such a thesis is unequivocally dismissed by Maxwell and Gill (1971) as 'positively misleading'; they instance books by Herbert Read and Hugh L'Anson Faussett as examples of 'psychological speculation . . . recklessly bandied about as hard fact', concluding that 'Neither writer shows any great acquaintance with the poetry' (pp. 171–2). They would doubtless have apoplexy over Margoliouth's conjecture that, had Wordsworth married Annette, he might have 'given up poetry to become a bishop' (1953, p. 12).

Yet the temptation remains, fuelled by the details of *l'affaire Vallon* that have been brought to light through the research of Harper (1916), Legouis (1922) and Moorman (1957), even though Gill, the poet's most recent biographer, unflinchingly asserts that such speculation erects foundations 'on sand' for the

interpretation of the next, crucial, years of Wordsworth's life
(1989, p. 59). Rader therefore offers the cautious observation
that 'the tragic theme of the unwed and deserted mother – as
expressed in such early poems as "The Thorn", "The Mad
Mother" . . . bears witness to his feelings of pity and remorse'
(1967, p. 101), and even Mayo, the champion of Wordsworth's
literary eclecticism, is prepared to admit that these lonely and
forsaken women '*may* . . . have had some personal meaning for
the author' (*WC*, p. 87). More precise and helpful is Mary
Moorman's statement that the authenticity of these ballads,
their 'sharpness of realism', is a direct reflection of the poet's
painful recollection of his desertion of both Annette and his
child. In support of this view, she detects a kinship between the
language of 'The Mad Mother' and some of Annette's letters
(1957, p. 385).

An interesting extension of this idea is advanced by Warren
Stevenson. Referring to a poignant letter in which Annette refers
to her 'husband', Stevenson maintains that Wordsworth was,
like the Ancient Mariner, a haunted figure, a *poète maudit* (Penn
Warren's phrase); that the killing of the albatross, in its 'violation of hospitality, gratitude and sanctity' paralleled Wordsworth's betrayal of lover and child; and that Coleridge's relation
to the poet was like the Wedding Guest's to the Mariner (1983,
p. 74). Such an interpretation acquiesces in Thomas McFarland's argument that the Mariner's kinship with the old men of
Wordsworth's poetry is evidence of 'a projection from the
psycho-dramatic center of *Wordsworth's* fantasy more than from
that of Coleridge' (1972, p. 274). Outlandish or not, this perspective at least offers an alternative to so many unflinching
equations of Mariner and creator; the pity is that McFarland,
warming to his theme, adduces a masculine Wordsworth and
masochistic Coleridge, thereby hinting at a latent homosexuality
in their relationship.

McMaster objects to the Read–Faussett scenario on grounds
that recall Mayo. That his remorse over Annette is 'the one key
to Wordsworth's life and work subsequent to 1792' (1972,
p. 264) conveniently ignores the *conventionality* of the pathos in
many of the poems. In any case, to stress the plight of exploited
women is consciously to pinpoint a specific *social* evil as well as
unwittingly expose personal conflicts. For Bateson these tensions
have a different source; Wordsworth is best understood in the

light of an only half-unconsciously suppressed incestuous feeling for Dorothy. This opinion, together with the view that the neurotic poet of *Lyrical Ballads* is 'a victim of psychical forces' (1956, p. 146) generated during childhood, a troubled spirit whose own disturbances and not his tranquil sense of joy in nature formed the subject and stimulus for his poems, puts him squarely in the camp of Prickett's psychological speculators.

One innovative addition to these ranks merits a mention. Though her approach yet again illustrates the hazards of categorising critics – the book has deconstructive and feminist overtones as well – B. A. Shapiro's *The Romantic Mother* (1983) argues that 'the poetry is largely concerned with the subjective experience of the solitary, isolated personality who feels abandoned and deserted as well as angry and rebellious' (p. xi). Her thesis takes account both of Kenneth Burke's belief that future criticism should give 'more emphasis . . . to matriarchal symbolizations as against the Freudian patriarchal bias' (1967, p. 284), and of Northrop Frye's perception that Romantic poetry *is* preoccupied with Mother Nature 'since alienated man is now cut off from Nature by his consciousness' (1983, p. 18).

Yet Shapiro takes issue with Richard Onorato, who sees Nature in 'Tintern Abbey' as compensatory, an *object* for 'an appetite: a feeling and a love' (l. 81) and unconsciously associated with the 'instinctual gratifications of infancy' (1971, p. 51). Not about a wish for oblivion, a return to the womb of the Earth Mother, 'Tintern Abbey' reaffirms the active links between Man and Nature. Drawing on the language of Freudian analysis, Shapiro discovers a maturing superego which enables the grateful poet to conclude that he has achieved greater self-knowledge, compassion for others and 'a powerful feeling of reintegration with Nature' (1983, p. 98). Such a predictable analysis at least offers a corrective to 'displacers' who negate the poem's celebratory aspects, and suggests that it may, after all, succumb to a psychoanalytic reading less wilfully idiosyncratic than Harold Bloom's.

More exciting in its trail-blazing potential as a Freudian–*feminist* critique is Adela Pinch's 'Female Chatter: Meter, Masochism and the *Lyrical Ballads*' (1988). Posing the vexed question 'why should feminine suffering be such a source of poetic pleasure and power to Wordsworth?', the author finds unlikely support for her analysis of 'Goody Blake and Harry Gill' in Freud's 'A Child is Being Beaten'. And that despite the admission that Freud's investigations of the workings of sexuality and the unconscious also constitute a radical break with that associationist (i.e. Hartleian) psychology so beloved of the poet. But what Wordsworth and Freud do have in common – 'their conceptions of the powerful effect of reading and their investments in the sufferings of the women they represent – can be seen working together in texts that describe how certain formal questions involve gender' (p. 837). In this context Wordsworth's explicit linking of metre to emotional control is significant; such regulation of excitement connects it with sexuality. Pinch quoted Wordsworth's own conclusions on the effects of metrical language as the pleasure which the mind derives from the perception of similitude in dissimilitude. This principle is the great spring of the activity of our minds and their chief feeder, determining the direction of the sexual appetite and all the passions connected with it. Pinch concludes that 'this curious passage' confirms that the pleasure of metre is linked to the 'heterosexist principle', according to which sexual difference, or 'dissimilitude', is essential to the reader's gratification.

Such a connection between metre, erotic pleasure and sexual difference is corroborated by the events of 'Goody Blake and Harry Gill' – the drama of 'a violence tinged with sexuality and masculine panic' (Pinch, 1988, p. 841). Goody Blake's curse, powerfully prophetic, is disarmed because it speaks through *Harry's* chattering. The effect of the curse is to transform Harry's body into a woman's and to change him into an 'automatic, seemingly agentless, generator of metrical sound – female "chatter" ' (p. 846). Put in psychoanalytical terms, 'the masculine subject's masochistic *introjection* ["a process whereby qualities that belong to an external object are absorbed and unconsciously regarded as belonging to the self" – Wright, 1984, p. 80] of a woman's suffering takes place in relation to the effects of a woman's voice' (Pinch, 1988, p. 845). This recalls Freud's assertion that 'the fantasy "A Child is Being Beaten" gratifies masochistic rather than sadistic desires because the children it represents are substitutes for the feminine subject' (p. 847).

Adela Pinch's analysis cannot be adequately summarised here. The article is densely argued and referenced, and repays close reading not just on account of its Freudian complexities, but also because it raises the issue of *gender* in relation to Wordsworth's principal sufferers in *Lyrical Ballads*.

'The Ancient Mariner' has attracted numerous Freudian interpretations, owing to the fascinating inconsistencies in Coleridge's personality, the supposedly symbolical nature of the poem, and Coleridge's self-confessed endeavour to 'transfer from our *inward* nature a human interest and a semblance of truth' (*BL*, ch. 14; emphasis added). Certainly the compelling, if limited, concept of the poem as personal allegory is hard to shift, in terms of its relevance both to Coleridge the man and to the well-springs of imaginative creation. For Kenneth Burke the psychology of this creative process constitutes the abiding interest of the poem: 'I am *not* saying that we need to know of Coleridge's marital troubles and sufferings from drug addiction to appreciate "The Ancient Mariner" ... I *am* saying that, in trying to understand the psychology of the poetic act, we may introduce such knowledge where it is available to give us material for discussing the full nature of this act. If we try to discover what the poem is doing for the poet we may discover a set of generalizations as to what poems do for everybody' (1967, p. 73).

Such reminders are important since critics have rushed in where angels might fear to tread, treating the poem as an abnormal product of an abnormal personality under abnormal conditions, and connecting each and every symbol to Coleridge's unhappy life or traumatised psyche. Two or three examples will suffice. Alethea Hayter, making a case for poppy power, suggests that the poet identified the 'Nightmare Life-in-Death' with the poisonous opiate that induced his nightmares (1968, p. 207), whereas for Empson 'Life-in-Death' with skin 'as white as leprosy' symbolises the Great Whore, or 'that bane of seamen, syphilis' (1964, p. 311). For David Beres (1951) the albatross is to be equated with the poet's mother – a source of protection and plenty (see also Frye, 1983; Onorato, 1971; Shapiro, 1983). The shooting of the bird, like the killing of Christabel's mother, reflects Coleridge's destruction of his mother in his unconscious mind; the ensuing thirst is the oral deprivation that inevitably follows her death. Blessing the water-snakes, themselves symbols of the phallic mother, leads to forgiveness through an acceptance of what was previously rejected. The reward is thirst-quenching rain. Such a Freudian interpretation, based on the biographical

assumption that Coleridge found his mother a profoundly ambi-
valent object, is questioned by Harding on the grounds that, in
seeking 'to understand the poet's fantasy in relation to his life
history', Beres had imported 'psychological doctrines' into the
interpretation, 'the facts of the poem being racked to make them
fit' (Coburn, 1967, p. 61).

If Wilson Knight's 'sexual' interpretation avoids clinical
terminology and merely hints at connections, it does draw on
Freudian ideas. Both men are frustrated – 'the wedding guest
agonisedly torn from human, and especially sexual normality
and conviviality', the Mariner (whose initial act is sadistic and
therefore arguably libidinal) the product of a 'sexually starved
existence in the modern world' where there is 'water, water
everywhere, nor any drop to drink' (1960, p. 86). The 'acceptance of the watery and reptilian' betokens a new and healthier
attitude towards sex, the guilt-laden vision of 'slimy things'
replaced by 'a spontaneous, unsought, upspring of love' (p. 89).
Though Knight admits the specifically sexual element is finally
'left unplaced', at least the ending offers a positive Wordsworthian association with earth and solid fact after nightmare and
transcendent vision' (p. 88). Bostetter, who maintains that
Coleridge's discussion of his dreams frequently brings him to
'the brink of Freudian discoveries', also sees 'shadowy sexual
implications' in the shooting of the Albatross and in the reaction
to the water-snakes, which 'suggests the transcendence of sexual
feelings or the absorption into feelings of benevolence' (1963,
p. 120). But he is more clear-cut than Knight in seeing sexuality
banished from the poem's conclusion; 'in the end it is significant
that the Mariner draws so sharp a distinction between marriage
and the church, placing the emphasis on sexual abstinence'
(p. 121).

In 'Sexual Personae', Camille Paglia follows a burgeoning line
of inquiry in expanding perceptions tossed off by earlier critics –
in this case Bostetter and Knight. She maintains that the
Mariner is the quintessential 'male heroine' – 'a prima donna
who triumphs through exquisite public suffering'. Reminiscent
of those original reviewers who castigated the poem's formal
inconsistencies ('flecked with passages so badly written as to
approach Lewis Carroll parody' – Paglia, 1985, p. 100), her
theory amalgamates psychoanalytical and feminist perspectives
in declaring 'the Bridegroom, Wedding-Guest and Mariner . . .

all aspects of one self, of Coleridge (p. 102). Thus the Bride-groom is the masculine persona, who 'comfortably integrated in society' is enviously glimpsed through the open door; the Wed-ding Guest is an adolescent supplicant 'aspiring to sexual fulfillment and collective joy' who needs merge with the Bride-groom to achieve it. But the spectral self of the Mariner, 'the male heroine or hermaphroditic self who luxuriates in passive suffering', will not allow this to happen. The Wedding Guest will never be the Bridegroom (the doorway to erotic bliss will *only* be breached by a transsexual strategy and in another poem – 'Christabel'). Yet Coleridge, alarmed by this chthonian horror story, 'vainly tries to turn his poem in a redemptive direction' (p. 106). Both Christian ending and tacked-on 'moon gloss' are attempts of the superego to obscure what has come from the amoral, daemonic and visionary id.

Perversely, Paglia discounts the albatross as 'the biggest red herring in poetry' – some mixed metaphor! – as a mere 'vehicle of transgression' (p. 102). It would certainly not fit smoothly into her chthonian scheme of things. How far she is out on a limb in making such a claim is evidenced by Whalley's consensus view: 'The Albatross must be much more than a stage property chosen at random or a mechanical device introduced as a motive of action in the plot. The albatross is the symbol of Coleridge's creative imagination, his eagle' (Boulger, 1969, pp. 84–5).

But other 'sexual' readings have, not surprisingly, also focused on the shooting of the albatross. Warren Stevenson's *Nimbus of Glory*, which catalogues many idiosyncratic interpretations, links the event to traditions in which the arrow is associated with the phallus, the bird with woman. 'It ate the food it ne'er had eat' becomes, by this token, 'a possible symbol of sexual intercourse' (1983, p. 73). At this point Stevenson is pursuing his speculation that the Mariner's act is linked in Coleridge's mind to Words-worth's seduction of Annette, but his main thesis (*pace* Shapiro, Frye) views the act as a violation of the sanctity of the Great Mother of the Gods (Cybele–Demeter), who presides over the poem. When love (blessing the snakes) supplants rape (shooting the bird), the Mariner's psychic reintegration can begin. 'Life-in-Death' a sinister variant of the usually beneficent god-dess, must disappear from a scheme of things in which she has no place.

The foregoing interpretations are mainly Freudian. Maud

Bodkin (1934), on the other hand, applies to the poem the Jungian principle that archetypes (universal symbols) recur in literature as manifestations of the collective unconscious or racial memory. Thus the theme of rebirth is pervasively present in a poem which celebrates harmony and renewal after discord and stagnation. Bodkin's expressive language charts Coleridge's mood-swings from apathy to ecstasy, fluctuations mirrored in the poem's archetypal symbols. Becalmed water thus equates with lassitude, wind with rejuvenation and creative activity. Elizabeth Wright regards this approach, which invites the reader to partake of a communal experience ('wander with it, muse, reflect and prophesy and dream upon it' – Bodkin, 1934, p. 29) as 'an analogous process to Jung's "amplification" ' and a step in the direction of reader-response criticism (Wright, 1984, p. 74).

Bodkin's startling conclusions have frequently been challenged. While accepting that metaphors of sailing strange seas are 'well-established parts of our cultural background' and that wind and calm probably do symbolise Coleridgean extremes of inspiration and inertia, Harding (1941) holds that Bodkin's discussion of rebirth is not adequately grounded in the text. Such a rash of examples finally obscures rather than clarifies. Abrams' essay 'The Correspondent Breeze' argues a similar case against Bodkin's inclusive vision whereby the rebirth archetype is revealed as 'identical in ultimate significance with tragedies, epics, novels and lyrics'. Such a procedure is finally reductive; to reduce a range of artefacts to 'variations upon a timeless theme' is to ignore the literary critic's primary concern with 'the particularity of a work' (Abrams, 1975, p. 51).

In taking these primordial images for granted and seeing high significance in their recurrence, Frye compounds, Wright believes, the Bodkin error. But, while discovering archetypal and mythic elements in 'The Ancient Mariner', Frye regards their origins as essentially *literary*; the practice of the poet is not to imitate nature but to tap the reservoir of archetypes and conventions that reside in the literary universe (Frye, 1957). As he has wryly observed, 'I am still often called a Jungian critic and classified with Maud Bodkin ... whom, on the evidence of that book, I resemble about as closely as the late Sarah Bernhardt' (Frye, 1976, p. 16).

One would be right to anticipate mythic emphases in Bostetter's essay 'The Nightmare World of the Ancient Mariner' (1962), which focuses on the poem's 'appeal to the irrational fears that lurk not far beneath the surface of modern consciousness' (Coburn, 1967, p. 76). We may be intellectually emancipated but these atavistic anxieties remain. It is this preoccupation that makes it difficult, in this post-Freudian, post-Jungian age, to detach the poem from psychological or mythic interpretations. As long ago as 1941, Harding admitted as much: 'If we accept the views of depth psychology, we have to consider the likelihood that . . . the poem has a symbolic significance the writer was not fully aware of . . . and did not . . . focus sharply' (Coburn, 1967, p. 64). So much for 'consistent' readings of the poem. Kenneth Burke reveals further benefits in biographical--*cum*-psychoanalytic approaches while disparaging the excesses of formalism:

> Only if we eliminate biography entirely as a relevant fact about poetic organization can we eliminate the importance of the psychoanalyst's search for universal patterns of biography . . . and we can eliminate biography . . . only if we consider the work of art as if it were written neither by people or for people, involving neither inducements nor resistances. Such can be done but the cost is tremendous . . . .   (1967, pp. 285–6)

Averill's *Wordsworth and the Poetry of Human Suffering* has a psychological cast of a quite different kind. On the one hand it insists that the most successful ballads challenge our stock expectations and therefore open avenues into the reader's own psyche (see also Danby, 1960; Sheats, 1973b). Thus the 'should you think / Perhaps a tale you'll make it' of 'Simon Lee' issues a psychological imperative to 'invest serious thought in the casual act of reading' (Averill, 180, p. 165). But, more specifically and uniquely, Averill detects in these same ballads evidence of Wordsworth's interest in those pathological conditions described in *Zoönomia* – that ponderous medical treatise by the fashionable poet–philosopher Erasmus Darwin. Thus Harry Gill's substitution of 'imaginations for realities' derives from the chapter on 'Diseases of Increased Volition' (Darwin, 1796, II, 356; quoted in Averill, 1980, p. 155); the Mad Mother's suckling recalls Darwin's analysis of post-natal depression where breast-feeding is declared the remedy; the shepherd's enforced sale of

his flock ('The Last of the Flock') reveals a 'maniacal hallucina-
tion' that overrides paternal emotions, (Darwin, 1796, II, 360;
quoted in Averill, 1980, p. 157). These poems thus become
'experiments' in a genuinely scientific and psychological sense –
poetical illustrations of pathological states of mind.

Marxist, historicist and problematic readings

'Marxism, of course, is not an entity. There is not one Marxism,
there is not one Marxist practice . . .' ('An Interview with
Jacques Derrida', in Easthope, 1988, p. 236). Such an assertion
by the darling of deconstruction perhaps explains my catch-all
title. Yet if we go back to Christopher Caudwell's seminal
Illusion and Reality (1937), we encounter an identifiably Marxist
critique that has anticipated a number of later materialist
readings. There Caudwell characterises Wordsworth as a revolutionary bourgeois whose rebellion takes the form of an
illusory return to natural man. Steeped in Rousseau he seeks
freedom and beauty – all that man now lacks because of the
alienating effect of the Industrial Revolution – *in* nature. Such a
retour à la Nature is accelerated by his growing sense of
disillusion in political alternatives. Revolution has offered no
enduring freedom; man must therefore return to his own best
nature.

   This sounds a pretty standard analysis. But Caudwell goes
further in asserting that the world of nature which Wordsworth
depicts in *Lyrical Ballads* is an idealised one in which industry
and its personal benefits are conveniently ignored. Wordsworth
the bourgeois poet exists on the *products* of industrialism while
celebrating a natural scene untainted by industry. But, argues
Caudwell, to get critics to see the palpable link between leisure
and economic activity, to admit that surplus produce has allowed
Wordsworth to live 'in austere idleness' in the countryside,
'would be to pierce the bourgeois illusion and expose the
artificiality of such Nature poetry' (1937, p. 98). Wordsworth's
Preface also embraces the mistaken theory that 'natural' (i.e.
conversational) language is preferable to artificial (i.e. literary)
utterance; on Caudwell's view, all language is both natural (the
products of man's struggle with nature) and artificial (directed
to social ends). In a single direct reference to the ballads them-

selves, he concludes (as have many from Coleridge on), 'under the spell of this theory some of Wordsworth's worst poetry is written' (p. 99). We hardly need to be told that he is probably thinking of the banalities of 'The Thorn'.

Maclean (1950) charges Wordsworth with elitism of a different kind. Proclaiming that 'to understand Wordsworth's reading of the peasant, we must look more largely at his performance as poet', he isolates two emotional modes: the first a concern with 'feeling as an imaginative response to the imagery of nature', the second with 'the affections – feelings that are homely and domestic' (p. 96). While *Lyrical Ballads* operates mainly in the second mode, Maclean detects elitism in the poet's implicit assumption that 'feeling as imagination . . . reserved for himself and the child ("best philosopher")' is 'something almost too good for the common people', a prejudice confirmed by the whole eighteenth-century school of 'rural reverie' (p. 96). Perhaps this now-venerable charge, which can only be levelled at 'Tintern Abbey' with any justification, goes some way towards explaining the poem's fascination for historicists.

Yet Maclean is quick to redress the balance when stressing how important for the progress of poetry the second mode of feeling proved. It helped create 'a new popular aesthetic which located the world of passionate feeling, not in mediaeval castle or renaissance palace but rather in the cottage, on the soil of common life' (p. 97). Such affections, linked to solitude and smallholdings (Bradley regards 'solitude' and 'soul' as synonymous in Wordsworth) pervade *Lyrical Ballads*; the book 'on which man's emotional life is written' is the first link in a chain that will in time join up Hardy, Lawrence and Heaney.

The tension that exists between society and Romantic artist is also explored in Raymond Williams' *Culture and Society* (1958). He sees the increasing emphasis on the twin and related notions of genius ('the autonomous creative artist') and art's superior reality (its 'penetration to a sphere of universal truth') as a reaction to an increasingly materialist world bent on denying such claims. In a discussion that recalls Maclean, he interprets Wordsworth's proclamation of the artist's role as 'upholder and preserver, carrying everywhere with him relationship and love' as a reaction to the aggressive individualism and economic ties of the new society (1987 edn, pp. 39–42). The Preface is evidence of such a reaction where it berates those who regard poetry as a 'source of amusement and idle pleasure', or art as a mere commodity. Williams believes that Wordsworth's view had important repercussions: in positive terms it provided the basis for a critique of industrialism (via the superiority of art); less happily it tended to isolate art and artist ('the free play of genius found it increasingly difficult to consort with the free play of the market' – p. 47).

Fascinating though it be, this analysis has only an oblique relevance to *Lyrical Ballads* and, as with Caudwell, take us to the ideas of the Preface rather than the ballads – to context, not text. Nor do such critiques entirely avoid what, for Eagleton, is the 'vulgar Marxist mistake of raiding literary works for their ideological content and relating them directly to the class struggle or the economy' (1976, p. 24) or the political conditions of the day. In any event, according to Lukács and Marcuse, ideology in art is transmitted through the form rather than through the work's abstractable content. Following this tack, Hamilton's *Wordsworth* (1987) maintains that the poet's choice of poetry (buttressed, it must be said by prose) as his instrument of persuasion in *Lyrical Ballads* is a political gesture. While he may be conservative in highlighting the unchangeable condition of suffering humanity, his choice of the traditionally contemplative mode of *poetry* to express this sympathy is a form of radicalism 'lending to poetry a significance rare in its history' (Hamilton, 1987, p. 4): modern society has generally relegated it to a 'marginal' status in the hierarchies of written expression. By this gesture, Wordsworth emerges as a 'revolutionary bourgeois' of a different kind.

Unlike Hamilton, Anthony Easthope sees in *Lyrical Ballads* the expression of a formal conservatism. Despite the pronouncements of the Preface, the poems themselves reaffirm the dominance of that essentially bourgeois metre, the iambic pentameter. Any programme that aims to imitate 'the real language of man' should, on Easthope's reasoning, 'tend logically to free verse' (1983, p. 133). This opinion, which ignores the fact that Wordsworth was inevitably a man of an age which had not yet heard of *vers libre*, needs to be set against Hamilton's insistence that the very use of poetry was a radical act; or Simpson's detection in Wordsworth's avoidance of dialect a deliberate refusal to draw on a language potentially divisive – because of its proletarian associations (Simpson, 1987).

In *The Correspondent Breeze* (1984), which identifies recent trends in Wordsworth scholarship, Abrams notes that 'problematic' readings of *Lyrical Ballads* proliferated in the 1960s. Tracing the immediate source of this critical propensity to structuralism and uncovering deeper roots in Hegel, Abrams saw its characteristic procedure as being to isolate problematic areas in the surface meaning and then seize on these as 'a clue to a deep structure manifesting an unspoken preoccupation of the poet' (p. 151). If such a 'procedure' now sounds familiar, particularly among critics who seek to undermine traditional interpretations, it is worth recalling that back in 1960 Paul De Man, in a seminal essay that has proved remarkably influential on newer generations of anti-transcendental commentators, observed a paradoxical dialectic, a problematic tension, in the attempts of Romantic poets to reconcile the polarities of consciousness (imagination) and what is not conscious (nature). In the conclusion to his essay De Man argues that Wordsworth's imagination 'marks ... a possibility for consciousness to exist entirely by and for itself, independently of all relationship with the outside world, without being moved by an intent aimed at a part of this world'. In fact, 'Wordsworth ... insists that the imagination can only come into full play when "the light of sense goes out" and when thought reaches a point at which it is "its own perfection and reward"' (De Man, 1960; in Abrams, 1972, p. 144).

Other books on Wordsworth published at that time reached similar, if less rigorously philosophical, conclusions. David Perkins undertook to 'go beneath the "surface"' of the poetry to explore the negative implications that ran contrary to the poet's overt intentions, and discovered, like De Man, a divide between human nature and the rest of nature that made inevitable a recourse to symbol in the poetry (Perkins, 1959, p. 22). David Ferry likewise alluded to 'the hostility between "surface" and "deeper" meanings' which reject or devalue the very experiences which express them (1959, p. 12). Geoffrey Hartman, the best and best-known of these pioneering 'problematists', saw in Wordsworth an un-Blakean rejection of total imaginative involvement and a constant yearning for the more solid realities of man or nature. It is this unresolved opposition between imagination and nature that, for Hartman, arrests Wordsworth's progress to fully fledged visionary poet.

These theories, it could be argued, are not very helpful to us. After all, *Lyrical Ballads*, like most art, represents an attempt to make sense of experience, to impose meaning upon it. Such approaches merely complicate or even obfuscate the processes of interpretation. Moreover, they only work with the solipsistic poetry, not with narrative and 'objective' ballads. It is entirely predictable that these critics (Miller and Bloom also) concentrate on *The Prelude*. None the less Hartman does tackle *Lyrical Ballads*, seeing its central problem as that of trying to reconcile reality to dream, to achieve what he calls 'supernatural naturalism' (1964, p. 143). He locates Wordsworth's attempt at this reconciliation in his dramatisation of *loss*, by emphasising both its physical and its spiritual dimension. 'Cleaving' is the abiding passion of the unfortunates that the poems portray; they 'cleave to one thing or idea in order to be saved from a still deeper sense of separation . . . from all that stands between the self and its nakedness' (pp. 143–3). In 'The Last of the Flock' the farmer 'cleaves' to sheep because possessions are also a spiritual need and, like all 'realia', serve to keep the imagination in check; the young girl 'cleaves' to the idea that seven *is* still seven, 'under the spell of a nature that still weaves a charm against her own, too powerful imagination' (p. 145). Elsewhere, for Hartman, Wordsworth complicates tone. In 'Simon Lee' and 'The Idiot Boy', the poet undermines the stock tradition of the 'moving accident' and instead concentrates on the *feelings* both of the characters (Simon and Betty) and of the intrusive poet/narrator. Such a 'displacement from incident to character, from plot interest to psychology' (p. 148) also characterises 'The Thorn'.

Hartman deserves space for two reasons. Alone of the so-called 'hermeneutic mafia' (T. Hillis Miller and Harold Bloom are the other members), he has pronounced at some length on *Lyrical Ballads*. Moreover the chapter in which he does so has, with its terminology of 'displacement' and 'problematic', proved very suggestive to newer cohorts of critics, both American and English, who focus on the literary text as a realisation of underlying systems. Hartman foregrounds 'cleaving' in a way that invites analogy with his own kind of critical perspective – such a *conscious* ritual is the palimpsest of a psyche covering up deeply ingrained but non-visible erasures in the sub-text about loss, separation and death.

But, though Hartman has responded to the stimulus of

post-structuralism (especially Derrida), he remains difficult to pigeonhole. Despite his watchword 'beyond formalism', he still combines close textual analysis with those deconstructive strategies already embryonic in his discussion of *Lyrical Ballads*. It remains a matter for regret that in *The Unremarkable Wordsworth* (1987), 'Wordsworth Revisited' alone returns to these poems, arguing that they are not conventional ballads of protest but post-crisis poetry, the expression of a mind restored to health after 'long sickness' (p. 4). In an analysis that recalls both Marxist commentaries and the poet's own pronouncements in the Preface, he diagnoses this malignancy as 'a disturbed relation between man and his environment caused by city life'. Such organic and social dissolutions, coupled with the deteriorating course of the French Revolution, convinced the poet that social liberty must be built on personal freedom. Like Lear, Hartman concludes, in a persuasive parallel, Wordsworth has been betrayed into 'autonomy, into self-dependence' (p. 5). The English countryside acting in concert with Dorothy and Coleridge would provide the restorative balm.

That comment is reminiscent of the conclusion of 'Tintern Abbey', a poem singled out not only by Hartman and his friend Harold Bloom, but by each and every American historicist (or materialist or theorist) discussed in the remainder of this chapter. Bloom's interpretation, based on his complex theory of 'misprision', is in fact his only contribution to the body of criticism on Wordsworth's poems in *Lyrical Ballads*. A 'strong' poem, 'Tintern Abbey' succeeds by virtue of its capacity to 'misread' and therefore devalue its predecessors. Behind its orotund effects lurks Milton; it is Miltonic sublimity, repressed out of the poem, which generates the poem's force. Such hermeneutic virtuosity, more Freudian than Derridean, needs to be analysed at source (Bloom, 1976, p. 56). So too Miller's brief foray into *Lyrical Ballads* in *The Linguistic Moment* (1985), which concentrates, idiosyncratically, on the extreme particularity of such poems as 'Lines Left . . . in a Yew-tree'. Such long-winded titles are evidence of the author's need to 'identify the act whereby the poem was given physical existence'; Wordsworth's concern with stones (the thorn is 'like a stone with lichens . . . overgrown') and inscriptions both symbolises the poet's wish for permanence and provides actual materials for its fulfilment (p. 81). Like Bloom, Miller has often been accused of ingenuity at the expense of direct engagement with the text: certainly it is a pity that his remarks are not amplified.

For the Marxist critic Frank Lentriccia, all these scholars are merely masquerading as innovators. In reality they are up-holders of an 'aestheticising and autonomising approach', quasi-formalists still 'concerned to demonstrate the history-transcending qualities of the text' (summarised in Salusinszky, 1987, p. 177). Undoubtedly more to his taste are critics who see works as inseparable from the conditions of their production and reception in history and who use a mix of methods and disci-plines to arrive at cultural and political conclusions. Simpson's *Wordsworth's Historical Imagination* (1987) provides a roll-call of such names, part of 'a field that one might think of as a collective project' (p. 20). Some – Aers, Cook and Punter (1981), Barrell (1988), McGann (1983), Butler (1981) and the earlier Woodring (1961), Thompson (1969) and Jacobus (1976) – feature in these pages. One could add Glen (1983) and Easthope (1983) to his list. What they have in common is not just the concept of a 'displaced' or 'alienated' text which, neither unitary or autotelic, operates largely in terms of what it suppresses, but the belief that the text thereby offers a critique of *society* at odds with its avowed statements. Unwilling to accept the post-structuralist 'commit-ment to the anarchic superficiality of language', Simpson's self-professed 'materialist approach' insists on going 'beyond and behind' its surface 'to discover a system of energies . . . not to be conjured away into merely additional fictions and substitu-tions. Mirror upon mirror is *not* all the show' (1987, p. 19). If Jordan is also temporarily corralled in this stockade, it is because his *Why the Lyrical Ballads?* (1976), shows what the poems were *not*: not topical statements, not a reflection of contemporary preoccupations with 'genre'. For Simpson these evasions are significant: we need to 'understand their *failure* or *reluctance* to decide between or among the variously available models for clear "political" statement' (1987, p. 20; emphasis added).

The language of many of these critics, heavily spiced with jargon, often rhetorically self-indulgent, does not always make for easy reading. Nor do they all toe a party line. McGann, for example, disapproves of 'Marxist critics, like Althusser' who would 'like to separate poetry and art from ideology' (1983, p. 12). Such a view is, in McGann's opinion, misguided, since romantic poetry 'both "reflects" and reflects upon those individual and social forms of human life which are available to the artist's observation'. But Romantic ideology suffers from a major illusion. Dominated by 'an uncritical absorption' in its 'own self-representation', it mistakenly asserts that 'only a poet and his works can transcend a corrupting appropriation by "the world" of politics and money' (p. 13). The 'real' message of 'Tintern Abbey' – a suitable case for treatment both by McGann and Marjorie Levinson – is that Wordsworth has 'lost the world merely to gain his own immortal soul' (p. 88). That he singles out 'Tintern Abbey' as a 'drama of displacement' is both a deliberate challenge to posterity's collusion in its 'greatness' and the product of his prejudice against the transcendental element in the poem and in the language of so much critical obeisance to it – Abrams is not alone among traditionalists in discovering in the poem the conception of an ordered, teleological universe. Only by suppressing the 'world' (the blood-letting of the French Revolution, the plight of the country poor) can the poet conclude, apparently harmoniously, on a note of reconciliation.

Simpson's historicist treatment of 'Simon Lee' is less sure of itself. Wordsworth's assault on literary 'decorum' (he is prepared to record the inconclusive, even inconsequential event of the uncut stump) is charted well enough, but Simpson's attempt to categorise the text as 'displaced' is tortuously pursued and issues in the inconclusive conclusion that the poem's uneasy mix of 'emotional release, honest sympathy, condescension and embarrassment . . . can be coherently related to the conflicting aspirations and anxieties in the Wordsworthian psyche' (1987, p. 153). In an argument that echoes Caudwell, Simpson equates the poet's dilemma with Simon's: cutting through the stump may give the momentary illusion of power and freedom but without patrons or help Wordsworth too is incapable of earning a living on his own (p. 153). Other critics, Simpson assures us, have also found the poem worryingly inconsistent in ways which point to 'a serious turbulence and insecurity in Wordsworth's mind, and in the public languages available to it' (p. 158). He cites Andrew Griffin's interpretation of the ending as a 'characteristically fumbling apology' (1977, p. 399) – which chimes with Hartman's and Danby's opinion that the uncomfortable platitudes cry out for a more purposive conclusion. More positively, Heather Glen finds in the poem an exploration of complexities in situations which the magazines reduced to mere clichés. Not summed up by the usual (magazine) appeal to pity, we have instead the awkward inconclusiveness of 'the present perfect continuous tense' emphasising irresolution (1983, p. 239).

Irresolution is a theme in Aers, Cook and Punter's compilation of essays. Arguing that Romantic texts can best be understood as part of 'a complex nexus of dynamic relations between literature, society and available ideologies' (1981, p. 2), they link 'The Ancient Mariner' to Coleridge's own unsatisfied creativity. His own career (the creator, *par excellence*, of *incomplete* poems) mirrors the circular progress of a Mariner unable to reconcile the 'contradictory identities of criminal and scapegoat' (p. 94). Yet, paradoxically, such unresolved contradiction gives the poem its power. The confines of a settled Christian community are not for the Mariner; instead the confidence in a theodicy is displaced by the poem's inconclusive ending.

Paul Hamilton's *Wordsworth* (1986) provides a useful encapsulation of these new approaches, announcing itself in the publisher's 'blurb' as the first book at student level 'to make available . . . the recent – and transforming – developments in Wordsworth studies that have come from new critical theories'. Undeniably accessible, Hamilton's book perceives the narrator–character tensions as supplying a unifying theme in *Lyrical Ballads*. Thus it is the adult speaker's failure to impose his view on the child in 'We Are Seven' which constitutes the poem's triumph. His analysis recalls Danby, Sheats and, more recently, Jacobus and Glen in highlighting Wordsworth's capacity – deliberately and artfully employed – to unsettle the preconceptions of narrator or reader. In this context, 'Lines Left . . . in a Yew-tree' (virtually ignored before the advent of these 'New Wordsworthians') is pivotal – an object lesson to the would-be reader of the volume. The poem's protagonist, reacting to public neglect by becoming yet more reclusive, thereby becomes alienated from those 'shared public responses which Wordsworth artfully shapes to his own ends throughout the rest of *Lyrical Ballads*' (Hamilton, 1986, p. 51). The solitary's pride in privacy is an illusory goal and leads only to an early grave: 'In this deep vale / He died, this seat his only monument'. It is up to us not to distance *ourselves* from the plight of the poor and thereby end up divorced from real human concerns.

Two studies deserve brief mention though their thrust is more general than specific. Siskin's *The Historicity of Romantic Discourse* (1988) claims, like Hamilton, an innovative role – this time in displacing 'Visionary Imagination with Revisionary Language and "Organicism" with "Irony"' (p. 5), though the revisions seem to encourage negativity. For him Romantic criticism (beginning with Arnold's 'surgical lyricization of Wordsworth') has mistakenly workshipped various shibboleths: the cult of literary personality, the primary poetic text, the capacity of Wordsworth to transcend 'the everyday world without unduly interfering with it'. By now such arguments will have a familiar ring; and, anyway, apart from 'Tintern Abbey' *Lyrical Ballads* contains little by Wordsworth that is transcendental. Indeed, for Marilyn Butler (1981) the volume is a *culmination* of thirty years of poetry based on popular metres and humble subject matter, fundamentally neoclassical in its rejection of adornment and its concern to reach a wide audience. It is in the very consistency of Wordsworth's application of such precepts and through observing *general* principles of simplicity and sincerity that the volume's originality resides, not in dramatic force (Parrish) or sheer excellence (Mayo). That these poems were later branded as subversive was the result of a growing conservatism in Coleridge which associated Wordsworth's 1798 experiment with the radical tendency of the Enlightenment. Though Butler's analysis refrains from discovering any radical displacements in the poems themselves, it is buttressed by the same wide-ranging concern for context as characterises other members of this 'school' of critics.

4

Lyrical Ballads: Criticism of the Major Poems

'The Ancient Mariner'

It is only one among innumerable ironies surrounding *Lyrical Ballads* that the most misunderstood poem in 1798 was 'The Ancient Mariner'. Wordsworth even considered dropping it from a second edition, to 'put in its place some little things which would be more likely to suit the common taste' (letter to Cottle, 24 June 1799, *EL*, p. 227). Yet it is now regarded as one of the supreme poems of any age, an inspiration to famous artists (Doré, Peake), frequently dramatised (recently by Peter Bogdanov at the National Theatre in London), and so exhaustively discussed that it can easily justify a critical survey on its own. Indeed, its status as part of a collective enterprise is usually conveniently forgotten, a process illustrated in the Casebook series. The *Lyrical Ballads* Casebook focuses exclusively on Wordsworth; 'The Ancient Mariner', along with 'other poems' by Coleridge, is accorded separate treatment.

This ascension to an exalted place in the canon is very much a twentieth-century phenomenon. It reflects a shift from the Victorian portrait of Coleridge the moral mess – Stephen (1892) talks of 'early promise blighted and vast powers all but running hopelessly to seed', and Pater of 'his faintness, his broken memory, his intellectual disquiet' (*Appreciations*, 1889, in *CC*, p. 111) – to Coleridge the major poet and celebrant of the imaginative life. By 1949 Lionel Stevenson was able to discern warring factions of 'Mariner' criticism:

To one school . . . it is an elaborate allegory of Coleridge's theories . . . to other groups of critics it is an incoherent transcription of the poet's opium-inspired dreams. The new psychoanalytical critics interpret it as an unconscious revelation of his guilt complexes and sexual repressions.

(1949, p. 34)

While such an analysis seems simplistic, this rekindling of academic interest in the poem, sparked off by J. L. Lowes' *The Road to Xanadu* (1927), is now a matter of critical history. A classic of early-twentieth-century criticism, the work's thrust probably owed something to the Imagist movement's predilection for concrete imagery. Thus the unique appeal of 'The Ancient Mariner' resided in clusters of vivid pictorial effects which the critic, in a stupendous effort of scholarship, sought to trace in the poet's 'cormorant' reading, using his 'Gutch-Memorandum Book' as starting-point. At the most basic level then, Lowes

firmly established the sources for the major images and scenes in the poem – the mariner, the albatross, the voyage, the water-snakes, much of the supernatural machinery – in two kinds of popular eighteenth-century reading, travel books of exploration and discovery, and popular ballads of the day.

(Boulger, 1969, p. 5)

But Lowes – no mere source-detector – concluded that Coleridge's main contribution to our understanding of the imagination and its creative process lay not 'in his metaphysical lucubrations on it after it was lost, but in the implications of his practice while he yet possessed the power' (1927, p. xii). But the 'Road' leads to yet wider vistas: it becomes a romantic celebration of 'the human spirit, and the imagination voyaging through chaos and reducing it to clarity and order' (p. 396). Such heady stuff, over 600 pages of it, began the poem's latest recuperation: students thronged to the lectures of this academic celebrity as he 'described, not how the "The Ancient Mariner" came about, nor the Mariner's destination, but the enormous range of interlocked reading out of which the poem set sail' (Coburn, 1967, p. 2).

Lowes' own breathless, highly wrought style betrays the same preoccupation with imagery as his scholarly method. Unsurprisingly, one of his favourite metaphors is the quintessentially Romantic one of the well, the 'deep well of unconscious cerebration' whose waters 'possessed of a peculiar potency' are where 'images and impressions converge and blend':

> The more kaleidoscopic the chaos of shattered fragments of memory, the more innumerable the reflections and refractions between the shifting elements. And in Coleridge's case there was assuredly God's plenty! Nightingales, and snake-birds, and footless birds of Paradise; the fauna of polar and of tropic seas, and of strange inland pools and subterranean streams; the daemons of the elements, stars and their angel guardians, maniacs and murderers and mutineers; shipwrecks and gibbets; dew-drops and dunghills and diamonds and lichened stones; haloes over frosty meadows, and rainbows in the spray, the ice-blink and the luminous wake of ships . . . .
>
> (Lowes, 1927, p. 56)

Critics have been unable to find common ground in regard to other reverberations generated by *The Road to Xanadu*. Coburn, noting the colossal range of annotation in the work – the index alone runs to forty pages, the notes to 170 – suggests that it gave students 'a new awareness ... that Coleridge's famous erudition was not to be divorced from the seemingly simple and effortless poems' (1967, p. 3) – that the philosopher had *not* killed off the poet. Beer, while stressing the element of 'detection' and Lowes' capacity to transmit 'the excitement of successful literary scholarship in action' (1971, p. 191), countered that the book's very emphasis on imagery at the expense of meaning did devalue Coleridge's status as a *thinker*. It has exacerbated the situation whereby 'many readers enjoy the poem without ever noticing that anything more than a simple, overt moral is intended; and this has led in turn to a conception of Coleridge as the naive poet of wonder' (Beer, 1959, p. 134). More recently Bostetter has also observed that Lowes merely renders the poem more 'palatable' and less profound. In arguing that Coleridge uses an ethical framework 'only to give the illusion of inevitable sequence to superb inconsequence', Lowes is manipulative and dishonest. He needs to be taken to task for refusing to admit that 'dreams reveal anything about dreamers or indeed have any relevance to waking life' (1962, in *CC*, p. 191).

It is a comment on the heavyweight presence of Lowes that subsequent critics frequently begin by quoting his conclusions. And, though no one has attempted precisely to duplicate his scholarly method – it is dauntingly difficult to emulate anyway – his central notion that the poet's reading fixed in his sub-conscious images that might resurface, magically crystallised, during the creative act has stimulated a number of more narrowly psychoanalytical interpretations of 'The Ancient Mariner' (see 'Psychoanalytical Perspectives' in Chapter 3).

In the forum of *post-war* discussion of the poem, Robert Penn Warren's 100-page essay occupies a similarly monolithic place. A jewel in the crown of 'New Criticism', its *formal* preoccupa-tions are considered elsewhere, but it does begin by taking issue with Lowes – who else? – and his stated refusal to consider the possibility of any didactic content because it would shatter the world of inconsequence and illusion which is the very essence of the poem (Lowes, 1927, p. 277). Warren's rejoinder, anticipat-ing Beer and Bostetter, is that such an imprecise reading implies that the poem has 'no reference to reality' (1946, p. 203), that themes thereby become mere structural devices and that the message is consequently devalued. These strictures offer clues to the direction of Warren's criticism – which regards the work as overtly didactic *and* richly symbolic. For him the primary theme, 'the outcome of the fable taken at its face value as a story of crime and punishment and reconciliation', is 'the theme of sacramental vision or the theme of the "One Life" ' (p. 214). The secondary theme of the imagination – 'the context of values in which the fable is presented' – is conveyed, in large measure, by a coherently organised set of symbols. Thus Warren's reading of 'The Ancient Mariner', while seeing its message as important (as Lowes does not), also sets great store by a unifying symbol-ism that literally as well as metaphorically sheds light on the narrative: moonlight (associated with creation and the second-ary imagination), the albatross (linked to both moon and fog) and the breeze (a 'creative' wind). This 'symbolic cluster' of wind, bird, fog and moon is closely related to the imagination: in killing the bird the Mariner commits a crime not only against the sacramental world of nature (his *other* theme) but also against the creative imagination. In this pattern, 'the bloody sun at

noon' (l. 108) is, on a realistic level, a malevolent force, a
harbinger of heat and drought; on a symbolic level it is, 'to adopt
the poet's later terminology, "that mere reflective faculty"
(reason without imagination) that "partook of Death" ' (Warren,
1946, p. 241).

Though Warren, himself a poet of substance, warned against
'a fixed system of point-to-point equation', Bostetter accuses him
(as do many other critics) of that very practice: of superimposing
upon the poem 'a rigid and consistent pattern of meaning which
can only be maintained by forcing certain key episodes into
conformity with the pattern and ignoring others' (1962, in *CC*,
p. 184). Whilst he concedes that most critics now accept the
Warren interpretation of sacramental vision as primary theme,
Bostetter reminds us of the opposition: of Griggs, who 'feels that
no moral meaning should be sought in the poem' (1934, p. 687)
and Lowes, who contends that "the moral" of the poem, *outside
the poem*, will not hold water' (1927, p. 300; in *CC*, p. 185).
Bostetter's own conclusion is somewhere in between: the poem
has *no* moral meaning 'beyond our fears and desires' (*CC*,
p. 196). 'Like the Mariner's experience, the universe is the
projection not of reasoned beliefs but of irrational fears and guilt
feelings' (p. 193). Taking the game of dice as pivotal, Bostetter
argues that *caprice* is the decisive factor in the Mariner's
punishment: it is symptomatic of a universe of unpredictable
forces where the punishment is as sadistic as the initial act. Such
arbitrary elements give the poem a sense of nightmare rather
than sacrament. Even the gnomic conclusion is seen as 'oppress-
ively puritanical', the final image that of an 'eternally alienated
Mariner alienating in his turn the Wedding Guest', now 'robbed
of his happiness and the spontaneous participation in the
marriage feast (which is really the "one life") and forced to share
the disillusioned wisdom and guilt of the Mariner' (p. 190).

But Coleridge, like his Mariner, has at least reached a
compromise; this inexorable morality pattern allows him to
complete what would otherwise be yet another inconclusive
fragment of poetry.

In part, the sweeping affirmation of the moral reflects the
excited relief and gratitude of both Mariner and Coleridge at
having reached even so partial a resolution of the Mariner's
problem as the conclusion of the poem presents. The Mariner

is allowed to live and to return to his own country; he is condemned (and privileged) to tell his tale; he has power and importance, a certain freedom of will and movement, a hope of salvation. He has arrived, at least, at a *modus vivendi*. And perhaps one reason why Coleridge was able to finish *The Rime* is that he had been able to work his way through within the structure of the narrative to a more or less positive resolution.

(Bostetter, 1963, p. 117)

Here Bostetter anticipates recent deconstructive approaches. Indeed, his end-game analysis finds an echo in the materialist interpretation of Aers, Cook and Punter (1981).

Of course there has always been controversy over the poem's meaning. If Coleridge's celebrated reply to Mrs Barbauld – that the poem's 'only or chief fault . . . was the obtrusion of the moral sentiment so openly on the reader as a principle or cause of action in a work of such pure imagination' – was intended to deter the message-hunters, it appears only to have intensified their zeal. Not that they necessarily approved what they found. Sir Leslie Stephen took issue with a moral 'which would apparently be that people who sympathise with a man who shoots an albatross will die in prolonged torture of thirst' (1892, p. 35). Irving Babbitt, on the other hand, objected to the proposition that the Mariner could be 'relieved of the burden of his transgression by admiring the color of water-snakes' (1919, quoted in Beer, 1959, p. 134). Beer in his turn has questioned the validity of a concluding injunction which he finds not only banal but alien to the rest of the work. 'The Mariner urges the wedding guest to love "all creatures great and small" and yet apparently disapproves of his attending the wedding feast – where such love might be expected to find high expression' (Beer, 1959, p. 135). Such a view runs counter to Humphry House's earlier claim that the conclusion *can* be seen in the total context, that 'after the richness and terror . . . it is no more a banal apothegm, but a moral which has its meaning, *because it has been lived*' (1953, p. 92).

These assertions are evidence of a flourishing line of critical inquiry, a process wryly observed by John Beer as 'several attempts to interpret it as something more than a racy ballad with a conventional moral' (1959, p. 133). Indeed, House takes for granted the poem's 'serious moral and spiritual bearing on human life' (1953, p. 92), enlisting the heavyweight support of Tillyard, Bowra and Warren. He might have added that as long ago as 1932–3 its message was being debated in the pages of *PMLA* by Professors Stallknecht and Nitchie!

But House refuses to fall into the trap of offering a precise interpretation. For him, the images 'gather their bearing . . . 'by gradual increment', by 'progressively rich associations'. The killing of the bird thus 'becomes a violation of a great sanctity at the animal, human and spiritual levels: but these levels are only gradually declared as the poem proceeds, just as the Mariner only gradually discovered the consequences of what he had done. Our enlightenment runs parallel with his' (1953, p. 97).

One of the more persuasive attempts to link the poem's meaning to Coleridge's philosophy is provided by R. L. Brett who takes issue with the commonly held dualistic view that Coleridge 'never fully brought creative experience and critical theories into relation' (House) and that in any case the theoretical positions were adopted too late to affect the poem's message. For Brett the gospel according to Lowes lacks credibility: Coleridge was *not* 'a sublime somnambulist spinning poetry from his subconscious mind'; 'The Ancient Mariner' offers a coherent system of belief that bears no relation to the irrational, nightmarish world of Bostetter's interpretation. The poem reveals not only the sequence of an orthodox religious experience ('a symbolization of the Christian experience of conversion'), but also the operation of the imagination, 'which can mediate between the individual mind and external reality'. The work of art is real life 'organised and shaped by the imagination into a pattern that will . . . provoke the understanding' (Brett, 1971, p. 107).

If Warren's essay became a stalking-horse for interpretations valorising the poem's paraphrasable meaning, it also provoked responses both from 'symbol-hunters' and from their opponents. Elder Olson (see 'Formalist Approaches' in Chapter 3) took issue with both Warren's conclusions (a symbolic poem) and his method (its susceptibility to systematic analysis), a position also taken up by Stoll (1948), who saw little sign of symbolist intent on Coleridge's part either during the poem's gestation or in later discussions, and by Elizabeth Schneider (1953), a Chicago critic like Olson. Her essay, which contains the additional, if questionable, argument that a 'ballad' could not have been the vehicle for serious ideas, provoked a ten-page refutation from Warren. 'The Ancient Mariner' was once more living up to its reputation for notoriety!

John Beer, in contrast, was prepared to find symbols while making the now-familiar noises about rejecting 'a rigid symbolic structure into which every detail can be fitted like a jigsaw puzzle' (1959, p. 173). He questioned, for example, Warren's pat equation of the moon with the creative impulse and instead linked it to both imagination *and* lunacy. Uncovering the poem's roots in occult sources as various as neoplatonism and Egyptian mythology, as well as in Berkeley and travelogues, Beer reasoned that the Mariner, in killing the bird, destroys the connection between sun (the world's inner harmony) and serpent. Both therefore become divorced from and alien to human nature – the serpent loathsome, the sun mere heat and wrath.

In the blessing scene the conjunction of snakes and moon *prefigures* the ideal harmony of the universe. But it is during the vision of his ghostly shipmates singing to the sun ('Around, around, flew each sweet sound / Then darted to the sun:' – ll.343–4) that the Mariner comes to a full awareness of the sun's real significance – a symbol both of God and of the image of God in human reason, the normative 'true sun' of mystics and poet alike.

Such mythic and symbolic discussions of the poem have proliferated since Bodkin's Jungian treatment (1934) and Warren's essay (1946). Warren Stevenson (1983), for example, regards the crime as perpetrated against the Great Mother (Cybele–Demeter), an allusive reading which, like Karl Kroeber's, is unnecessarily recondite. Kroeber (1957), like Boulger, foregrounds its roots in epic rather than ballad. He maintains that the poem is a stylised quest epic; the killing of the bird is related to the slaying of the sun god's oxen in the *Odyssey*. No charge of abstruseness can be levelled against Frye, who sees 'alienated man cut off from nature by his consciousness' as 'the Romantic equivalent of post-Edenic Adam' (1983, p. 18). The Mariner, 'compelled recurrently to tell a story whose moral is reintegration with nature', is a pivotal part of this myth; his redemption is his recovery of this original unity with nature which 'being born as a subjective consciousness has broken'. This idea both explains the presence of mother-centred symbols,

and Wordsworth's appeals to 'Mother Nature' (for instance, the
'Mother Earth' of 'Expostulation and Reply'). The links with
'mother-centred' interpretations of 'Tintern Abbey' (Shapiro,
Onorato) and 'The Ancient Mariner' (Warren Stevenson,
Empson, Paglia, Knight) are obvious.

Elliott Gose's 'Coleridge and the Luminous Gloom' (1960)
likewise betrays a preoccupation with the poem's allegorical
possibilities, but in predominantly Christian terms. By blessing
the water-snakes the Mariner 'regains harmony with God' and
thereby nullifies the moon's vengeance (not the *sun's*, we note),
which has rendered the Mariner incapable of love. But only by
mixing with *humanity* will he complete his penance for violating
the 'one life'. Coleridge accepts that man's relation to nature is
subject to time and must be constantly reaffirmed throughout
the Mariner's life; his soul's relation to *God*, 'fixed once and for
all' in the blessing scene, is *timeless* and absolute (Gose, 1960; in
Bloom, 1986, p. 18).

Christian readings of the poem – like those that find an
analogue for the Mariner in Cain or the Wandering Jew – are of
course commonplace. As Frederick Pottle has argued, they are
sustainable despite – perhaps because of – the dramatic
presentation of the story 'through the lips of a mediaeval,
superstitious, and possibly deranged old man':

> It is, after all, not unlike a story from the Old Testament
> recording the exceeding fierce wrath of the Lord; for example
> how he smote the men of Bethshemesh because . . . they had
> looked into his ark. . . . The poem runs the gamut of genuine
> guilt and remorse, suffering and consolation, hate and forgive-
> ness, grief and joy. Since the emotions are so true to universal
> human experience, we accept the events that are advanced as
> their cause.   (1960, p. 264; in Boulger, 1969, p. 113)

Of 'the poem as confessional' critiques, George Whalley's 'The
Mariner and the Albatross' (1946–7), a piece of self-styled
innovation at the time of its first publication, remains one of the
most persuasive. Indeed, the essay has been reprinted both in
Coburn's collection (1967) and in the Macmillan Casebook of
the poem (*CC*). The albatross is 'a symbol with profound
personal significance' (Coburn, 1967, p. 33); its wanton destruction parallel's Coleridge's expressed awareness of the wilful

atrophy of his 'shaping spirit of imagination' ('Dejection; An Ode', l. 86). Bringing to bear a wealth of confessional 'evidence' from the poetry and prose ('I have played the fool and cut the throat of my own happiness, of my genius, of my utility' – *BL*, ch. 1), Whalley contends that Coleridge would be haunted all his life by the realisation that he had killed his own 'pious bird of good omen' (Coburn, 1967, p. 48).

The poem, then, is 'both an unconscious projection of Coleridge's early sufferings', his loneliness, his passivity and his horror of nightmare, and a 'vivid prophecy of the sufferings that were to follow'. The poem was probably not originally intended to be a personal allegory; but that is what, in Coleridge's eyes, it later beame 'as the prophecy was slowly, inexorably, and lingeringly fulfilled' (Coburn, 1967, p. 49). Whalley's essay dovetails nearly with Geoffrey Yarlott's chapter on the poem in *Coleridge and the Abyssinian Maid* (1967). Yarlott, like Bald (1940) and Whalley, draws attention to the frequent references to the poem in Coleridge's notebooks. More interestingly, as John Beer has observed, while modifying Whalley's theory of the poem as personal myth, Yarlott does explicitly link the process of self-identification to Coleridge's 1804 voyage to Malta. This 'voluntary exile from the people he loved most' – and, incidentally, the poet's first long sea-trip – prompted later revisions to the poem, 'notably the stanza describing the ghostly light from the helmsman's lamp' (Beer, 1971, p. 193).

Writing in *Scrutiny* in 1941, D. W. Harding had already reached similar conclusions concerning the poem's exploration of inner discordances. The nub of 'The Ancient Mariner' was, he declared, 'a private sense of guilt, intense out of all proportion to public rational standards' (Coburn, 1967, p. 55); such an experience mirrored Coleridge's irrational depressions. But, though the Mariner's partial reintegration (his 'reunion with the very simple and humble kinds of life') reflects the poet's own social needs, it means that the *self-assertiveness* of the Mariner/poet, paradoxically both a requirement for creative achievement *and* destructive of affection and sociability, has gone for ever. William Empson agreed – though elsewhere his essay is predictably iconoclastic. In concentrating not on the act or its consequences but on the *voyage*, he confronts those critics who are relieved that 'the fanciful reverie is so free from politics' (1964, p. 298).

The effect on literature of their maritime empires was to make the explorer a symbol of scientific discovery ... thence of intellectual adventure in general, and at last for the highest event in ethics, the moral discovery, which gets a man called a traitor by his own society. (1964, p. 305)

Empson doesn't adequately expand his thesis, and some of his perceptions, though fascinating, are pretty far-fetched (the spectral woman as prostitute – her skin is as 'white as leprosy'; 'Life-in-Death' as syphilis, a disease of retired sailors and originally brought from the New World). One might say the same of J. R. Ebbatson's discussion (1972), which, like Empson, questions Tillyard's and the consensus view that the poem is not political – despite the political consciousness of its author. For Ebbatson the Mariner anticipates all those subsequent voyages of exploration and discovery whereby Europe imposed its imperialist, slave–master mentality on the New World (p. 176). If nothing else, Empson and Ebbatson illustrate the ever-increasing difficulty of saying anything new about 'The Ancient Mariner' without becoming outlandish.

'Tintern Abbey'

'Lines Composed a Few Miles above Tintern Abbey' – to give the poem its full title – has ever been a shrine at which Wordsworthians must genuflect. Characteristically, Beatty, promoting it both as the culmination of the collaborative enterprise (written last and placed last) and as a propaedeutic piece, (anticipating in its themes the supreme Wordsworth work, *The Prelude*), gave a scholarly fillip to this process of enshrinement:

It is to be noted that we find in 'Tintern Abbey' the first clear indication of a characteristically Wordsworthian method of poetic procedure, that is the method of reminiscence or retrospect, combined ... with the method of the three ages of man. (1922, p. 107)

Thus to the 1963 editors of *Lyrical Ballads* it is still the 'most considerable of Wordsworth's poems in the volume', summing up 'beliefs formed over the five previous testing years' (B&J,

p. xxiv). Their claims have the same confident ring as Hough's consensus statement that the 'slighter pieces' of the collection are 'the data on which this great reflective poem is based' (1953, p. 50). Mayo, while predictably stressing not its subjectivity but its Augustan roots, none the less felt that, if its reception signalled reader recognition of a stock 'genre', its novelty lay in its excellence. Abrams, on the other hand, found evidence of genuine originality – as befits a first trial in the 'extended lyric' – while conceding its poetic antecedents in eighteenth-century loco-descriptive verse, of which there were at least 2000 published examples. His term for the poem – a paradigm of a new genre – is 'the greater Romantic lyric', a form in which meditation on a scene leads to insight or resolution: 'Often the poem rounds upon itself to end where it began, at the outer scene, but with an altered mood and deepened understanding which is the result of the intervening meditation' (Hilles and Bloom, 1965, p. 528).

Traditionally, critical connivance at the poem's greatness has gone hand-in-hand with a belief in its affirmative nature. Abrams extols the imagination as a redemptive and unifying force in 'Tintern Abbey', and Hough concurs on the disturbingly fragile basis that 'verse of such serene loveliness carries with it its own guarantee of authenticity' (1953, p. 50). Yet another 'affirmatist', James Benziger (1950) trenchantly dissociates himself from minority critics beginning to question such assumptions of infallibility. No 'superb expression of unwisdom' (Foerster, 1941, in *WC*, p. 234), the poem is a triumphant congruity of form and content; not just a unified pattern of images but a whole *paysage moralisé* which proclaims the unity of a universe in which the human and divine worlds are linked through the meditation of the natural world. In its twin progressions to serenity ('from din to murmur to silence and from human life to vegetable life to the cliff and sky'), 'Tintern Abbey' is a moving expression of Wordsworth's quietistic philosophy (*WC*, p. 239).

An emphasis on the poem's coherence, both structural and phenomenological, has dominated many other interpretations – and laid some open to the charge of 'hermeneutic circling', whereby the critic imposes his/her own interpretative coherence on works that may resist such attempts at symmetry. None the less, the poet's earlier reflections on the significance of the Wye landscape do appear to mirror the stages of his lifelong response to *nature*: the 'glad animal movements' (l. 75) associated with the physical pleasures of boyhood are succeeded first by the visual delights of youth and finally by the undoctrinal pantheism of a spirit that 'rolls through all things' (l. 103).

Following a new and adventurous tack, Heather Glen remarks the poem's positive observations about the perceptual process itself: 'a landscape to a blind man's eye' (l. 25) is a clear allusion to the then much-debated 'Molyneux problem'. For Wordsworth 'These forms of beauty' (l. 24) are *not* the 'meaningless chaos of sense impressions' that a blind man newly restored to sight would probably experience, but a visible pattern of life's unity – human habitation in a natural environment (Glen, 1983, p. 253). Glen however, uncovers contradictions which reflect uncertainties elsewhere in the volume. Not so much anticipating *The Prelude* as terminating *Lyrical Ballads*, 'the still, sad music of humanity' must be seen in *that context*. Here 'meditatively distanced' by the poet's trance-like state, the 'music' sounds less harmonious, and the 'confident' closing exhortation less secure, when juxtaposed, as the poem physically is in the collection, to the 'harsh' and 'grating' (l. 93) presences of convicts, deserted women and hapless old men:

> For in face of what they present, the relatively peaceful, socially unproblematic experience of looking at a beautiful landscape – an experience of delighted recognition, in which perception and creation seem to be fused – hardly seems an adequate paradigm for all intercourse with that which is external to the self: certainly not for those exchanges in the interpersonal world in which others may prove less amenable than 'These plots of cottage-ground, these orchard tufts'.
>
> (Glen, 1983, p. 259)

For Glen such problems, here suppressed, will be creatively confronted in the eighteen-month gestation of *Lyrical Ballads* 1800.

It is worth remembering that Glen's book is relatively recent. For this dissonant note, out of tune with harmonious interpretations of 'Tintern Abbey', dominates newer studies. Already in 1963 Gérard was wondering why this should be so. Citing as an example Bateson's dismissive '*rhetorically* it is superbly assured and persuasive' (emphasis added), he concludes that 'the present age feels only contemptuous dislike for what is "superbly assured": hence the reaction against "Tintern Abbey" ' (Gérard, 1963, p. 103). Whatever the reason, Hartman certainly became a catalyst in this as in other critical processes when noting a disparity between the poet's exultation and the sober appearance of the scene: 'The objects do arouse a sense of beauty but the emotion of the mind in beholding them is far too strong to make this evident beauty its explanation, too sincere to make this independent beauty its function. There is a paradox inherent in the human and poetic imagination: it cannot be, at the same time, true to nature and to itself' (1954, p. 7).

On the other hand, David Ferry is baffled by ambivalences in the *conclusion*: the address to Wordsworth's 'dear, dear sister' (l. 122) is moving precisely because it conceals a basic insecurity. Though her unfettered delight in nature will, according to Wordsworth, make her immune to 'evil tongues' or 'the dreary intercourse of daily life' (ll. 129–33), 'he is the living proof', as a consequence of his own traumatic experiences, that 'this is *not* true' (Ferry, 1959, p. 111). 'He has returned to the Wye to seclude himself from that world, to participate again as much as possible in its wildness, for what he has learned is not only that love of man which is another form of the love of nature, but a corresponding hatred and fear of the ordinary experience of men.' John Barrell, a self-professed 'cultural materialist', also regards the brother–sister relationship in the poem as problematic. An extension of Gérard's observation that in the poet's 'anticipation of Dorothy's future as identical with his present' there is an omission which ... has passed unnoticed', both 'puzzling and significant' (Barrell, 1987, p. 66), Barrell's analysis also has feminist overtones. Thus he sees Wordsworth's refusal to explain or tone down the *abstract* language of 'Tintern Abbey' ('thought' and its variants occur nine times) as a masculine strategy intended to place him above women and children and their concrete way of saying things. Dorothy *will* mature and develop the capacity to use these same abstractions which now chart and vindicate Wordsworth's own progress. But her achievement will threaten 'the notion of gender on which the difference between them is founded' (p. 15). In his heart of hearts, the poet hopes that Dorothy's maturation will not happen.

Students may well turn with relief from these gestures of

critical puzzlement. In fairness, however, summaries can
scarcely do justice to such complex arguments. And at least they
offer more than Bateson's dismissive 'series of concessions to
irrationality' (1956, p. 141), Empson's conviction that 'Tintern
Abbey' is an irretrievable muddle, or even Leavis's influential
observation that the poem embodies a recurrent Wordsworth
strategy: it 'produces an emotional experience' that it seeks to
explain, but the shortcomings of that exposition are concealed by
the 'convincing success of the poetry' (1964 edn, p. 134). We are
back in the territory of Foerster and Bateson, but a more
expansive Leavis might have been more illuminating.

Gérard, whose essay summarises some of these arguments,
concludes that this 'whirlpool of interpretative contradiction'
probably results from the ambiguities of the opening section
(1963, p. 94). While 'ambiguity' may be too deferential a word,
Gérard suggests, perceptively, that critics, following Coleridge
and Hazlitt, tend to hear *one* of Wordsworth's characteristic
voices in the poem to the exclusion of the other – either the voice
of the visionary *or* the matter-of-fact voice of the commonsensical
northerner ('an old half-witted sheep / Which bleats articulate
monotony' – J. K. Stephen). Such polarisations explain the
wide-ranging reactions to 'Tintern Abbey' and provide the key
for unlocking its meaning. Gérard traces the poem's symmetrical
pattern as it is woven between these poles: a movement from
'objective data' (observed phenomena) to 'subjective inference',
culminating in the sublime passages about unity of being. But
Wordsworth is all too aware that he might be cut off from nature
and Gérard approvingly quotes Danby on this process: 'The
ecstatic harmony is only a phase in a larger movement that
passes on, in individual experience, to eventual loss' (Gérard,
1963, p. 94). Nature can both offer a transcendental experience
and take it away. The poem records both this moment and the
inevitability of its disappearance, or at best 'lodgment in the
memory'.

Harold Bloom's *Poetry and Repression* (1976) is more adamant
about the poem's ultimate inconclusiveness. Wordsworth wanted
a far more positive statement than the one he actually made, but
'the defensive process of repression' prevented it from happening
(p. 56). Such an interpretation appears to dovetail with the belief
of Bloom's friend Meyer Abrams that the poem inaugurates
what Wordsworth was to call the 'two consciousnesses', whereby

the remembered landscape fails to match the now-revisited scene; 'a sad perplexity' compels the ensuing meditation (1984, p. 83). Yet Abrams' reading is – finally – an affirmative one: the poet's tragic alienation from the natural world *is* resolved – 'the poem ends at the time of its beginning' (p. 79).

These apparent suppressions have attracted a new generation of transatlantic theorists. McGann (1983) who argues that poetry is produced and reproduced within concrete historical contexts, concentrates on the significant dating of 'Tintern Abbey' (the eve of Bastille Day) and on the crucial developments (the bloody course of the French Revolution and the worsening plight of the rural poor) that occurred during the five years bridged by the poem. The 'vagrant dwellers in the houseless woods' (l. 21) *are* there, incongruously juxtaposed to 'pastoral farms' (l. 17), but, since their jarring presence threatens the poem's movement towards reconciliation, that observed landscape is superseded by another, the interior landscape of Wordsworth's mind and feelings. The picture *in* his mind (a ruined abbey, a haven for vagrants) becomes 'in a spiritual displacement', a 'picture *of* the mind' (l. 62) as past associations with disaster are replaced by hope (1983, p. 88).

But this gain is illusory. Wordsworth has, paradoxically, forsaken the real world 'to gain his immortal soul'. The poem's success 'lies in the clarity and candor with which it dramatizes not merely this event, but the structure of this event' (1983, p. 88). It is perhaps worth a brief aside to recall that one strand in this sequence of erasures – the idea of an isolated and therefore solipsistic self – is unravelled in 'Lines Left . . . in a Yew-tree'. As Thomas McFarland remarks, that poem clearly warns against egotistic solitariness. The ensuing loss of all love was an abyss that 'loomed before Wordsworth as an absolute limit on the possibilities of the egotistical sublime and generated a special anxiety' (1981, p. 155).

The fullest discussion of 'Tintern Abbey' as palimpsest is provided by McGann's compatriot Marjorie Levinson (1986). To her it is inconceivable that the public events of 1797–8 – the Irish rebellion, the first execution in England for treason, the invasion threat – 'did not influence "Tintern Abbey" in the profoundest ways'. Making capital of McGann's arguments – she pays fulsome tribute to him as he to her – she asserts that all these factors (including a date that marks three French anniversaries: Wordsworth's first visit, Bastille Day, the murder of Marat) are suppressed in the poem. Instead the project is to render 'Tintern Abbey' a 'portable resort and restorative' ('a mansion for all lovely forms') (Levinson, 1986, p. 24). Philosopher poet, priest and hermit take over from the political enthusiast; the poem becomes 'less interesting than the subject thereby overwritten' (p. 34). The disturbing aspects of the scene – 'a national monument overrun with a morally and materially unfixed class', a spoiled ruin indicating religious loss, the urban contamination – are all erased by a poet all too aware of their significance (p. 35).

Simpson (1987) also discovers in these displacements evidence of 'a desire to tame or deflect social and political realities' by privileging the personal vision of affirmation and transcendence (p. 109). But these suppressions are 'covertly admitted and signified' both by the date and location given in the title and by the deliberate language of surprise ('as *might* seem' – 1. 20). Moreover, the conviction of the positive passages is 'unsettled by their contiguity to other passages, and by the general rhetoric of hypothesis' (p. 113). The conclusion proposes two solutions, one deriving from natural and the other from human contact (Dorothy), but the negative utterance and Wordsworth's sudden turn to his sister imply tensions (compare Barrell) that are not resolved.

Siskin (1988), whose book is the final unit in this American tetrad of historicist analyses, believes that this abrupt introduction of Dorothy is a strategy for transferring the poem's task to her and thereby eliminating Wordsworth himself from the poem. This process anticipates Roland Barthes's celebrated insight that 'the interpretative search for transcendental meaning can end only with the "birth of the reader . . . at the cost of the death of the Author"' (Siskin, 1988, p. 111). Siskin's deconstructive sally also finds an echo in Easthope's statement that 'Tintern Abbey' gives 'the effect of a presence of a speaker by denying its presence in the poem' (1983, p. 132). As Easthope makes abundantly clear, such disjunctive readings cross swords with traditional humanist interpretations such as Beer's, which continue to eulogise the poem in terms of a powerful authorial presence in which all the elements expressively combine 'to reveal the persona of a poet who has learned to devote himself to the affections of the heart and who invites the reader, by participating in the same processes, to share what he has discovered' (Beer, 1978, p. 74; quoted in Easthope, 1983, p. 132).

Stephen Gill, the most recent in a long line of distinguished Wordsworth biographers, admits, perhaps out of deference to these 'displacers', that the actual scenic details – the river traffic, the charcoal-burners and the Abbey beggars – are 'passed over'. Significantly though, he sides with tradition in discerning harmony in a poem which marries 'the elegiac and the triumphant, so that the coloration of both moods mingles but does not dissolve' (1989, p. 152). That all these conflicting opinions have been aired in the recent past suggests that this particular debate will run and run.

But it is salutary to recollect the words of Wordsworth's fellow Romantic Keats, who, in a letter of 1818 to J. H. Reynolds (1960 edn, pp. 147–8), described stages of imaginative growth that not only shed light on the sequences in 'Tintern Abbey' but also alert us to what is inherently elusive and finally unanalysable in the poem. Likening life to a 'large Mansion of Many Apartments' through which we pass, Keats says that the first or 'thoughtless Chamber' leads to 'the Chamber of Maiden-Thought', where one is initially 'intoxicated with the light and the atmosphere' (compare Wordsworth's 'Their colours and their forms, were then to me / An appetite' – ll. 80–1). 'However among the effects this breathing is father of is that tremendous one of sharpening one's vision into the heart and nature of Man – of convincing one's nerves that the World is full of Misery and Heartbreak, Pain, Sickness and oppression' (Wordsworth's 'still sad music of humanity' perhaps). The chamber darkens and its many doors open, 'all leading to dark passages – We see not the ballance of good and evil. We are in a Mist – *We* are now in that state – We feel the "burden of the mystery", To this point was Wordsworth come . . . when he wrote "Tintern Abbey" and it seems to me that his Genius is explorative of those dark Passages.'

'The Thorn'

Posing the vexed question, is it 'about a man, a woman or a tree?', Gérard (1964) observes that 'an uncommon amount of

critical dissention characterises interpretations of "The Thorn" '
(*WC*, p. 215). The arguments began early. Such squibs as
Southey's 'he who personates tiresome loquacity, becomes tiresome himself' (*Critical Review*, October 1798) had already been
anticipated by Wordsworth's defence of his favourite that 'The
Thorn' was 'not supposed to be spoken in the author's own
person: the character of the loquacious narrator will sufficiently
shew itself in the course of the story' (Advertisement). In 1800 he
amplified these remarks, commenting that the narrator – a
retired man rendered 'credulous and talkative from indolence' –
would likely be superstitious. Wordsworth wanted a picture
'consistent with the character that should describe it' and which
'adhered to the style in which such persons describe', whereby
words 'which in their minds are impregnated with passion,
should likewise convey passion to Readers who are not accustomed to sympathise with men feeling in that manner or using
such language'. This approach would, the poet argued, inevitably make for verbal repetition as the character, conscious of his
own inarticulateness, strove to 'communicate impassioned feelings'. But such 'repetition and apparent tautology' was not only
psychologically accurate: it had the additional virtue of being
aesthetically right – frequently producing verbal 'beauties of the
highest kind' (Note to 'The Thorn', 1800, in B&J, pp. 288–9).
Coleridge, with his friend's explanation in mind, offered an
interpretation based on the centrality of the talkative sea captain's role, a reading later adopted by Wordsworth's editor de
Selincourt and in varying degrees by most subsequent critics. In
fact this on-going debate has overshadowed discussion of other,
equally fascinating aspects of the poem. At times Martha, the
'wretched woman' of the tragedy, has been as much an object of
rejection by the critics as by her lover Stephen Hill.

   The convolutions of Wordsworth's ballad demand a simple
summary of source and plot. The only piece in *Lyrical Ballads*
inspired by a natural object – a Quantock thornbush – this
familiar presence is transformed into 'an impressive object' by a
real storm (compare the wind-animated daffodils of 'I wandered
lonely as a cloud') and subsequently becomes a central ingredient in this domestic tragedy. Told by a rambling old sea
captain, Wordsworth's tale is of Martha Ray, jilted on her
wedding day and temporarily unhinged by the experience.
Rumour has it that she has subsequently given birth to a child

and that her lonely vigil beside the blasted thorn and its 'beauteous hill of moss' is a self-imposed penance for infanticide. More lurid still, village gossip links this 'scarlet hill' to the spilt blood of her baby. While both nature and narrator reject such malicious stories, Martha's ritual despair is palpable enough.

Helen Darbishire believes that 'The Thorn' derives its power from its treatment of essential human emotions – 'love of maid for man, agony at the lover's desertion, love of mother for child, misery of the distraught mind which seeks relief in the wild or calm companionship of Nature' (1950, p. 43). Yet, oddly, no poem has been so plagued by a solitary couplet, 'naive lines which brought Wordsworth more critical vituperation than any others he wrote' (Hamilton, 1986, p. 57). None the less Hamilton is prepared to defend lines which, while 'best read as disingenuous', do 'comically discredit the language of measurement' – Martha's tragedy cannot be so conveniently weighed in the scales of justice – and stress the literal-mindedness of a narrator involved in a 'misguided investigation': 'I cannot tell how this may be / But plain it is' (ll. 243–4).

Even Darbishire, a key figure in the mid-twentieth-century resurgence of *Lyrical Ballads*, admits that the offending 'I've measured it from side to side, / 'Tis three feet long, and two feet wide' (ll. 32–3) perhaps tips over the 'edge of bathos' (1950, p. 43). None the less her sympathetic and extended treatment of a 'great and remarkable poem' has proved more durable than judgements on its failure to transmute 'intractable and embarrassing autobiographical material into impersonal art' (Campbell and Mueschke, 1933, p. 23). Darbishire compares the circular process of conversation with the 'circling of the imagination round one centre', twin movements in a poem which fuses 'the human passion and the natural scene so that each expresses itself in and through the other: the misery and love of the woman, and the bleakness yet beauty of the tree, pond and mound' (1950, p. 44).

The level of informed debate has been further raised by the availability of material about the gestation of 'The Thorn', in Dorothy's *Journal* and Wordsworth's subsequent reminiscence in the Fenwick Note (*PW*, ii, p. 511). In fact Jordan, skirting the familiar obsession with narrator significance, believes that the moment of the poem's conception on the Quantocks constituted an epiphany for the poet, as the storm animated the inherently prosaic thorn and charged it with feeling. 'What he learned was that *everything* can be poetic, if it is perceived poetically, felt poetically' (1976, p. 158).

Following Wordsworth's and Coleridge's early lead, Stephen Parrish (1973) roundly declared that the poem was a 'dramatic monologue' in which the psychology of the *speaker* was paramount. The poem's events have little if *any* 'existence outside his superstitious imagination and the way his imagination works is the subject of the ballad' (p. 100). Such an unequivocal interpretation, which clearly marginalised the role – not to say discounted the existence – of the jilted Martha Ray, attracted swift reactions. Arguing that 'interest in the character of the retired sea-captain is the last thing that could explain the poem's hold' (1960, p. 36), Danby admitted that, while the narrator might direct our sympathies, he was an insufficient end in himself. Martha Ray may remain an enigma but she is a palpable victim of man's inhumanity to woman, part of a larger context of 'anti-vital and elemental forces' in which the tree, mound and pond are both symbols *and* agents of human misery. The pond, for example, is both watery grave and a mirror in which the villagers see their 'poisonous fancy' – Martha the jilted child-murderer (p. 71).

'The Thorn' is the only Wordsworth ballad in the collection to reward such a symbolic approach. Four years later Gérard (1964) tried the same tack, attempting a 'global analysis' (*WC*, p. 216) which married the three interdependent motifs to a compelling formal unity of mood and structure. The 'burial' mound becomes image both of 'natural beauty' and 'innocence'; the storm-blasted thorn and pond are like Martha, part of the 'world of experience, of suffering and endurance' (*WC*, p. 223). But Gérard's essay confirms another shift of critical attention: not only from dramatic to symbolic but also from narrator to victim. Martha is the *central* mystery, protected, both by nature's ministrations and by the poet's compassion, against fact-finding villagers or readers. 'The Thorn' is 'yet another treatment of the theme of undeserved suffering and of the motif of the abandoned mother' (p. 215). But what gives the tragedy such poignancy is the sympathy accorded Martha by both inanimate and human nature. Mother Nature seems to consecrate maternal love by fostering the growth of beautiful mosses on the burial mound. But nature's *miraculous* final intervention is more compelling because it is accepted as evidence by the sea captain. 'On the plane of the story's moral, she is rescued by the narrator's attitude which makes itself felt in his manner of presenting his tale' (p. 231).

Since critical opinion usually reinforces or modifies earlier views, a sequential survey of analyses of 'The Thorn' will inevitably sail close to the reefs of tautology and risk that very hazard that Wordsworth was reluctant to recognise in his own poem. But, although Averill adroitly summarises this process as stressing *either* 'what is told (Martha's story) or the way it is told (the sea-captain's role)', his own approach does have the benefit of novelty – despite his overall dismissal of the poem as 'barbaric yawp' (1980, p. 172). Again foregrounding Darwin's *Zoönomia*, important both as source material for the ballads and for the definition of 'experiments', he links Martha's condition, like the mad mother's, to 'erotomania'. This occurs when a lover's ultimate rejection is 'instantly followed by furious or melancholy insanity' (Darwin, 1796, II, 363; quoted in Averill, 1980, p. 167). Such a quasi-psychological view of Martha's condition is juxta-posed to biographical 'evidence': the actress Martha Ray, a victim of 'erotomania', was the grandmother of Wordsworth's ward Basil (see 'Anecdote for Fathers') at Alfoxden. Averill therefore concludes that the two Marthas, one real and one imaginary, occupy a central role in a poem 'about the uncertain ground between the misery we read about in books and that which we see too clearly in the world around us' (1980, p. 168). Travelling a very different route, Averill has arrived at the Hartman-like conclusion that 'The Thorn' is about 'the process of mind by which pathetic poetry is produced'; it accommodates Hartman's view that the double plot of narrated action and the progress of speaker/poet's mind operate in tandem – 'a carica-ture of Wordsworth's own imagination-in-process' (1964, p. 148). The effect of this procedure is to distract the reader from the emphasis on mere incident that Wordsworth now abjured. But Averill has no wish to marginalise a subject who is recognis-ably the sister of the Female Vagrant. The narrator has no tangible identity apart from his obsessive interest in Martha Ray; for all his strange loquaciousness he is less a psychological study than 'a hyperventilation of Wordsworth's usual self-projection' (Averill, 1980, p. 170).

When both Glen and Jacobus discern in 'The Thorn' evidence

of Wordsworth's reaction against existing models, respectively
the simplistic formulae of magazine verse and the vicarious
obsession with violence that characterises Bürger's ballads, they
inevitably emphasise the poem's sense of mystery and complexity. Jacobus (1976), in a circling metaphor that recalls
Darbishire, establishes woman, thorn, pond and mound as
the fixities around which the poem revolves, and discovers,
in contrast to the sensationalism and knowing conviction of
maternal guilt in Bürger's 'The Lass of Fair Wone', a meditation
on the mystery of sorrow and its comprehension. Likewise for
Glen the poet advances no clinching moral, and the narrator's
plodding loquaciousness deliberately diminishes the poem's
capacity for melodrama (1983, p. 42). Such an analysis is
modified by Hamilton, who, accepting that our sympathy for
Martha is invoked *in spite of* the narrator's prurience, sees in the
captain's evasions – his refusal to disclose the 'facts' of
child-murder – a 'pleasure in preserving the *frisson* of a
sensational mystery' (1986, p. 57). This evasion is evidence
enough, for Averill, of a pathological condition; the captain's
cravings for the stimulation of fiction distance him from the
poet's own voice. 'Mystery' and 'fiction' are words that reverber-
ate through this debate; fittingly they become our final epithets
on 'The Thorn'. We are back with Gérard's rhetorical question:
is it 'about a man, a woman or a tree?'

'The Idiot Boy'

> 'The Idiot Boy' leads the reader on from anxiety to distress,
> and from distress to terror, by incidents and alarms which,
> though of the most mean and ignoble kind, interest, frighten,
> and terrify, almost to torture, during the perusal of more than
> a hundred stanzas.
>
> (*Monthly Review*, June 1799, in B&J, p. 323)

The learned Dr Burncy's mingled air of fascination and bewilderment was typical of contemporary reactions to Wordsworth's exploratory poem. But the author was, on the face of it,
far more hurt by Southey's contemptuous 'No tale less deserved
the labour that appears to have been bestowed upon this'
(*Critical Review*, October 1798, in Reiman, 1972, I, 308), retort-

ing that Southey was all too aware that 'I published these poems for money and money alone' (*EL*, p. 267).

Wordsworth's riposte – that he wanted to make commercial capital from the venture – is very different from the response that Southey's comments on 'The Thorn' provoked, and flies in the face of his own enthusiasm for the poem. As de Selincourt observes, the 'importance that Wordsworth attached to the "The Idiot Boy" is shown by the fact that in the *Lyrical Ballads* 1800 it and *The Ancient Mariner* are the only poems which are given a separate title-page', and in *The Prelude* only 'The Idiot Boy' and 'The Thorn' are mentioned by name (*PW*, II, 478). Indeed Wordsworth was at pains to stress the profundity of the subject when he wrote back to that precocious seventeen-year-old John Wilson to rebut his opinion that it was 'almost unnatural, that a person in a state of complete idiotism should excite the warmest feelings of attachment in the breast even of his mother' (letter from J. Wilson, May 1802, in B&J, p. 335). The poet's reply is worth quoting at length:

> I have often applied to Idiots, in my own mind, that sublime expression of scripture, that *'their life is hidden with God'*. They are worshipped, probably from a feeling of this sort, in several parts of the East.
>
> Among the Alps where they are numerous, they are considered, I believe, as a blessing to the family to which they belong. I have indeed often looked upon the conduct of fathers and mothers of the lower classes of society towards Idiots as the great triumph of the human heart. It is there that we see the strength, disinterestedness, and grandeur of love, nor have I ever been able to contemplate an object that calls out so many excellent and virtuous sentiments without finding it hallowed thereby and having something in me which bears down before it, like a deluge, every feeble sensation of disgust and aversion.   (*EL*, p. 357)

None the less Wordsworth was less solemn when recollecting the circumstances of the poem's composition:

> The last stanza – 'The Cocks did crow to-whoo, to-whoo, And the sun did shine so cold' – was the foundation of the whole. . . . Let me add that this long poem was composed in

the groves of Alfoxden, almost extempore; not a word, I believe, being corrected, though one stanza was omitted. I mention this in gratitude to those happy moments, for, in truth, I never wrote anything with so much glee.

(FN, *PW*, ii, 478)

It was a long time before *critics* were able to muster much cordiality for the poem. Coleridge didn't help by preferring two charges against it – first its failure 'to preclude from the reader's fancy the disgusting images of *ordinary morbid idiocy*', and secondly its portrayal of maternal feeling:

the idiocy of the *boy* is so evenly balanced by the folly of the *mother*, as to present to the general reader rather a laughable burlesque on the blindness of anile dotage, than an analytic display of maternal affection in its ordinary working.

(*BL*, ch. 2)

That verdict of 'laughable', heartily endorsed by Byron, was an unconscionable time a-dying. Danby, one of the first to question such a simplistic response to a complex poem, quotes Hutchinson, himself drawing on an earlier tradition represented by Hazlitt:

The humour and pathos of 'The Idiot Boy' are sadly marred by his clumsy attempts at mirth. Hazlitt, in his pen-portrait of Wordsworth, speaks of a certain 'convulsive inclination to laughter about the mouth, a good deal at variance with the solemn, stately expression of the rest of his face'. Not less awkward and incongruous, surely, are the heavy pleasantries in which the poet of . . . 'The Idiot Boy' seeks an occasional vent for his exuberant cheerfulness. 'At rare times in his poetry Wordsworth shows an inclination for frolic: it is the frolic of good spirits in the habitually grave, and he cannot caper lightly.'   (Danby, 1960, p. 48)

Danby is rightly dismissive of this Victorian incapacity to marry the serious and the comic; it is precisely the oracular tone which he finds so compelling in a poem 'beautifully mock-solemn and yet indulgently ready with its sympathy' (p. 50). Wordsworth here takes on the role of 'satirist of feeling': Betty's sentimental and fatuous vision of her idiot son as potential hero; Susan's miraculous cure 'as she frets more and more about the others'. Johnny however is not 'on the see-saw of passion' himself. Comically ineffectual in getting the doctor, he none the less both inspires 'the grandeur of love' in Betty and Susan, and himself manifests a kind of uncomprehending joy:

> Burr, burr – now Johnny's lips they burr,
> as loud as any mill, or near it,
> Meek as a lamb the pony moves,
> And Johnny makes the noise he loves,
> And Betty listens, glad to hear it.
>
> (ll. 107–11)

The backdrop to his comedy of errors is the natural world; it incarnates all the values denied the human participants – 'energy and calm, permanence and process, spontaneity and order, ranging from the stars in the sky to the nearby birds' (Danby, 1960, p. 56).

Danby's remarkable revaluation of a remarkable poem more-or-less coincided with David Ferry's. Again highlighting the poem's deceptive virtues and taking due account of Wordsworth's own pronouncements, Ferry essays a different tack in arguing a close affinity between the idiot boy and Mother Nature.

Rejecting a psychological interpretation based on the processes of a mother's worries, he offers the telling perception that the boy's state of mind can best be understood if we think of him as 'stripped' of intelligence, 'so that there is between him and the natural world *nothing* but his capacity to discover in it its deep hidden secrets. Nature speaks to him directly because there is nothing in his mind to be gotten out of the way' (1959, p. 98). But Betty Foy is also in harmony with her moonlit surroundings. 'In thinking of Johnny rather than Susan', she is 'paying a deep obligation to the irrational force in nature, to the life which is "hidden with God"', and, since nature never did betray the heart that loved her, Susan is cured as the sign of nature's approbation of Betty's choice' (pp. 97–8).

Sheats, Jacobus, Averill and Glen all comment on the poem's ability to expose the stock response and to invite our participation in the feelings of the characters. For Sheats this process recalls 'Simon Lee'; here the reader's 'condescending pity and indeed disgust' is supplanted by 'an affirmation of the dignity and autonomy of the boy's existence' (Abrams, 1975, p. 138). The agents in this process of elevating our response are Betty Foy, through her consuming love for her son, and the narrator, closer here to the poet than in 'The Thorn' – 'encouraging us to apprehend and to participate in the boy's feelings for their own sake' (p. 138). Jacobus, in apparent disregard of Ferry's strictures about Betty Foy's psychology, suggests that, in portraying her excessive emotional reaction, the poet 'presents love almost as a form of unbalance' (1976, p. 258) – the view recalls Danby – before reaffirming the poem's power to enable us to 'see afresh what is familiar, and value fully what is simple in our own experience' (p. 261). None the less Jacobus finds, like Glen, no sentimental resolution along the lines that readers of magazine verses on madness would have anticipated in 1798 – an opinion reinforced by Averill's statement that 'The Idiot Boy' discounts 'all romance, whether . . . supernatural or pathetic, as irrelevant to human concern' and neutralises the potentially 'exploitative relationship of poet and reader to suffering' (1980, p. 193). By this token, the inconclusive ending provides yet another displacement of reader expectation and prompts the observation that perhaps the idiot's very inscrutability first attracted Wordsworth to the subject.

No one since Danby has more convincingly demonstrated this complexity than Angus Easson. In an extended essay which mirrors current critical preoccupation with the poem, he reaffirms its concern with *what constitutes a story* as well as with

> the fluxes and reflexes of feeling – Betty's varying emotions – conveyed primarily through external gesture and markers: speech, bodily movement, the sound of clocks; while the business of narrative is carried on by a poet who comes up against the problems of poetry and of being a poet, the very narrative he is supposedly creating (for he is clearly conscious of his readers and of telling a tale, whether tedious or delightful) raising questions about poetic and comic form.
>
> (1980, p. 6)

Among the plethora of newer Wordsworth studies, a number have mercifully avoided this issue of reader response. For J. R.

Watson the idiot is in the tradition of Wordsworth's outcasts; unlike the others, Johnny 'has the best of both worlds' (1982, p. 116). He is a kind of simple mystic but he 'also has the joy of being surrounded by human love'. In this unstructured and yet caring community 'strange and marvellous things happen; it is a world of natural intuitions, primary affections and spontaneous recovery from illness'. The doctor's logical behaviour, is a reminder of 'all the features of society which the poem is *not* about'; he is necessarily 'cut off from the happiness in which Johnny and Betty find the recovered Susan' (p. 117).

While agreeing with Mary Jacobus that 'The Idiot Boy' presents maternal love 'almost as a form of unbalance', David Pirie stresses another tension: what he sees as a calculated balance between 'the fluctuating misery and joy of Betty and 'Johnny's undiscriminating joy in himself, his pony and the world' (1982, p. 129). The plot *literally* separates mother and son so that this distinction can be explored without obvious contrivance. In a suggestive conclusion Pirie proposes a parallel with the 'Immortality' ode. There Wordsworth confronts the irresistible changes that impels us 'towards a bleakly emptied world where "nothing can bring back the hour of splendour in the grass, of glory in the flower" ([ll.] 178–9). Johnny remains securely spellbound "in his glory", confidently asserting as facts the intimate incongruities of his dream-like vision' (p. 146). Unhappily for us, such a blissful state of innocence has already vanished.

While focusing on the poem's linguistic procedures, J. P. Ward also asserts the 'adult–child balance', expressed through a 'continuous spate of binary contrasts'. Thus Betty has instructed her son

> Both what to follow, what to shun,
> What do, and what to leave undone,
> How turn to left and how to right.
> (ll. 64–6)

These contrasts are 'climaxed' in the final stanza, where Johnny's celebrated 'The cocks did crow, to-whoo, to-whoo / And the sun did shine so cold!' are, in Ward's opinion 'remarkably prophetic of Lacan's example, 'Le chien fait miaou, le chat fait oua-oua', which illustrates the creative perceptions very young children *impose* on their environments by the same means' (1984, pp. 118–19). More interesting still, it seems to me that Johhny's concluding view of his world is an illustration of Jakobson's observation about modified aphasia (impairment of the capacity to understand and articulate), a condition which generates metaphoric utterance of this kind (1956, p. 69ff.). The idiot boy's 'idiocy' might now be thus diagnosed. But the stanza, and indeed the poem as a whole, seems also to reflect Wordsworth's own thoughts on those associative processes that he recognised as part and parcel of the act of poetic creation.

Comparing such searching appraisals with those dismissive early reviews is to remind ourselves how far the critical wheel has turned in the case of Wordsworth's poem. Margaret Drabble movingly remembers a personal *volte-face*:

> at school . . . we were taught to think them [*Lyrical Ballads*] ludicrous, and at 'The Idiot Boy' even Mary Scott had laughed. But now I do not laugh, I weep, real wet tears, the same tears that I shed over newspaper reports of air disasters . . . for they have as high a content of uninflated truth. And I weep partly as an apology for my past ignorance, from which I might never have been rescued.   (1966a, p. 171)

5
The Poet as Critic:
The Preface (1800)

It could be easily argued that authorial criticism has no place in this survey. The Preface to *Lyrical Ballads* is, after all, more self-justification that self-criticism; Coleridge's *Biographia Literararia* (1817) has the knowing air of being wise after the event. None the less such exclusion would be to deny the significance and uniqueness of the poets' comments both to their contemporaries and to us, now able to evaluate them as documents both precipitating and reflecting a crisis in English poetry. Not only do they provide a crucial gloss on the creative chore of producing innovative poems; they have also helped determine the direction which poetry in general has since taken. And, though the Preface was written to accompany the second edition (1800), it does have a powerfully retrospective function in confronting the original reviews of the 1798 volume. Indeed, some perceptive recent commentators have chosen to focus on the prose statements rather than the ballads themselves.

These documents do not, however, always reflect creative unanimity. Wordsworth protested that the Preface was written to please Coleridge (whose inclination was to prose anyway), but, as Brett and Jones remind us, 'it is hard to believe that he wrote six thousand words for this reason alone' (B&J, p. xliv). That he failed in this endeavour to please his friend is endorsed not only by subsequent strictures in *Biographia Literaria* (ch. 14) but by Coleridge's much earlier confession to Southey that the Preface was 'half a child of my own Brain . . . yet I am far from going all lengths with Wordsworth' (*CL*, II, 811; in B&J, p. xliv).

Coleridge's lack of enthusiasm for the Preface has not rubbed off on scholars, who have divined in its pages everything from an advocacy of neoclassical principles to a vatic and crusading spirit presiding over a new temple to the muses. Bloom and Trilling thus liken Wordsworth's admonitory role to that of Cromwell addressing the Rump parliament: 'a rebel general . . . announcing the terms on which he will accept the leadership of the state whose corrupt government he is about to overthrow: "It is not fit that you should sit here any longer . . . you should now give place to better men" ' (1973, p. 593).

Put more soberly, the main object of the Preface was to develop the position adumbrated with some inconsistency in the Advertisement. If the Advertisement was just that (a public announcement), intended to anticipate and deflect criticism and to offer a pretty unconvincing rationale, the Preface was altogether more consistent and considered, its imperatives moderated by lengthy explanations and illustrations that were, in large part, a measured response to the doubters. What did brand the project as militant was its crusading sense of cultural crisis, its awareness that 'a multitude of causes, unknown to former times' were 'now acting with a combined force to blunt the discriminating powers of the mind' and reducing it to 'a state of almost savage torpor'. Among these causes were 'the encreasing accumulation of men in cities, where the uniformity of their occupations' had produced 'a craving for extraordinary incident' hourly gratified (B&J, p. 249).

It was against this background of an urban and industrial society and its concomitant demands for a vicarious sensationalism ('this degrading thirst after outrageous stimulation') that Wordsworth composed his poems – around 'incidents and situations' taken, in the main, from 'low and rustic life' (B&J, p. 245). Such offerings were intended as a corrective to all these 'deluges of idle and extravagant stories in verse' (p. 249). They would be based on fundamental and enduring emotions proven on the pulse of country living ('in that situation our elementary feelings exist in a state of greater simplicity'), and couched in direct and sincere language (the product of 'repeated experience and regular feelings' – p. 245). For receptive readers, this meant nothing less than a re-education in their primal sympathies, in their capacity to empathise with the people in the poems and their predicaments, and a willingness to discover how 'our feelings and ideas are associated in a state of excitement'

(p. 247). What has become a critical commonplace – that Wordsworth foregrounded only *rural* victims – is hardly to the point. Among the urban poor, both deep feelings and their very expression, were, in his view, already at risk if not atrophied beyond recall. In the cities the drudgery of mindless occupations had reduced workers to 'a state of savage torpor'. Unredeemed by the countryman's contact with 'the beautiful and permanent forms of nature', they now sought only the cheap thrills of 'frantic novels' and sensational incidents, real or imagined (p. 249).

The poet's explanations were a riposte to these reviewers who had so recently complained of the banality of his material, an answer to the charge of a matter and manner unworthy of high art. For Wordsworth the elemental character of these 'ballads' allowed no compromise. It was the poet's task to discover inspiration in 'the manners of rural life', in profound feelings that found expression in 'a plainer and more emphatic language' (p. 245). The recollection 'in tranquility' of emotions generated by such observations and experiences engendered a 'spontaneous overflow of powerful feelings' that was the very stuff of poetry (p. 266).

Admittedly some parts of the Preface are hard to defend. Coleridge's view was that mountainous districts do not necessarily produce high-minded inhabitants, that rustics do not naturally speak a pithy and lucid language. Even Wordsworth's justly famous diatribe against urbanisation and divided labour has come under recent fire from materialists such as Simpson, who there discerns 'the seeds of . . . later fears about the possibility of universal suffrage and popular radicalism' (1987, p. 63). Nor does Wordsworth offer the reader much hard evidence to support his theories. None the less the insistence that poetry should aspire to the condition of unspoiled nature, both human and non-human, that it should derive strength from 'the beautiful and permanent forms of nature', remains a cornerstone both of the Preface and of Wordsworth's subsequent thinking.

This notion of 'permanence' is singled out by W. J. B. Owen, that assiduous commentator on Wordsworth's prose utterances. In *Lyrical Ballads* Wordsworth seeks

to write a poetry the subject matter of which shall be of permanent interest; he seeks, similarly, to use a language which shall be permanently intelligible, or as near that as possible. . . . Such a subject-matter Wordsworth thinks he can find in rustic subjects because . . . 'rural occupations' (as he thinks) have been, are, and will continue to be . . . the mainstay . . . of humanity; in a word because 'rural occupations' provide us with food and clothing and other 'animal wants'. (1969, p. 12)

Perhaps this concern in the Preface with nature's permanent aspects has another dimension. It provokes in man (both poet and peasant) a sense of his own insignificance; it inevitably generates a modesty and humility that informs speaker and character alike in so many of the ballads.

The debate about style shows Wordsworth inveighing against the 'curiously elaborate' excesses of fashionable poetic diction. His avowed aim is to 'keep my Reader in the company of flesh and blood' – the personifying of abstractions and the employ-ment of cliché ('expressions in themselves proper and beautiful but . . . foolishly repeated by bad Poets' – B&J, p. 251) are inimical to his purpose. Here, as far as we are concerned, he is preaching to the converted. But Wordsworth then puts forward the argument, controversial to modern readers brought up on the primacy of the image, that the best poetry differs from the best prose not in terms of verbal potency, but because of its commitment to a metre that is needed either to inject some life into jaded verse or for 'tempering and restraining the passions by an intertexture of ordinary feeling'. 'Such regular impulses of pleasurable surprise from the metrical arrangement' thus prevent Shakespeare's pathos from becoming unendurable (p. 264). Wordsworth's final exhortation reminds the reader of the value of a 'genuine' response (the word is used twice): in terms reminiscent of the Advertisement, he hopes that his poems will also pass the test of genuineness and that their high moral seriousness will mean they are 'well adapted to interest mankind permanently' (p. 272). So far, it seems, so good.

Such a summary does scant justice to the length and complexity of the Preface; at best it reveals facets of Wordsworth in an unfamiliar role – that of the critic. It was not a theoretical posture wholly endorsed by Coleridge seventeen years later in *Biographia Literaria*, where, for the first time, the 'controversy' concerning their respective views achieved the status of public debate. Not that Coleridge was unequivocally hostile: for a start, he already saw in the continuing popularity of *Lyrical Ballads* evidence of that very permanence so desired by Wordsworth. Moreover, his friend's espousal of 'a reformation in our poetic diction' and 'the truth of passion', his insistence on 'dramatic propriety' in figurative language and his delight in the 'pleasurable confusion' created by 'an unaccustomed train of words and images' were all stances deserving of support. What Coleridge could *not* stomach was embedded in the kernel of the Preface: the solemn pronouncements about rustic life and its attendant benefits in terms of essential passions, more durable manners and their 'incorporation with the beautiful and permanent forms of nature' (*BL*, ch. 17). Coleridge, more cerebral, more elitist and more urban, (even his terminology is strikingly different) believed education and independence to be the keys to mental improvement. Mountains, to some locals, might offer no higher stimulation than 'pictures to the blind and music to the deaf'.

Nor could he accept the *'real* language of men' argument. There was no such thing as a common language; nothing illustrated the matter more clearly than the gulf between 'the language of Mr Wordsworth's homeliest companion' and that of 'a common peasant'. 'Ordinary' language, yes – 'real' language, no. And the proviso 'in a state of excitement' made the case no more tenable. Passion did not of itself create; it simply 'increased activity'. If it resulted in 'unmeaning repetitions, habitual phrases, and other blank counters' as the poet wrestled with the muse, then the poet should at least ensure that such tautologies did not take over the poem. Perhaps Coleridge had 'The Thorn' in mind.

While this agitated view of passion implies a temperamental divide, an emotionality singularly different from the slow burn of Wordsworthian feeling, it is clear that Coleridge did present a critique that is both lucid and incisive – ample proof, if proof were needed, that in the realm of discursive prose the younger man was very much the master. But in fairness to Wordsworth the circumstances were no longer the same. The Preface was an original exploration of the creative process, a justification of Wordsworth's own innovations: Coleridge was writing long after the event, when the dust of critical skirmishing had begun to settle.

Wordsworthians have been reacting ever since in evaluating

or explaining the Preface. Owen belongs squarely to the eluci-
dators, but other recent initiatives have not only unearthed
apparent inconsistencies but tried – with mixed results – to
relate precept to poetic practice. Roger Sharrock explains it thus:
'Wordsworth's revolt against the poetic diction of the later
eighteenth century, and the expository convenience of this for
the purposes of the literary historian, have obscured the more
iconoclastic notes of the Preface of 1800' (1953; in *WC*, p. 157).
Of these perhaps the most startling is the poet's admission (in
1802, not 1800) that his capacity to 'imitate passions' is 'mechanical', a poor substitute for 'substantial action and suffering'
(B&J, p. 256). As Sharrock points out, 'Wordsworth's sense of
the poetic richness of nature is balanced by a melancholy
concern with the limitations of language' (*WC*, p. 159). In this
respect the Preface hints at a kind of neoclassical emphasis at
odds with, say, Keats, for whom 'the poetry of the word is a
simple reflection of the poetry of the world' (p. 159). Elsewhere
inconsistent, the Preface returns to this 'photographic (or phono-
graphic) conception of the languge proper to poetry' (p. 162).
Pledged to renounce literariness, the poet's skill inheres in his
ability to recognise and select the 'language really used by men'
(B&J, p. 241) and thereby to convey things 'as nakedly as
possible' using 'the words of the original participants in the
action' (*WC*, p. 161). Such an extreme realism (as Garrod has
noted, the 'imagination' is only mentioned twice in the Preface)
informs 'The Thorn', where the sea captain's banal repetitions
are an apt 'medium for an experience which defies language by
its tragic poignancy' (*WC*, p. 164). But ultimately this stress on
anti-literary realism is limiting, because such a 'technique of
commonplaces' does not allow much in the way of unifying-
symbolism.

While one could argue, *contra* Sharrock, that much of the
strength of 'The Thorn' does in fact derive from its symbolic
structure, in general the ballads lack the linguistic enrichment
that symbols can provide. Easthope maintains, much more
assertively, that the attempt of the Preface 'not to allow that life
and art, experience and the poetic representation of experience,
are different' is finally indefensible (1983, p. 124). 'In denying
the difference between experience and the imitation of experience, the Preface means to efface enunciation altogether'
(p. 125). The result is not only that poetry is to be 'so wholly

transparent to experience that it is virtually identical to it', but that any self-conscious literariness must – in Wordsworth's book – constitute bad poetry.

Stephen Land's earlier analysis similarly emphasises Wordsworth's profound mistrust of words. Naturally devious things, they need to have their potentially distorting effects limited by the creative strategy of keeping to a simple vocabulary. The human models for such simplicity are those least corrupted by a commercial economy and by urban living (1973, p. 163). Put in political terms, Wordsworth's alternative to poetic diction is a 'republican alternative' but *not* one that embraces the potentially divisive use of *dialect*. Usually bent on consigning its speakers to the realms of comedy or unintelligibility it is 'an indicator of social difference' and therefore harmful to readers encouraged to 'meditate upon the essential similarities between man and man' (Simpson, 1987, p. 102).

Perhaps the last, if not the latest, word on the Preface should be Donald Davie's:

> Wordsworth was his own worst critic. Coleridge was right. The Preface to *Lyrical Ballads* is great literature; but it is great as a personal testament, not as criticism, or if as criticism, then criticism at its most theoretical. . . . It is theoretical in the sense that it is wise about the nature and function of poetry and poetic pleasure, and foolish about poetic techniques. To be particular, Wordsworth invites us to approach his poems by considering their diction; whereas most of these poems by-pass questions of diction altogether. . . . The early poems, when they succeed, do so by virtue of invention; the language is as nearly irrelevant as it can be in poetry.
>
> (1952, pp. 111–13)

6
Personal Perspectives: The 'Other' Lyrical Ballads

It seems that whenever we pick up a book or article on *Lyrical Ballads* we encounter paradox. Hazlitt, whose remarks retain their freshness and percipience to this day, began the fashion by divining in the revolutionary origins of the volume a reaction to 'servile imitation and tamest commonplace', generating verse of 'the utmost pitch of singularity and paradox' (1818, 1944 edn, p. 247). Arnold felt that the route to Wordsworth's psyche lay through his 'paradoxes'. More recently Beer has confessed that the power of *Lyrical Ballads* remains 'something of a puzzle' (1978, p. 56), and Hartman has referred us to the 'paradox' of a mind unwilling to transcend natural fact (1964, p. 39). Colin Clarke has even gone so far as to entitle his study *Romantic Paradox* (1962).

Contradictions are woven into the very fabric of *Lyrical Ballads*. The volume was a joint enterprise, yet the table of contents conveys the air of a random collocation of disparate items. The decision to bring together poems on natural and supernatural subjects seem, on the face of it, like an attempt to mix oil and water. Coleridge's supernatural masterpiece was not to Wordsworth's taste, but then Coleridge had reservations about his friend's matter-of-fact ballads, later asserting that he had been 'far more alive' than his detractors to Wordsworth's 'faults and defects' (*CL*, IV, 780). In fact the very *title* has proved enduring problematic: not only does it couple an unwilling pair of generic bedfellows; it fails to do justice to the range of poetic 'experiments' in the collection. And are they 'experiments' anyway? I hope the survey of criticism has revealed the gulf –

with all sorts of islands in between – that separates the views of those who talk of a 'revolution in poetry' and those who, following Mayo's sober lead, see the volume as conforming 'to the taste and interests of some segments of the literary world in 1798'. Ironically evaluations of *Lyrical Ballads* have been frequently geared directly to the criterion of *originality*, a Romantic concept that is now a cornerstone of appraisal for all the arts in the Western world.

Whatever one's views on the volume's trail-blazing virtues, it is clearly a very mixed bag. We will all judge the contents differently, but some poems are palpably uneven in quality and a few (Coleridge's 'other' contributions for example) have been pretty much ignored. Even the famous Preface is sometimes short on lucidity and consistency, prompting the sacrilege that its fame may not be independent of an opacity that has necessitated much 'clarification' by critics. Abrams voices a commonly held view about the divide between precept and practice when he affirms that *Lyrical Ballads* succeeds precisely where the Preface and Advertisement fail, in making the transition from an Augustan view of man and nature. That is reason enough to take account of authorial 'intention', despite its dismissal as an irrelevance by formalists, in the following discussion. Contextual considerations may in turn prompt thoughts about the overall unity of *Lyrical Ballads*, but it is at best a fragile unity, as even its proponents (Prickett, Beer, etc.) admit. That is an issue best left to the final pages of this book.

Without going to the other extreme, that of seeing the enterprise as an arbitrary yoking-together of heterogeneous elements, I am concentrating my critical gaze in this chapter on the individual poems of the volume, forging connections where they seem justified by internal 'evidence' – certainly the poems do seem to fall naturally into groups – but also conscious that each piece is an autonomous entity, separately created and deserving of discrete treatment. Four poems – the longest and the most assured in the judgement of posterity, and in three cases so judged by Wordsworth too! – have already been subjected to the spotlight of scrutiny by coveys of critics. Now it is the turn of the remaining nineteen – one baulks at saying *less well-known* pieces, though that *is* the case – to submit to interpretation. Most are considered independently, though the 'Yew-tree' lines and the prison poems ('The Convict' and 'The

Dungeon') are relegated to the final chapter's discussion of unity and diversity.

I wish to declare my own critical hand at once. It is a pluralist not a purist one. If writing this book has taught me anything, it has made me aware that, in the current free-market economy of criticism, each and every approach has something to commend it. I have no hesitation, for example, in including relevant extrinsic matters – circumstances of composition, authorial pronouncements, and the like – though they assume greater importance in relation to the issue of unity. While the disciples of an absolute formalism – do they still exist? – might disapprove, stated intentions can prove a helpful first step to understanding, even when, as so often happens, the original objective is modified, perhaps metamorphosed out of recognition, during the creative process. But formalist procedures, with their insistence on close textual analysis and their preoccupation with tone and structure, have left too indelible an imprint on modern criticism to be ignored – indeed, some of the most penetrating interpretations of individual ballads foreground Wordsworth's skilful role as ironist. Sometimes unintended, more often conscious and subtle strategies, these ironies embrace a whole range of personalities engaged in the poetic experience – be it poet, persona, 'gentle reader', narrator or protagonist. Problematic and post-structuralist procedures, with their emphasis on the accidental, on erasure and sub-text, have also helped me get to grips with these elusive poems; such procedures discern in *Lyrical Ballads* prescient intimations of a modernity that demands flexibility rather than uniformity of attitude, respect for the dissonances of life and art rather than for harmonious feelings and their predictable expression. For the uncertainty of *tone* in these ballads, despite what post-structuralists or historicists may decree, is as much conscious as accidental; their simplicity is often *deliberately* dissembling. Both collectively and individually they upset our complacency and undermine our anticipated responses.

Three Ballads

'The Female Vagrant'

'The Female Vagrant' is undoubtedly one of the poems that

appear to emphasise the *ad hoc* nature of the compilation. Admittedly, the title hardly suggests inconsonance. After all, this particular vagrant is part and parcel of a 'mixed rabble' of destitutes: the 'noble savages' of 'The Foster Mother's Tale'; deprived Goody Blake and ailing Simon Lee; the speakers, overwhelmed by personal loss, of 'Old Man Travelling' and 'The Last of the Flock'; the abandoned characters of 'The Thorn', 'The Mad Mother' and 'The Forsaken Indian Woman'. Of these soul-mates, five are women.

The clue to difference lies not in subject matter but in dating. In its original (1791–2) version this poem formed part of 'Salisbury Plain', which makes it, by some distance, the earliest contribution. Such dating confirms its immaturity – as Wordsworth recognised. For, though Coleridge had been much affected on hearing 'The Female Vagrant', Wordsworth never took to it. Indeed, judged by the subsequent pronouncements about ordinary language in the Advertisement and the Preface, the poem fails to measure up. Why, then, did the author neither discount it or at least eliminate the most studied poeticisms? Arguably appropriate to the reflective pieces, they fail to justify their presence here.

In fact 'The Female Vagrant' is shot through with poetic diction; with the kind of artificiality that Southey immediately praised and Wordsworth soon abhorred: the periphrasis of 'fleecy store' (flock), 'snowy pride' (fleece) and 'dewy prime', the arch personification of 'journal time', and the tautology of 'sad distress' – all without a built-in excuse such as we find in 'The Thorn'. Add to these devices the reverberating sound without sense of 'equinoctial deep' and the stilted measures of a Spenserian stanza which allows only three rhymes in a nine-line unit, and one has some idea of the poem's sense of contrivance.

To be fair, Wordsworth was aware of the linguistic impurities of 'The Female Vagrant', stating that the 'diction of that Poem is often vicious, and the descriptions are often false, giving proofs of a mind inattentive to the true nature of the subject on which it was employed' (*EL*, p. 328). Revealingly he sent Anne Taylor a substantial list of revisions in the same letter of April 1801, since the poem 'did not conform to the principle laid down in the Preface that he had "at all times endeavoured to look steadily at my subject" ' (Gill, 1989, p. 191). Just how far Wordsworth had moved in the direction of a convincing simplicity and in adopting the language of 'repeated experience and regular feeling' (B&J, p. 245) can be seen by comparing this poem with the austere but altogether more authentic effects of 'Old Man Travelling' or the measured but convincing speech of the 'statesman' in 'The Last of the Flock'. Six years is a long time in a young poet's life.

Yet, however artificial and even sub-Augustan the language, the substance of the poem *is* revolutionary and makes for a disparity between the mode of expression and the ideas expressed, between signifier and signified. Wordsworth had told Francis Wrangham in a letter of November 1795 that 'Adventures on Salisbury Plain' (of which 'The Female Vagrant' was a part) was written 'partly to expose the vices of the penal law and the calamities of war as they affect individuals' (*EL*, p. 159). Thus it *is* a product of the poet's revolutionary phase, the most politically daring and explicit of the pieces of *Lyrical Ballads* in its exposé of a culture to whose poetic manners the ballad paradoxically pays homage. It is significant that the 'apostate' Wordsworth – now distanced from Godwinian necessarianism or Jacobinical ideas – altered the text in 1802 and again in 1805 in an effort to tone down his attack on the inequities of society; in 1842 the version published as stanzas 23–50 of 'Guilt and Sorrow' almost mitigates the social criticism out of existence.

So what is the poem about? The narrative, though 270 lines long, has some of the folk ballad's directness and economy, if not its simple quatrain or studied impersonality and understatement. The woman who tells her tale has grown up a child of nature, in harmony with her surroundings and secure in her 'hereditary nook'. Like the speaker of 'The Last of the Flock', her father is 'a good and pious man' who here combines the time-honoured Lake District occupations of farming and fishing. But their twenty-year idyll is threatened. A new acquisitive landowner, that bane of the agrarian revolution in general and of Cumbria in particular, tries to buy them out. Failing in that endeavour, he none the less forces them into poverty – forfeiture of fishing-rights followed by the loss of their 'dear-loved home' (l. 63) – and desperate emigration to America. There, in a calamitous year of 'sword / And ravenous plague' (ll. 132–3), the unwilling exile loses her entire family. She returns, desolated, to England; close to death, she is admitted to hospital; and after leaving she is befriended by a 'wild brood' of gypsies. Encountered

by the poet three years on, she has become, like the Mariner, a
hopeless wanderer; unlike him, she has been stripped of everything that makes life worth living.

> And now across this moor my steps I bend –
> Oh! tell me whither – for no earthly friend
> Have I. – She ceased, and weeping turned away,
> As if because her tale was at an end
> She wept; – because she had no more to say
> Of that perpetual weight which on her spirit lay.
>
> (ll. 265–70)

Such a summary inevitably – perhaps unfairly – stresses the
'sensational' nature of the subject. For the ballad burns with
social indignation both against grasping 'townee' landlords out
of harmony with their human and natural surroundings, trying
to ride roughshod over rural values with 'proffered gold' (l. 46) –
a situation Wordsworth knew at first-hand – and against the
horrors of a war that sets man against man ('the brood that lap
... their brother's blood' – l. 126). Society offers no redress. It
maltreats the poor, turns them into outcasts and then forgets or
criminalises them. This is precisely Godwin's stance in *Political
Justice*, where crime is seen as the inevitable concomitant of
social oppression: 'A numerous class of mankind are held down
in a state of abject penury, and are continually prompted by
disappointment and distress to commit violence upon their more
fortunate neighbours' (1798, I, 12).

In the context of the poem only the gypsies, outcasts themselves, offer a temporary haven to the vagrant. What for
Wordsworth compounds society's injustice is the fact that she
has done no wrong; despite her sense of guilt she is the innocent
victim of an increasingly corrupt system, driven by Mammonite
rather than Christian principles. And principles, despite her
experience, are what she values most; what she regrets is the
inevitable compromising of personal standards ('my inner self
abused' – l. 259) in the desperate search for survival. It is this
message, along with the natural process whereby these values
are inculcated, that is the most enduringly Wordsworthian
element in the poem. While the 1802 excision of the passage
about British soldiers in America is symptomatic of the growing
conservatism of the poet, the poem manages to sustain a more

positive note (as in the Preface, the credal lyrics and 'Tintern Abbey') – that 'Nature' is the best 'teacher'. The twenty formative years of happiness passed 'beneath the honeyed syca-more' (l. 30) cannot be forgotten or the values then implanted entirely uprooted. What also emerges – with typical force – is the poet's bottomless capacity for sympathy: his ability to empathise with the family as their rural heritage crumbles around them; to make us too feel 'that perpetual weight which on her spirit lay' (l. 270).

While the poem *is* technically flawed – Wordsworth was, after all, only twenty-two at most when he wrote it – it therefore remains interesting on two counts. First, it anticipates what will become a motif in *Lyrical Ballads*: the portrayal of individual distress, coupled with a Godwinian sense of indignation at societal oppression – 'protest' hand-in-hand with an 'interest in the workings of human feeling' (Jacobus, 1976, p. 147). Second, this strident political message – already displaced by a more personal and enduring pantheism – is packaged in a poetic diction that Wordsworth was soon to announce, in the Preface, he had 'taken as much pains to avoid ... as others ordinarily take to produce it' (B&J, p. 251). In one way the poem marks a fertile beginning, in another an unpromising cul-de-sac.

'The Last of the Flock'

The story of 'The Last of the Flock' is unfolded by a shepherd who, rather like the woman of 'The Female Vagrant', associates his happiest memories with the possession of 'fifty comely sheep' (l. 33). In both poems the pastoral idyll (eighteenth-century style) has been shattered by an apparently uncaring society – in this case not by an eighteenth-century developer but by a system that refuses 'relief' to a parishioner of obvious substance, despite the onerous claims of ten children. In both situations, the speaker – inherently virtuous, as Wordsworth is at pains to stress – is forced by circumstances to consider crime (here, 'To wicked deeds I was inclined' – l. 71); in both the confession is delivered to a listener whose sympathies, now recorded without a trace of overt sentimentality, are complicit with those of the poet.

But the obvious parallels end there. 'The Last of the Flock' is part of the *annus mirabilis*, a product of that three-month burst of creative activity in the spring of 1798 that spawned most of the poems in *Lyrical Ballads* ('The Female Vagrant' dates from 1791–2). The fact that it subsequently underwent little revision reflects its complicity with the statements of Advertisement and Preface. Hence its calculated ordinariness of vocabulary, in line with the Advertisement's apologetic but unrepentant warning of 'expressions' that may seem 'too familiar, and not of sufficient dignity', and the Preface's advocacy of 'plainer and more emphatic language' (B&J, p. 245). There are no words in this poem of more than two syllables ('The Female Vagrant' has at least fifty of three or more, many of them Latinate), and there are only two figurative tropes: 'like blood-drops' and 'melt like snow away' (ll, 59, 64) – both of them 'ballad' similes which do not draw attention to themselves and impede the narrative flow. The syntax too is in keeping with the direct utterance of the 'statesman': short, pithy sentences and reiterated phrases (Wordsworth defends functional tautology in his note to 'The Thorn') with the minimum of subordination.

More significant, the poem illustrates the tenets of the Preface in 'making interesting the incidents of common life . . . by tracing in them . . . the primary laws of our nature: chiefly as far as regards the manner in which we associate ideas in a state of excitement' (B&J, p. 245). Wordsworth has chosen a real situation, one in which his rustic character speaks a simple but impassioned language, born of his obsessional sense of loss. The elegiac note rings true. Here is no overwrought Godwinian tale, like 'The Female Vagrant', designed to propagandise the evils of an indifferent society and couched in an adjectival language ('illimitable' – 1. 175; 'remorseless' – 1. 131; 'incessant' – 1. 151) that ill suits the character of the teller. Instead the reader is presented with a compellingly direct tale in which the 'elementary feelings' do 'exist in a state of greater simplicity' (B&J, p. 245). Consequently our own emotions are more fully involved. If all effective poetry is the 'spontaneous overflow of powerful feelings', then here, indubitably, is the sense of speaker, poet and reader alike experiencing such a groundswell of emotion. Not that the poet/observer allows himself the least demonstration of sentimentality: after the manner of the traditional ballad, he simply observes and records. Dr Burney identified himself with the shepherd in just the committed and ingenuous way that Wordsworth hoped the bulk of his readers would: 'If the author

be a wealthy man, he ought not to have suffered this poor
peasant to part with the last of the flock' (B&J, p. 322).

Of course, much of the poem's strength derives from its roots
in reality. Much later (1843) Wordsworth revealed that 'the
incident occurred in the village of Holford, close by Alfoxden'
(FN, *PW*, II, 476). Not as extreme in situation as 'The Female
Vagrant', the poem 'confronts not death but destitution – the
plight of the labouring poor' (Jacobus, 1976, p. 202). Therein
lies its potency: as a veracious elegy about the human condition,
something to which the earlier poem aspires but – too meretricious by half – only fleetingly achieves. And the image of a
weeping shepherd, his cheeks wet with tears, resonates in the
mind with biblical force.

None the less the poem's morality is not as straightforward or
even as laudable as it appears. That word 'paradox' comes to
mind again. On the face of it, the ballad proposes a direct
refutation of a Godwinian truth embodied in 'The Female
Vagrant' and subsequently stated thus by the poet:

> The man who holds with Godwin that property is the cause
> of every vice and the source of all the misery of the poor
> is naturally astonished to find that this so called evil,
> the offspring of human institutions, is a vigorous instinct
> closely interwoven with the noblest feelings. It represents
> familiar and dearly-loved fields, a hereditary cottage and
> flocks, every animal of which has its own name.
>
> (FN, *PW*, II, 476)

The poem is critical, moreover, of a system of parish relief which
permits a man of property no benefits at all.

Such views certainly coincide with Wordsworth's growing
conservatism. His assertion not only of man's right to *own*
property but also of its stabilising emotional influence hints at
what his detractors were to label 'apostasy'. Yet this reading
displaces another message threatening to surface in the poem:
that the man's values are deeply suspect because he places
chattels before children. Only after four stanzas and thirteen
references to his beloved sheep does the shepherd actually deign
to mention his 'ten children' (l. 41). Even then, his primary
feelings are directed not towards his *offspring*, admittedly now
nourished on the proceeds of his first sale, but to the potential

loss of a flock. It is *this* loss which provokes the poem's solitary irruption of melodramatic language: 'It was a vein that never stopp'd / Like blood-drops from my heart they dropp'd' (ll. 63–4). While it is true that the loss of all fifty sheep (now anticipated in the last line) prefigures financial ruin, it does not mean starvation for a family who will now, presumably, be cared for by the parish.

Indeed, the reference to a flock 'as dear as my own children be' – an odd inversion in the context of a poem that constantly puts the sheep at the centre of the speaker's consciousness and of his love for his own kith and kin – is delayed until the penultimate stanza and then is compounded by the revelation that loss of sheep breeds resentment of those nearest and dearest responsible for the loss: 'I prayed, yet every day I thought / I loved my children less' (ll. 87–8). The final image is of the last lamb cradled like a child – but not a child ('and here it lies upon my arm' – l. 97); the concluding remark ('It is the last of all my flock') reinforces a sense of *Angst* that has little to do with parental love and much to do with material deprivation.

Lest such a reading be considered eccentric, consider the following passage from Darwin's *Zoönomia* (1796, ii, 360) on the subject of 'Diseases of Increased Volition':

> When a person becomes insane, who has a family of small children to solicit his attention, the prognostic is very un-favourable; as it shews the maniacal hallucination to be more powerful than those ideas [paternal feelings?] which generally interest us the most.

We know from the Advertisement that Wordsworth had been reading Darwin's treatise, and, though we cannot be sure that he had this precise passage in mind, it does reinforce my belief that there are antithetical currents in his poem. Certainly its primary message is that rural property – like Yeats's 'spreading laurel tree' – gives us roots and a sense of belonging. On the other hand, this obsession with ownership can, in pathological cases such as this, reflect, in its suppression of parental love, a peculiar form of incipient insanity. Perhaps this displaced meaning reveals a tension, overt or latent, in the poet's own psyche – a vacillation both personal and political that was still shaking his being in the spring of 1798.

'Old Man Travelling'

That this poem has elicited a host of diverse reactions reflects a deceptive simplicity. Southey found it so unsatisfactory that he produced a new and altogether more predictable 'version' – 'The Sailor's Mother' – in his *English Eclogues* of the following year. Glen argues that even Wordsworth – who tacked on the five lines of the conclusion and then later suppressed the direct speech – found the poem 'in some way disquieting' (1983, p. 226). Yet for Hartman it is 'one of the perfect pieces of the collection' (1987, p. 147). Such varied responses confirm its obliquity. An anti-war statement *may* be intended by the juxta-posing of natural decay and unnatural mutilation, but there is nothing stridently pacifist or overtly propagandist after the manner of 'The Female Vagrant'. Even the shepherd's obvious distress ('weep in the public roads' – l. 4) and the poet's compassionate inquiry ('What ails you?' – l. 16), so strongly and unsentimentally rendered in 'The Last of the Flock', are here merely implicit.

Wordsworth's own gloss provides a useful starting-point. Recollecting the poem's genesis as 'an overflowing from "The Old Cumberland Beggar"' (FN, *PW*, IV, 447–8), de Selincourt follows the poet's suggestion that 'it split off as a study of the inward state of the old man expressed in his outward form: "resigned to quietness" in the margin of ll. 7–8 (in the MS.) expresses the spiritual core of it' (*PW*, IV, 448). Like 'The Last of the Flock' and 'The Female Vagrant', the poem adopts the well-tried formula of an encounter between listener and teller, poet and stranger, in which the speaker's observations prompt a question, about 'the object of his journey', and answer: that he is 'going many miles' (l. 17), to see his dying son, mortally wounded in a naval battle. Another of Wordsworth's simple solitaries on the *via dolorosa* of life.

Yet the experience of reading the poem is, finally, an un-settling one, which the sub-title, 'Animal Tranquillity and Decay', fails to dispel. In 'The Female Vagrant' the mismatch between poetic diction and 'revolutionary' content appeared to indicate a lack of real imaginative involvement on the part of the immature poet; in 'The Last of the Flock', where the language for the most part manages that very ordinariness which Words-worth sought, the surface message subverts another and more disturbing moral, which, for all its efforts at repression, the poem does not entirely expunge. In 'Old Man Travelling', however, tension seems to reside in the disparity between opening description and concluding explanation; guilty here neither of incompetence or of dishonesty, Wordsworth appears bent – as he always does in the best of these ballads – on the active manipulation of our feelings as we engage with the situation in the poem.

At first the title adequately prefigures the poem's sombre and stoical mood: 'tranquillity' suffuses the 'settled quiet' (l. 8) of the old man's outward demeanour and measured progress towards an unknown destiny. The traveller has moved beyond conventional responses, beyond the need to exercise patience in a self-conscious way ('a thing of which he hath no need' – l. 12). He is part and parcel of that natural world which, for most of us, remains ever impenetrable; he has achieved a serenity which even 'the young' (including, presumably, the young poet 'behold with envy' (l. 14). His bodily decrepitude – the outward and visible sign of life's downward spiral – and his tranquil acceptance of it provoke mixed emotions in poet and reader: intimations of mortality as well as admiration for the traveller's fortitude.

But the old man's brief explanation of his journey's tragic purpose comes as a shock, a jarring juxtaposition to what has gone before:

> Sir! I am going many miles to take
> A last leave of my son, a mariner,
> Who from a sea-fight has been brought to Falmouth
> And there is dying in an hospital.
>
> (ll. 17–20)

Such an abrupt termination may make *us* question – as did the poet – the advisability of including it *at all* (Wordsworth excised it in 1815). After all, does the reply provide anything more than a note of intrusive discord? My answer, which is indebted to Heather Glen's valuable interpretation, is that Wordsworth wanted to make a point about 'decay' of another kind – the cutting-off of a young man in his prime by the murderous hand of war. The 'decay' of the subtitle thus acquires another resonance, that of a dissolution less acceptable because more unnatural in one so young. The inevitable concomitant of man's inhumanity to man, it is, in the last analysis, the decay of putrifying wounds. The old man appears in a new light, no longer 'led to peace so perfect' but despairingly and perhaps unsuccessfully trying to embrace his son before he dies. He is led 'by nature' (l. 12), but it is human nature *in extremis* cleaving to its own; the 'peace' now becomes the 'peace' of a *son*'s death which he anticipates with anguish, the stoicism of his appearance paradoxically at odds with his inner feelings.

A subtle manipulation of our feelings has taken place. Taken early into the confidence of the observer, we have *apparently* been privy to the old man's innermost thoughts, however abstractly described in such phrases as 'insensibly subdued to settled quiet' (ll. 7–8). The conclusion, on the other hand, provokes the sharp realisation that the poet has not pigeonholed his character's feelings in the predictably sentimental terms that we – or, still more, the readers of fashionable magazines of the day – would have expected. 'Mild compromise' and 'long patience' suggest authorial omniscience, but such omniscience is, finally, an illusion. We, like the poet, only *know* the deserving poor via their own speech, by listening to their own 'spontaneous overflow of powerful feelings'. The poet's silence after the old man's reply is significant; like his readers, he is at a loss for words – and platitudes will not do. The poet has questioned the validity of a single controlling authorial viewpoint, and the contradictions, once revealed, refuse to go away: a slow and 'tranquil' decline is juxtaposed to a premature and violent end and the grief it engenders; polite but misguided assumptions about the deserving poor are confounded by real exposure to suffering humanity – father and son. Wordsworth has shattered our complacency.

It is no coincidence that the 'plainer and more emphatic language' of the old man holds the emotional key to the poem. As with all the rustic speech of *Lyrical Ballads*, these direct utterances are crucial contributions to the poems' significance – whether it be the simple curse of Goody Blake or the 'traveller bold' of 'The Idiot Boy' offering his two-line verdict on nocturnal escapades. No longer a rambling, melodramatic tale like 'The Female Vagrant', the traveller's reply offers a pithy encapsulation of profound emotion that goes far beyond tub-thumping pacifism or stock reader expectation. We are educated in the feelings – and Wordsworth has been our teacher.

Two Laments

'The Complaint of the Forsaken Indian Woman'

Of the foregoing triptych of poems based on an interaction between observer and observed, two are grounded in actual experience and bring the everyday world into art. Superficially this 'complaint' is very different. Written in a well-established poetic genre, it has a 'bookish' inspiration – like 'The Ancient Mariner', the product of reading and not of a personal encounter. Indeed, one might be forgiven for asking why it is here at all. The answer certainly does not lie (as with 'The Female Vagrant' and 'Old Man Travelling') in its arbitrary annexation for such purposes; there is no gainsaying Wordsworth's unequivocal statement that it was 'written in Alfoxden in 1798, where I read Hearne's Journey with deep interest. It was composed for the volume of *Lyrical Ballads*' (FN, *PW*, II, 474).

The Preface of 1800 elaborates on this decision. There Wordsworth singles the poem out as a pivotal example of his self-imposed artistic brief to 'follow the fluxes and reflexes of the mind when agitated by the great and simple affections of our nature' (B&J, p. 247). The woman's mind *is* 'agitated'; here 'maternal passion' is laid bare 'at the approach of death', still 'cleaving in solitude to life and society' (p. 247). The source, as both Preface and epigraph make clear, was Hearne's *Journey from Hudson's Bay to the Northern Ocean* (1795, p. 202). Such travel books were more Coleridge's meat than Wordsworth's; their appeal lay in their exotic locales and customs. For Wordsworth, however, it was the human dimension that was disturbingly memorable in Hearne. The conflict between a grim necessity (the abandonment of the old or infirm) and instinctive human feelings left an indelible impression on the poet: 'At length, poor creature! she dropt behind, and no one attempted to go back in search of her' (*PW*, II, 475).

The evidence of 'Old Man Travelling' confirms a Wordsworth conviction: namely, that in extremity the human mind attains a single-mindedness, honesty and power that is denied it in more mundane circumstances. That the speaker here is Amerindian in no way invalidates his point; Wordsworth's capacity for compassionate involvement – what Coleridge referred to as 'ventriloquism' and Keats might positively term 'negative capa-

bility' – allows him to empathise with the victim and her
predicament. Nor does the exotic setting necessarily diminish
the poem's relevance to Wordsworth's pronouncements about
'humble and rustic life'. This *is* humble and rustic even if it is
North American; here strange customs are superimposed upon
the bedrock of a common humanity. Readers of *Lyrical Ballads*
would have had no difficulty in relating to this kind of 'ballad'.
While the homely and everyday was one side of the coin of
eighteenth-century primitivism, the exotic was the other. As
Mary Jacobus reminds us, Hugh Blair's *Lectures on Rhetoric and
Belles Lettres* (1763) gave Wordsworth every justification for
going beyond his own experience in the perennial search for
subject matter; Blair, privileging the primitive origins of pure
poetry, singled out American Indian song as a peculiarly vital
tradition for the lamentation of 'public and private calamities'
(II. 314–15; quoted by Jacobus, 1976, p. 189). In fact this poem
charts the most inevitable and extreme calamity in the volume:
deserted by companions and forcibly separated from her child,
the Indian woman pleads for a death which cannot arrive too
soon.

   None the less it can be argued that the complaint is not
unrelievedly gloomy or consistently successful. Despite the cutting of that physical bond which still links mother and babe in
'The Mad Mother', this ballad hints at the existence of another:
that between the human and natural worlds. That 'cleaving'
(which Hartman argues is the central emotion in these ballads)
to tribe and child is thus, in Beer's opinion, partially replaced by
a 'basic magnetisation . . . to the energies of the universe' (1978,
p. 69) as revealed in the 'crackling flashes' of the Aurora
Borealis. They haunt both dreams and waking moment. But
indubitably the most powerful bond is between mother and
child: she recalls how, at the epiphanic moment of separation,
the child seemed suddenly galvanised in a forlorn attempt to
protect her ('Through his whole body something ran / A most
strange something did I see' – ll. 35–6).

   In this ineffectual attempt to locate instinctual feelings of
protection in an unlikely source (though the heightened sensi-
bilities of the child is an issue addressed elsewhere: in 'We Are
Seven' or 'The Nightingale', for example) Wordsworth stresses
his belief that natural energies exist in both microcosm and
macrocosm; the Indian would more readily embrace death if she

were in contact both with nature and human nature. That, alas, is not to be. 'Fire', the most pervasive image in the poem, is a potentially vitalising and redemptive force. But, now glimpsed only far off in the 'crackling flashes' of the 'northern gleams', it can no longer provide a companionable warmth. The ashes are 'stiff with ice', the water has turned 'snowy white', and the premonitory implications of 'my fire is dead' (l. 55) are all too obvious.

Averill maintains that the focus of interest is psychological – a study of 'the effects of isolation and alienation upon the confusion of a dying mind' (1980, p. 152). But, though the poem offers some basic psychological insights and provides what might be construed as an outlet for personal feelings of guilt, its barely relieved stoicism, and a predictability threatened only by this bizarrely rendered telepathy between child and mother, make it a less compelling portrayal of 'confusion' then we are given in 'The Mad Mother'. Perhaps the absence of genuine ballad inspiration and the 'exotic' locale *do* make its trite and static effects feel more contrived; at all events Wordsworth's attempt to impose a massive weight of pathos upon unfamiliar material has not entirely succeeded.

'The Mad Mother'

Placed next in the collection to 'The Idiot Boy', where a wretched mother is driven frantic by her missing son, 'The Mad Mother' offers another insight into derangement and unbalance. Yet, superficially at least, it is closer in spirit and substance and probably chronology to 'The Complaint of the Forsaken Indian Woman'.

Both poems are about solitaries, the one physically, the other imaginatively distanced from the temperate climes of Somerset; both are portraits of abandoned women for whom 'maternal passion' remains the most powerful and elemental feeling, even when their own lives are poignantly at risk. In their choice of mother and child as victim, both elegies appear to give expression to deep-seated feelings of remorse over the Annette Vallon episode. Mary Moorman even notes 'a similarity between the language of some of the stanzas ... and that of Annette's letters': for example, 'If her features are altered ... her heart is unchanged' becomes 'if it's true / Be changed ... / 'Tis

fair enough for thee' (1957, p. 385). However, the poem's literary
ancestry, despite the employment of tetrameters and a ten-line
stanza (the same scheme as in the 'Complaint'), is to be sought
in such folk ballads as 'Lady Bothwell's Lament', where the sole
audience for the woman's outpourings is her own baby. Certainly
the poem's sentiments and phrasing would seem to reinforce this
connection. As with the Indian 'Complaint', the poet encountered
the experience at second hand, though – significant for the
poem's success – not from a book but from another human
being: 'The subject was reported to me by a lady of Bristol who
had seen the poor creature' (FN, *PW*, II, 476). One can
reasonably assume that the sheer poignancy of the story, again
stirring a dormant sense of guilt, prompted a creative response.
Whichever poem came first, it is clear from the reiteration of the
concluding rhymes ('die' and 'away' end stanzas in both pieces)
that the poet either had the first piece in mind while writing the
second, or was working on both at the same time.

There are further points of contact. In both poems the
dominant emotion is of a mother for her baby son. Though in
'The Complaint' this ultimate source of solace has been forcibly
wrenched from her grasp, the sense of kinship between them has
led to a miraculous if barely credible moment of revelation when
the clairvoyant child anticipates a manhood in which he can
protect his mother. A similar sense of the extraordinary nexus
between mother and son informs 'The Mad Mother'. Here,
while mature feelings are again attributed to the infant ('Oh!
love me, love me little boy!' – l. 41) it is the therapy of actual
physical contact that the poet valorises – that natural connection
between breast and lips that, like a healing poultice, draws out
the inner sense of pain and despair ('It cools my blood; it cools
my brain' – l. 32). There seems no reason to doubt Averill's
conclusion that the poet had been reading Darwin again and had
noted his specific suggestion that in cases of acute post-natal
depression 'the child should be brought frequently to the
mother, and applied to her breast, if she will suffer it . . . by a few
trials it frequently excites . . . maternal affection and removes the
insanity' (1796, II, 360; quoted in Averill, 1980, p. 156).

Yet there are significant differences here which argue that
Wordsworth intended a palinode rather than a companion piece,
one which built on lessons learnt in composing the 'Complaint'.
The Indian woman's all-too-realistic sense of hopelessness

makes death welcome ('oh let my body die away!' – l. 2), for she has lost the companionable presence of the one thing that would make life worth living; conversely, the mad mother's pathetic cleaving to a fantasy world of pastoral delights shows how out of touch with reality she is and gives the lament a psychological complexity that recalls 'The Idiot Boy'. Admittedly her child still suckles at her breast, but the naïveté of her language and the attendant simplicity of her vision are an ironic reminder of a stark truth: that she and her child are doomed. The Indian woman, while clearly a victim, is both pragmatic in her attitudes and a victim of pragmatism, of tribal necessity. The mad mother's case is poles apart: she has been exploited by an uncaring husband who has callously (so we are told) deserted his little family. And, though her 'madness' seems to anticipate this desertion and may even be linked to post-natal depression, this betrayal has unbalanced her further and prompts her obsessional references to him. Wordsworth makes no attempt to suggest this derangement through the conventional literary methods of fragmented syntax or dislocated imagery; instead it emerges in child-like confessions of secret hideaways, descriptions of landscape that at times recall the wood-lore of a Caliban ('I know the poisons of the shade, / I know the earth-nuts fit for food' – ll. 95–6) but more often issue in a rose-coloured view of a benevolent and exotic nature which though savage is essentially harmless, or in a picture of a father who, against all the evidence, is weighed down by guilt.

There are more sinister and elusive overtones. What are the references to the 'fiendish faces' that 'hung at my breasts and pulled at me'? (ll. 23–4). Is Wordsworth suggesting the manic excesses of puerperal depression – for which Darwin proposes the very remedy supplied by the poem? Or is the very grotesqueness of the language a comment on the earlier unnatural but necessary practice of suckling other people's children in order to survive? The conclusion adumbrates yet more disturbing possibilities: the potential transference of resentment from husband to child ('that look so wild / It never, never came from me' – ll. 87–8); and, following the disturbing reference to 'poisons of the shade' (l. 95), continuation of the pointless search for a father who, wherever he may be, is clearly *not* 'in the wood' (l. 98). Finally the reader is left with the haunting, incantatory and Blakean 'Now laugh and be gay, to the woods away! / And there, my babe; we'll live for aye (ll. 99–100). Ultimately elusive in terms of time and mood, the poem actively engages the reader in constructing meaning in a way that 'The Complaint of the Forsaken Indian Woman' does not; our sympathy and curiosity are involved as we read a poem whose simplicity is only skin-deep.

'Goody Blake and Harry Gill'

Of all the Lyrical Ballads, none has a more clearly established provenance than 'Goody Blake and Harry Gill'. One of only four poems referred to by name in the Advertisement, it is there described as 'founded on a well-authenticated fact which happened in Warwickshire', an event already recorded for posterity in Erasmus Darwin's *Zoönomia* (1796). This book was, as we know from Averill's study (1980), an important source of material for Wordsworth's rustic ballads, a fact borne out by the poet's urgent request for a copy early in 1798 – the very time when *Lyrical Ballads* was in gestation. Beer draws our attention to the 'urgency of the underlining' in Wordsworth's request for the original version of the tale – his appetite doubtless already whetted by Coleridge. 'I write merely to request (which I have very particular reasons for doing) that you would contrive to send me Dr. Darwin's *Zoönomia by the first carrier*' (letter to Cottle, 28 February 1798, *EL*, p. 199).

We can allow ourselves the same luxury as Wordsworth was about to enjoy by going straight to his source:

A young farmer from Warwickshire, finding his hedges broke, and the sticks carried away during a frosty season, determined to watch for the thief. He lay many cold hours under a haystack, and at length an old woman, like a witch in a play, approached, and began to pull up the hedge; he waited till she had tied up her bottle of sticks, and was carrying them off, that he might convict her of the theft, and then springing from his concealment, he seized his prey with violent threats. After some altercation, in which her load was left upon the ground, she kneeled upon her bundle of sticks, and, raising her arms to Heaven beneath the bright moon then at the full, spoke to the farmer already shivering with cold, 'Heaven grant, that thou

mayest never know again the blessing to be warm.' He
complained of cold all the next day, and wore an uppercoat,
and in a few days another, and in a fortnight took to his bed,
always saying nothing made him warm; he covered himself
with many blankets, and had a sieve over his face as he lay;
and from this one insane idea he kept his bed above twenty
years for fear of the cold air, till at length he died.

(Darwin, 1796, quoted in PW, IV, 439–40)

It is not difficult to understand the passage's appeal for Wordsworth. It contains most of the ingredients he could work into a
ballad. About a poor and lonely old creature ('This woman
dwelt in Dorsetshire, / Her hut was on a cold hill-side' – ll. 29–
30), it gave him an opportunity to express his concern for the
plight of rural communities in Dorset, elsewhere reflected in
Dorothy's remark that 'the peasants are miserably poor; their
cottages are shapeless structures (I may almost say) of wood and
clay – indeed they are not at all beyond what might be expected
in savage life' (*EL*, p. 162). The poet himself had, already, on 24
October 1795, observed that such grinding penury was a
seedbed for crime: 'the country people here are wretchedly poor;
ignorant and overwhelmed with every vice that usually attends
ignorance in that class, viz. lying and picking and stealing, etc.'
(*LL*, III, 1334; quoted in B&J, p. 283). As Brett and Jones remind
us, this association of vice and ignorance is pure Godwinianism:
hence Wordsworth's attack against farmers (a young drover in
the poem), who were 'enjoying unusual prosperity while the
peasants were suffering severe hardships' (B&J, p. 283).

Not only on the breadline, Goody is, like Simon Lee, a victim
of advancing years and inclement elements ('But when the ice
our streams did fetter / Oh! then how her old bones would
shake' – ll. 41–2). Worse, she is alone and has in Harry a most
unneighbourly neighbour hellbent on punishing her. But Wordsworth further softens and humanises the story. The Darwinian
version, which dispenses with the intimacy of names, tells of a
destructive woman who intends to 'pull up the hedge' and of a
farmer finding his hedges 'broke'. The poet, on the other hand,
directs the reader to an old hedge whose dead sticks, unremoved,
would actually impede new growth. More to the point, Wordsworth's Goody has a record of unremitting industry ('All day she
spun in her poor dwelling / And then her three hours work at

night' – ll. 25–6). This is allied to a cheerful disposition that still contrives to surface in summertime. 'Then at the door the *canty* dame / Would sit as any linnet gay' – ll. 39–40). Moreover, the Darwinian simile 'like a witch in a play', with its suggestions not only of evil and black magic but also of unreality, is expunged; instead Wordsworth builds up a compassionate picture of Goody's predicament (compare the Female Vagrant's mendicancy in the adjacent poem) that forces her into what is, quite literally, a *life-saving* activity. She knows that, according to the letter of the law, she is in the wrong (her act a 'trespass') and that she risks detection, but the frost is 'past enduring'. *In extremis*, she is in that 'state of excitement' that Wordsworth felt revealed so much about the human psyche.

What Wordsworth finds equally fascinating is 'the psychology of fear' (Mary Moorman's phrase 1957, p. 383) – here demonstrated by the 'punishment' of Harry. The poet is, of course, only too aware that the focus of Darwin's account is the *curse* and its effect. It is a study of what today would be diagnosed as psychosomatic illness – Darwin's 'one insane idea' whereby Harry, reacting literally to the curse of 'O may he never more be warm', is metamorphosed into the shivering wreck that confronts us at both the beginning and the end of the poem. But characteristically the poet sees the phenomenon not in clinical terms, as a species of insanity, but as a manifestation of the potency of our imaginative faculty, a demonstration of the 'truth that the power of the imagination is sufficient to produce such changes even in our physical nature as might almost appear miraculous. The truth is an important one; the fact (for it is a *fact*) is a valuable illustration of it' (B&J, p. 267).

Cursed like the Mariner by his victim(s), Harry has only himself to blame. But at least there is a grim irony in the fact not only that Harry's punishment fits the crime (Goody's hypothermia is transferred to him), but that his obsession initially drives him to endure nocturnal 'frost and snow' in order to wreak vengeance on his pathetic victim. In a sense, he has already *chosen* to be cold. Already there is more than a hint of that unnatural behaviour which will issue in a pathological condition. But his *froideur* goes deeper than that. It bespeaks an absence of warmth toward his fellow human beings, the complete negation of that concern and sympathy that Wordsworth seeks to instil in readers of his ballads.

As Mary Jacobus and, more recently, Richard Gravil have revealed, this element in the poem is 'openly parodic' of a current fashion (exemplified by Hannah More's *Cheap Repository for Publications on Religious and Moral Subjects*) whereby verse was utilised for the conveyance of 'moral truths to the lower orders. Such poetry chastises intemperance, improvidence and impatience in the name of solid bourgeois virtues' (Gravil, 1982, p. 48). Turning the tables on such values, Wordsworth's poem has the stalwart Harry (he of the 'cheeks as red as ruddy clover') worsted by a 'highly improvident old woman whose way of life recalls . . . the parable of the foolish virgins' (p. 48). The tone of the concluding apophthegm ('Now think, ye farmers all, I pray / Of Goody Blake and Harry Gill') echoes modish sententious verse but proposes a neat reversal of its values. Now it is the farmer, not the thief, who needs to think again. Yet to leave things there, as Gravil does in his excellent essay, may be to ignore another ironic dimension to the poem. Certainly the respectable farmer is cast throughout as the real villain of the piece. But Wordsworth hints that such a black-and-white reaction on our part is too simplistic – that we should no more condemn Harry out of hand than we would the 'baddie' of a moralistic tract. After all, his crime doesn't amount to much more than safeguarding his own property. So, while Darwin's heavily melodramatic conclusion sees his protagonist pining away on his sickbed for twenty years with 'a sieve over his face', in the poetic version Harry is still up and about. And, anyway, village gossip, as we know from 'The Thorn', is notoriously unreliable and given to exaggeration. By employing a homely ballad simile, Wordsworth ensures that our final response will be one in which our sense of justice done will be meliorated by amusement:

> 'Twas all in vain, a useless matter,
> And blankets were about him pinn'd;
> Yet still his jaws and teeth they clatter,
> Like a loose casement in the wind'
> (ll. 113–16)

True, Harry is the prototype of a man 'so concerned with his property and possessions, and so unmindful of the needs of others, that he never becomes fully human' (J. R. Watson, 1982,

p. 62). But, since, as in the Mariner's case, the penalty exceeds
the crime, the use of the present continuous tense hints that his
state may be no more permanent than the sailor's nightmare
ordeal. Even the Harry Gills of this world deserve a modicum of
our sympathy. If he 'never becomes fully human', we as readers
should not fall victim to the same state of mind.

'Simon Lee'

Infirmity, that most irreversible of all deprivations when coupled
with old age, is the unequivocal subject of 'Simon Lee'. As in
'Goody Blake and Harry Gill', Wordsworth asks his readers to
ponder the miseries of senility and to empathise with its victims,
particularly those uncushioned by wealth, friends or patrons
('His master's dead, and no one now / Dwells in the hall of Ivor'
– ll. 21–2). Once again the poet purposes a re-education in the
feelings of his 'gentle reader'. Lest we should be in any doubt,
the Preface gives clear notice of his intention to 'place' the
'Reader in the way of receiving from ordinary moral sensations
another and more salutary impression than we are accustomed
to receive from them' (B&J, p. 248).

Of all the rural ballads in the 1798 collection, 'Simon Lee'
gives us least in the way of a story to compel the attention.
Indeed, Wordsworth specifically counsels his readers *not* to
anticipate a thrilling yarn. Instead we should reflect on the
human issues raised by the chance encounter and thereby arrive
at profounder truths, truths which a varnished tale could
scarcely embody. Just as 'Goody Blake and Harry Gill', is, *inter
alia*, a parodic riposte to improving verse, so this ballad, by
playing down suspense and melodrama, undermines, as Hartman has noted, the stock convention of the 'moving accident'
('Hart-Leap Well'). None the less the 'accident' which inspired
the poem was one which shook the impressionable Wordsworth
to the roots of his being – so much so that he was able, nearly
half a century later, to recall it in remarkable detail:

> This old man had been huntsman to the Squires of Alfoxden,
> which at the time we occupied it, belonged to a minor. The old
> man's cottage stood upon the common, a little way from the
> entrance to Alfoxden Park. But it had disappeared. Many

other changes had taken place in the adjoining village, which I could not but notice with a regret more natural than well-considered. Improvements but rarely appear such to those who after long intervals of time, revisit places they have had much pleasure in. It is unnecessary to add, the fact as was mentioned in the poem; and I have, after an interval of 45 years, the image of the old man as fresh before my eyes as if I had seen him yesterday. The expression when the hounds were out, 'I dearly love their voices' was word for word from his own lips. (FN, *PW*, IV, 412–13)

Oddly the prose reminiscence makes no mention of the poem's concluding – and conclusive – incident. But it does remind us of that passage of time which has now put nearly half a century between Wordsworth and the encounter, and which now ironically threatens to undermine his own physical powers. But, if such thoughts of personal senescence are in the poet's head, they do not obtrude. Instead the septuagenarian's allusion to a subject as 'fresh before my eyes as if . . . yesterday' implies a vigorous old age denied Simon Lee. The recollection does however, underscore another concern of the poem – that of the enclosure of common land and its effect on farm labourers. Kenneth Maclean makes the point that, between 1799 and 1844, 1,765, 711 acres of common were enclosed by Act of Parliament, thus depriving the poor, in many cases, of free pasture (1950, p. 20). Happily, Simon Lee still has his patch, it appears; unhappily, he is too weak to work it. Here the irony resides in the fact that *nature* has reclaimed her own, as she inevitably does when man relinquishes the capacity to tame and husband her resources. It would have been easier to endure a *landless* old age than constantly be reminded – by the plot's untilled presence – of his own infirmity:

> This scrap of land he from the heath
> Enclosed when he was stronger;
> But what avails the land to them,
> Which they can till no longer?
> (ll. 61–4)

Simon's current plight (his body dwindled and 'awry') is rendered still more pathetic because of his earlier heyday as

huntsman and athlete, when he 'all the country could outrun'.
But Wordsworth is aware – as he was not in 'The Complaint of
the Forsaken Indian Woman' – of the dangers of piling on the
pathos too soon. We are some way into the poem before the
intimate revelations of 'ancles swoln and thick' begin to invest
the account with the seriousness that Wordsworth intends to be
its abiding impression. Initially the jaunty rhythms of the
opening section had seemed to subvert the prospect of any
problems linked to Simon's advancing years:

> Of years he has upon his back
> No doubt a burden weighty;
> He says he is three score and ten,
> But others say he's eighty.
>
> (ll. 5–8)

But the growing catalogue of misfortunes steadily challenges our
complacency and enlists our sympathy despite – or perhaps
because of – the matter-of-fact way in which they are recounted.
Finally confronted, like Simon, with the stump of rotten wood,
we are profoundly relieved when the speaker comes to his rescue.
We share the same sense of desperation as the old man. It is in
all of us to want to help.

What makes the incident even more affecting are *symbolic*
resonances rare in these ballads. Simon is himself a venerable
object, like the root now physically decayed to the core. So total
is his disintegration that even a mere unfeeling stump defeats his
efforts. Like that of the once proud tree, his decline has been
similarly unheralded; unlike the stump he must now live constantly with the painful awareness of his inexorable decay. There
is no quick release, no instant severance from *his* condition.
None the less his gratitude is palpable:

> The tears into his eyes were brought,
> And thanks and praises seemed to run
> So fast out of his heart, I thought
> They never would have done.
> – I've heard of hearts unkind, kind deeds
> With coldness still returning.
> Alas! the gratitude of men
> Has oftner left me mourning.
>
> (ll. 97–104)

But the concluding homily is less straightforward than it seems, a fact evidenced by diverse critical reactions to its meaning. Legouis, for example, offers the opinion that it is a riposte to Godwin's view, expressed both in *Caleb Williams* and *Political Justice*, that 'if by gratitude we understand a sentiment of preference which I entertain towards another, upon the ground of my having been subject of his benefits, it is no part of justice or virtue' (Legouis, 1896, pp. 309–15; quoted in B&J, p. 284). Certainly Wordsworth, unlike Godwin, is prepared to concede the virtue of a gratitude based on favours. It is surely better than repaying 'kind deeds' with 'coldness'. And in one sense Simon's effusive thanks make the speaker all too aware how desperate is a plight that involves a Herculean effort of body and will to attempt even the most mundane chore. *That* is cause for 'mourning'. But paradoxically this fulsome response widens the gulf that already exists between them, a gulf which the poet has attempted to bridge by his act. Simon's gratitude is profoundly felt – he has benefited hugely – but his sincerity is manifestly over the top, since all it has taken is a single blow on the part of the poet. Wordsworth is forced to the conclusion that he cannot fully empathise with Simon's predicament: they inhabit different worlds with different values. That too is a cause for 'mourning'.

Alas, so too is the insensitivity of his own response. Finally it hints at condescension and impatience – provoked it seems by the unending stream of 'praises' that 'never would have done'. Such feelings are quite unworthy of that initial sense of profound pity that precipitated his act of kindness. He would have had more excuse for irritation if he *had* encountered the 'coldness of ingratitude'.

The poem is a minor *tour de force*. It is as though Wordsworth had challenged himself to make poetic capital out of the most trivial of incidents (by comparison 'The Complaint of the Forsaken Indian Woman' appears positively suspenseful and melodramatic). True, it constantly runs the risk of teetering over into pathos, especially in such lines as 'For still, the more he works, the more / His poor old ancles swell' – ll. 67–8). Indeed we are tempted, like some of those first reviewers, to regard it as altogether too ludicrous a proposition for high art. However, as Danby has observed, the poem 'plays with ambiguities of tone' (1960, p. 39). 'It is as though the reader were being challenged to recognise his first impulse to laugh, get it over at the outset, and dismiss it for the rest of the poem' (p. 40). Once we encounter the abrupt mid-verse shift of tone in the third stanza ('Men, dogs and horses, all are dead'), we are suddenly in no doubt that we are about to become embroiled in a private tragedy framed 'in the larger social tragedy of the decaying countryside' (p. 43).

But it is the subversions of the conclusion which produce the most disarming 'ambiguities of tone'. Here it is not the 'gentle reader' but, ironically, the poet/speaker who has lectured us on our responses who now needs to reappraise his reactions. He is in danger of making those very mistakes that he has counselled his readers not to make. 'Mourning' becomes a richly connotative termination. He mourns not only for the unfortunates of this world but also for the ingrates. His own immunity is not guaranteed.

Two Expostulatory Pieces

'Expostulation and Reply'

No serious attempt to interpret *Lyrical Ballads* can marginalise the so-called 'expostulatory' poems. Such a title is a comment on their formulaic nature: they are dialogues – literally an expostulation ('remonstration or protest') and a reply. But they could just as easily be categorised as expository poems – key statements of 1798 Wordsworthian doctrine. Odd then that the poet should, in these of all pieces, opt for that very ballad quatrain he studiously avoids in the obvious 'ballads' of the volume, the more so since the abstract nature of these poems demands a relatively sophisticated vocabulary. One is tempted to conclude that Wordsworth is, once again, unsettling reader expectations about 'genre'.

While Wordsworth's authorial gloss that 'Expostulation and Reply' 'is a favourite among the Quakers' (FN, *PW*, IV, 411) is not particularly illuminating, the Advertisement does offer a useful clue to its provenance (and that of 'The Tables Turned'): the poems, we are told, 'arose out of conversation with a friend who was somewhat unreasonably attached to modern books of moral philosophy'. The 'friend' – Matthew of the poem – was Hazlitt, who visited Wordsworth at Alfoxden in May–June 1798; in his essay 'On My First Acquaintance with Poets'

(1823), he recalls how he 'got into a metaphysical argument with W., while Coleridge' – it is tempting to think that he was preoccupied with 'The Nightingale' – 'was explaining the different notes of the nightingale to his sister, in which we neither of us succeeded in making ourselves perfectly clear and intelligible' (quoted in *PW*, IV, 411).

If Wordsworth intended his poem to impose order on these conversational confusions, he only partially succeeds. True, the inquisitor's argument is familiar enough. Why 'dream your time away' (l. 4) – the poet's lapses into reverie were well known to friends and villagers – when you can be imbibing 'the spirit breath'd / From dead men to their kind' (ll. 7–8) through reading books? In replying – and here there can be no presumption of a wide gap between poet and persona, since they have the same name – William apparently declares himself an enemy to the rational processes that one brings to the study of literature.

Yet such an interpretation is to misread the emphasis of the poem. What Wordsworth is doing is to argue that the conscious search for knowledge is not the only way to the palace of wisdom and that a real and inclusive insight gained through experience of life is more profound than encapsulated, ready-made knowledge acquired from books. The ironic potentialities of Matthew's original reference to the words of 'dead men', quite unintended by that speaker, become increasingly apparent. A sincere and open receptivity to *life's* processes is what is required; in that frame of mind, the powers that nature has at her disposal will operate, willy-nilly, upon all the human senses:

> The eye it cannot chuse but see,
> We cannot bid the ear be still;
> Our bodies feel, wher'er they be,
> Against, or with our will.
> (ll. 17–20)

The calculated oxymoron of 'a wise passiveness' indicates the continuing influence of Hartley (and perhaps Locke): it pays lip service to his idea that simple 'sensations', gleaned from our contemplation of a natural world that, like the human brain, is, despite its calm appearances, in a constant state of animation, do eventually give rise to complex ideas. Put in more modern parlance, if we tune in to the good vibrations of nature, we will hear its deeper harmonies ('this mighty sum / Of things for ever speaking' – ll. 25–6)). What the poet *is* objecting to is a 'barren and divisive rationalism' (Jacobus, 1976, p. 98), a philosophy that, in the hands of such thinkers as Godwin, has devalued the primal sympathies of love, gratitude and pity. Wordsworth has now reached a state of uneasy calm ('a wise passiveness') after the anguish of the French Revolution and the intellectual rigours of necessarianism. In that progress towards serenity, nature has had a central role to play. That poetic licence should paradoxically permit the transference of the setting from Alfoxden to his beloved lake of Esthwaite only reinforces Wordsworth's claim. Tangible presence *or* tranquil recollection (like Yeats's Lake Isle of Innisfree), nature's favourite places never fail to do their stuff – they 'feed' and 'impress . . . this mind of ours / In a wise passiveness' (ll. 23–4).

'The Tables Turned'

The sub-title 'An Evening Scene, on the Same Subject', indicates the kinship between this poem and 'Expostulation and Reply'. Here the speaker denies the same acquaintance the right to reply: warming to his 'green' theme, he exhorts his friend (Hazlitt) to 'quit your books / Or surely you'll grow double' (ll. 3–4), to come into the open air – whether Cumberland or Somerset makes no essential difference – where the emanations from the vibrant world of nature will calm and restore.

Once again the reader should not take the poet too literally: the poem's brief compass allows little scope for qualification. Hazlitt was writing an 'Essay on the Principles of Human Action', so it is reasonable to assume that Wordsworth's strictures were directed against analytical works in general in which the 'meddling intellect' proves a murderer by dissection, and not against works which make demands on the imagination. Moreover, the much-quoted 'impulse from a vernal wood' stanza requires us to interpret its sentiments in the liberal spirit intended by the poet. The song of a thrush is uplifting to the human ear, but the bird doesn't literally 'preach' any more than spring woods counsel 'Of moral evil and of good'; indeed our post-(Charles) Darwinian consciousness sees nature as at best morally neutral, at worst – as Tennyson declares in *Maud* – 'one with rapine'. (Aldous Huxley found Wordsworth's vision of a temperate nature conveniently narrow, a parochial view totally at odds with her rioting tropical manifestations.) But Wordsworth is using rhetoric and hyperbole to make his point: the imperative of a total commitment by man to the non-human world around him. Reading books on ethics probably won't make you a better person; a walk in the country will always prove beneficial.

Where 'The Tables Turned' improves on its companion piece is in the quality of its language. 'Expostulation and Reply' employs a vocabulary that, because abstract and finally vague, jars on the professed sentiments of the poem. However, 'The Tables Turned' is direct and straightforward, drawing on a sunshine world of throstles and linnets (songsters both) to evoke a colourful and harmonious natural cosmos that contrasts with the grey and potentially misshapen world of the intellect. That linnets are not woodland birds seems beside the point. The abiding instinct of Mother Nature is for harmony and reciprocity, a reciprocity which permits man – in the right frame of mind – to join in the celebration of universal concord.

But more is demanded of man than 'Expostulation and Reply' has required. Reanimated by his theme, the poet decrees that, to receive, man must unstintingly reveal those personal qualities that nature's own 'lore' so cherishes – 'chearfulness', spontaneity, a sane and heartfelt attitude to the green world. Approached in this positive way, nature will repay abundantly from her ever-replenished store of 'ready wealth':

> She has a world of ready wealth
> Our minds and hearts to bless
> Spontaneous wisdom breathed by health,
> Truth breathed by chearfulness.
> (ll. 17–20)

The simple equivoques of the conclusion (leaves = book leaves/ tree leaves; love = human erudition/nature's intuitive lessons) ironically *do* reveal the workings of a rational mind that still perceives difference. But, in privileging the natural associations, these puns reinforce the richly orchestrated theme: openness not closure, fertility not barrenness, spontaneity not pedantry. This theme, restated in the music of the credal lyrics, will find its most amplified expression in the antiphonal effects of 'Tintern Abbey'.

Two Credal Lyrics

'It is the First Mild Day of March'

Since Wordsworth subsequently grouped this lyric in 'Poems of Sentiment and Reflection' along with 'Expostulation and Reply' and 'The Tables Turned', we can assume that he wished to foreground its kinship with that pair of poems. It was almost certainly composed during the same burst of creative activity – towards the end of May 1798. But here there is no dissenting voice to take issue with the speaker's joyous pantheism: in telling his sister Dorothy to 'put on with speed your woodland dress', he is preaching to the converted. To use the formula of expostulation ('to reason earnestly . . . in order to dissuade or remonstrate' – Longman *Dictionary of the English Language*) would here be an irrelevance.

The lyric – the expression of a now-familiar creed – encapsulates positive values. It is a seasonal offering that signals an end to winter's barrenness and welcomes the first signs of a burgeoning springtime that revives and inspires both human and non-human nature. This celebratory tone, coupled with the erasure of discordant opinions and a language reminiscent of eighteenth-century hymns, gives the poem a more vibrant rhythmical impulsion than any other lyrical ballad (in 'Lines Written in Early Spring' the regretful note of the conclusion tempers the 'songs of spring').

The opening stanza initially provides some unexpected resonances. The dating is significant. It is, after all, only 'the first mild day of March' – not fully fledged springtime. The robin revives memories of winter snow; both trees and mountains are still 'bare'. But the occasion is memorable for it carries with it the first intimations of seasonal renewal ('There is a blessing in the air / Which seems a sense of joy to yield' – ll. 5–6). Indeed the moment is so charged with significance that the emotion generated by the day and 'recollected in tranquillity' some two months on becomes a paean of praise to the opening of the year. As Hartman reminds us, this poem, like the other credal lyric, is one of 'thanksgiving, marking or creating a *date*, excerpting from the flow of time a particular moment . . . part of the "living calendar" kept by Wordsworth and his sister from the time of Alfoxden when the poet's A. D. truly began' (1964, pp. 151–2).

Striking the same anti-rationalist note as 'The Tables Turned' with its closing-up of 'barren leaves', the speaker/poet declares redundant the mechanical figures of an officia! record: 'No joyless forms shall regulate / Our living Calendar' (ll. 17–18). Moreover, this is no mere Christian almanac. The apprehension of nature's 'universal birth', the moment when 'love' – initially manifested in the territorial mating-song of the redbreast – steals 'From heart to heart', constitutes an event in which all nature worshippers must share. Coleridge espouses similar views in 'The Nightingale' when hearing the 'love-chant' of the bird and seeing the 'love-torch' of the glow-worm. Hence it is important that mutual bonds should be forged and strengthened. Dorothy, Edward and William will venture forth together to 'feel the sun' – primal source of all life – and Dorothy, as a gesture of solidarity with the green world, will put on her 'woodland dress'. Just as love visited the Mariner when he blessed the water-snakes 'unaware', so now love is 'stealing' – the verb is important – 'From earth to man from man to earth' (l. 23).

The lesson, as in 'Lines Written in Early Spring', is clear. If man opens his heart to Mother Nature, she will open hers in return, particularly at such epiphanic moments as this – the '*hour* of feeling' (emphasis added) when 'one moment now may give us more / Than fifty years of reason' (ll. 25–6). What makes the moment so important is that both human nature (man, woman and child – the same range of human experience is invoked in 'The Nightingale') and non-human nature recognise its consequence. In a deliberately mixed metaphor, Wordsworth valorises sensual apprehension over cerebration: 'Our minds shall *drink* at every pore / The spirit of the season' (ll. 27–8; emphasis added).

The poem rises to a crescendo of praise in the penultimate stanza, employing language that could come straight from a hymn by Isaac Watts.

> And from the blessed power that rolls
> About, below, above,
> We'll frame the measure of our souls:
> They shall be tuned to love.
>
> (ll. 33–6)

But it is worth reminding ourselves that Wordsworth's calendar is a natural and not a Christian one. Though any specifically sexual elements are displaced from the poem, the resurrection is both in body and in soul; it involves the total being ('every pore') as well as all aspects of the cosmos ('an universal birth'). The joy is the joy of a faith reaffirmed, but it is a faith that contains none of the self-abnegation or exact chronology of a precise religious creed.

'Lines Written in Early Spring'

Another 'credal lyric' – the term derives from the poem's conclusive allusion to the speaker's 'creed' – 'Lines Written in Early Spring' is the shortest of these expository poems. Like 'It is the First Mild Day of March', it employs a near-balladic stanza that Wordsworth obviously found congenial: the only thing that differentiates it from the common measure of the ballad quatrain is the injection of a tetrameter in the second line. But its perspective, once again subjective if not wholly solipsistic, is as far removed from the impersonality of the best ballads in Percy's *Reliques* as are its hymn-like passages. This feature is not lost on Hartman, who observes that the lines 'sustain until the last stanza an antiphonal structure as if they were a hymn or catechism' (1964, p. 152).

Alone among this group, the poem owes its inspiration to a moment of solitary contemplation: not 'recollected' later, it was composed while the poet (as he remembered in 1843)

> was sitting by the side of the brook . . . a chosen resort of mine. The brook fell down a sloping rock so as to make a waterfall . . . and across the pool below had fallen a tree, an ash, if I rightly remember, from which rose perpendicularly boughs in search of the light intercepted by the deep shade above. The boughs bore leaves of green that for want of sunshine had faded into almost lily-white; and from the underside of this natural sylvan bridge depended long and beautiful tresses of ivy which waved gently in the breeze that might poetically speaking be called the breath of the waterfall. The motion varied of course in proportion to the power of water in the brook. (FN, *PW*, IV, 411)

If nothing else, the description shows the poet as a close *observer* of nature, something he is not always credited with being. Moreover the scene, with its own intimations of sadness – the stricken ash-tree, its leaves 'faded into almost lily-white', and the cascading ivy perhaps helped to induce a sombre mood in the poet. But, in the poem itself, nature is an avian choir singing in joyful unison – the voices 'blended' (a word much used in hymns) harmoniously for the benefit of the solitary member of the congregation. It is a song of praise that touches the heart strings of the hermitic poet.

The time of year is late March or April, and the harmony of nature is evidenced not only by the birdsong (compare Coleridge's nightingale or the redbreast of the companion piece) but by the active and collaborative *dance* of fauna and flora – birds that 'hopp'd and play'd', periwinkles that grew in company with primroses, 'budding twigs' that 'spread out their fan' to caress the breeze. While the natural world is not unaware of its own mortality – the periwinkle that 'trail'd its wreathes' echoes the 'dependent' ivy tresses of the prose description – its sounds are predominantly melodic, not dissonant, its mood active not passive. In one of a number of observations that flirts with the pathetic fallacy, the speaker asserts 'that every flower / Enjoys the air it breathes'.

All these manifestations of a joyous natural world responding to the promptings of another spring provoke in the reclusive poet – like the Yeats of 'Sailing to Byzantium' unable to join this 'sensual music' – sad thoughts of a human world which should be happy but which is, alas, torn by strife. Nature's harmony makes the contrast all the more poignant:

> To her fair works did nature link
> The human soul that through me ran;
> And much it griev'd my heart to think
> What man has made of man.
>
> (ll. 5–8)

The speaker – whose positive 'creed' is firmly based on the intuitive lessons provided by a green world – 'grieves' and then 'laments' at 'what man has made of man'. The antiphonal note is the concluding and conclusive one. It is tempting to read the poet's innermost thoughts. There had been events in France murderous enough to daunt the most libertarian spirit. And the victims of war, human folly and injustice, the jilted women and indigent men that people *Lyrical Ballads* are hardly a positive advertisement for the state of the English nation in 1798. Nature is always adept at erasing its bleak moments and coming up smiling. Would that man could follow suit. The best he can do is to contemplate, sadly and passively, what might have been.

Two Anecdotes

'We Are Seven'

According to the poet, 'We Are Seven' was written during the 'spring of 1798, under circumstances somewhat remarkable'. Inspired by a 'little girl' he had 'met within the area of Goodrich Castle' in the year 1793, he 'composed it while walking in the grove at Alfoxden . . . last stanza first, having begun with the last line'. Short of a 'prefatory stanza', Wordsworth sought Coleridge's help,

> mentioned in substance what I wished to be expressed, and Coleridge immediately threw off the stanza thus:
>
> A little child, dear brother Jem –
>
> I objected to the rhyme, 'dear brother Jem', as being ludicrous but we all enjoyed the joke of hitching-in our friend, James Tobin's name, who was familiarly called Jem.
>
> (FN, *PW*, i, 362)

To what extent Wordsworth embroidered the facts of his chance meeting with the Goodrich 'heroine' we have no way of telling. But the stated circumstances of composition are revealing: while there was genuine collaboration here between the friends, the fact that Wordsworth so magisterially applied the word 'ludicrous' to part of Coleridge's quick-witted response shows that he was very much the boss. A second creative stimulus for the piece was the poet's own remembered fixation about death when a child:

> Nothing was more difficult for me in childhood than to admit the notion of death as a state applicable to my own being . . . I

was often unable to think of external things as having external existence, and I communed with all that I saw as something not apart from, but inherent in, my own immaterial nature. Many times while going to school have I grasped at a wall or tree to recall myself from this abyss of idealism to the reality.   (FN, *PW*, IV, 463)

Two different kinds of experience, one a conversation, the other a pervasive memory from childhood, thus created the germ of the poem. But, while the first supplied a narrative framework, the second provided the deeper resonances. It may, indeed, be indicative of Wordsworth's closeness to the material that he felt quite unable to frame the stark question which sets the tale in motion. After all, the reason why the conversation with the 'little girl' registered so indelibly on his consciousness was that her views revived those of the child Wordsworth.

The lyric's seventeen stanzas (sixteen employing strict common measure) convey an elusive charm that characteristically flirts with bathos. As Beer reminds us, 'the possible effect of absurdity was in fact pointed out to Wordsworth by Tobin, who ' "earnestly entreated" him to cancel it from *Lyrical Ballads* on the grounds that, if published, it would make him "everlastingly ridiculous" ' (FN, *PW*, I, 362). We should be grateful that, like the child of the ballad, the poet stuck to his guns. In fact the 'simple and unelaborated expressions' are abundantly justified by the poem's context – a conversation between an eight-year-old 'cottage girl' and an adult intent on 'talking down' to her: 'church-yard' and 'porringer', both familiar objects to the child, are the longest words in the ballad. And a ballad the poem undoubtedly is, not just in terms of its employment of refrain and repetition, but on account of its straightforward language and vigorous narrative line.

But, despite the condescension of the well-intentioned adult and the fact that he gives himself the last word, it is a tribute to Wordsworth's irony that the conviction of the 'little maid' wins *us* over. And this victory is achieved notwithstanding that in conventional and literal terms she is guilty of telling a white lie – there *are* no longer seven in her family, only five. 'Brother John' and 'little Jane' lie side-by-side in the local churchyard a mere dozen steps from her front door. But, for her, conventional distinctions of life and death, of actual or imagined presence (after all, she lives apart from her other brothers and sisters), simply do not apply. Later she will presumably come to accept, in adult fashion, the horrid fact of mortality; for the moment, like the young Wordsworth of recent memory, she cannot. Even when visiting the grave-side she resists the evidence of physical extinction: in a moment that echoes such visits in traditional balladry she declares, 'I sit, / And sing a song to them'. For her the worlds of inner and outer reality coalesce.

Herein resides one of the least obtrusive ironies in the poem. It is a common critical assumption that the speaker in all these doctrinal lyrics is Wordsworth, the author speaking *in propria persona*. Such an assumption, always dangerous in view of the poet's ironic strategies, is here positively misleading. It is much safer to assume that Wordsworth's sympathies – like ours – are with a child whose instincts are to 'commune with all'. Gravil's persuasive essay on 'Wordsworth as Ironist' is instructive: 'the speaker is characterised by a blend of pertinacity and obtuseness, qualities which the hasty and unsympathetic reader often projects upon Wordsworth, having been brought up to read him as both didactic and solemn – as, indeed, identical with the figure in Beerbohm's cartoon' (1982, p. 44). That the wisdom of the adult dwindles before the superior wisdom of the child dwelling in his own world of instinct and imagination is clear evidence that Wordsworth aligns himself with his own childhood rather than with a rational maturity.

'Anecdote for Fathers'

The companion piece 'Anecdote for Fathers' uses a formula that is, at least superficially, akin to that of 'We Are Seven'. Both are cautionary tales about encounters with actual children in which the moral is pointed early on, 'What should [a child] know of death?' (l. 4) being here replaced by the subtitle 'how the art of lying may be taught'. In both, a do-gooding, literal-minded adult comes up against the instinctive and elusive consciousness of a child; in both, as Gravil reminds us, 'there is a Blakean tactic of reversing the thrust of the didacticism; it is the presumptuous adult at whom the moral finger is wagged' (1982, p. 45). But Gravil's interpretation of the speaker as 'an ironic portrait of a compound adult persona – compounded of Wordsworth, Watts (the hymn-writer) and the reader' is particularly perceptive. Granted the poet's own recollections of childhood, there seems at best only a parodic smattering of Wordsworthian obtuseness in the literal intransigence displayed by the speaker.

The circumstances of composition again provide a useful entry-point for interpretation. As in 'Lines Written at a Small Distance', the child of the poem is Edward. His father, Basil Montagu, was at Cambridge with Wordsworth; after the death of his wife in childbirth, Edward (or Basil as he was known) went to live with William and Dorothy, becoming 'a continual reminder to the poet of his own childhood'. Wordsworth none the less initially had strong reservations about the boy, who, as he confided in a postscript to Wrangham (7 March 1796), 'Among other things . . . lies like a little devil' (*EL*, p. 168). Two years on, however, the poet had developed, like Dorothy, a deep affection for the boy.

Certainly he intended nothing so damagingly scurrilous in his 1798 'Anecdote': rather he was interested in the much more subtle business of revealing 'the injurious effects of putting inconsiderate questions to Children, and urging them to give answers upon matters either uninteresting to them, or upon which they have no decided opinion' (*LL*, I, 253; quoted in B&J, p. 285).

The subject, then, is again an intuitive child, 'a boy of five years old' known to the poet. A father-figure *in loco parentis*, the speaker can assume – perhaps wrongly, granted the subsequent events of the poem – that 'dearly he loves me'. The vocabulary and modified ballad quatrain again seem appropriate for such an encounter, in which the stubborn rationality of the adult confronts the intuitive nature of the child. But the tone of moral hectoring is here altogether more insistent than in the other cautionary tale. The speaker not only grabs the boy's arm but also repeats his second question no fewer than five times.

'Little Edward' is first asked whether he would rather be 'here at Liswyn Farm' or 'At Kilve's smooth shore, by the green sea'. He offers the instant observation that he prefers Kilve. It seems to have escaped critical notice that this is where the boy begins intuitively (his reply is, according to the poem, in 'careless mood') to outwit his interrogator or, at the very least, to lose patience with these boring adult intrusions into his private world. He really *would* rather be somewhere else! Now badgered insistently to *explain* his preference, the boy seeks inspiration from

his surroundings before he finally 'unlocks' his tongue and offers
a tart reply born of exasperation:

> Then did the boy his tongue unlock,
> And thus to me he made reply;
> 'At Kilve there was no weather-cock,
> And that's the reason why.'
>
> (ll. 53–6)

The final stanza is the narrator's chance to get his own back –
in a moralistic conclusion after the manner of a topical cautionary
tale. However, in a stated ironic reversal that highlights the
speaker's emergent self-awareness, the adult concedes his error.
Before indifferent to his own bullying manner, he suddenly
experiences a revelation – a Joycean epiphany – of his
thick-skinned, inquisitorial posture. Far more significant than
the stated platitude of the poem ('showing how the art of lying
may be taught') is the adult (in *both* senses of the word)
realisation that a child's intuitive wisdom, devoid of what Keats
calls any 'irritable reaching after fact or reason', is vastly more
meaningful than the orthodox knowledge of so-called maturity.

> Oh dearest, dearest boy! my heart
> For better lore would seldom yearn,
> Could I but teach the hundredth part
> Of what from thee I learn.
>
> (ll. 57–60)

Here is a lesson that he must now try to live his life by. The 'lore'
seems of a quite different kind from the woodland lore privileged
in the expostulatory and credal lyrics. But the intuition of the
child and his close kinship with natural forces make him another
exemplar of that 'spontaneous wisdom' which we ignore at our
peril.

'The Nightingale'

In comparison with Coleridge's albatross, his nightingale has
suffered from critical neglect. Indeed, on encountering it in
Lyrical Ballads, one may at first wonder why the poem is there at

all. In fact its inclusion – as a last-minute replacement for the already published 'Lewti' – was primarily a practical gesture designed to protect the volume's anonymity. And, suitable or not, a Coleridge contribution was sorely needed to maintain his slender presence in the volume, at a time (April 1798) when the balance of forces in the relationship was shifting more and more towards Wordsworth.

Nothing indicates that power-shift more clearly than Coleridge's grovelling ditty of explanation that accompanied the poem to Alfoxden – proof, if proof were needed, of his burgeoning deference to the older man. The verse-letter's tone of self-recrimination may also help explain why critics ever since – Brett is a notable exception – have been reluctant to sing the praises of 'The Nightingale':

> In stale blank verse a subject stale
> I send *per post* my *Nightingale*;
> And like an honest bard, dear Wordsworth,
> You'll tell me what you think, my Bird's worth.
> My opinion's briefly this –
> His *bill* he opens not amiss;
> And when he has sung a stave or so,
> His breast, and some small space below,
> So throbs and swells, that you might swear
> No vulgar music's working there.
> So far, so good; but then, 'od rot him!
> There's something falls off at his bottom.
> Yet, sure, no wonder it should breed,
> That my Bird's Tail's a tail indeed
> And makes its own inglorious harmony
> Æolio crepitû, non carmine.
>
>   (*CL*, I, 244)

The term 'conversation poem', unique in *Lyrical Ballads*, is Coleridge's own. Sub-title to the poem, it was quickly fastened onto by the *British Critic* (October 1799), which announced, 'The Poem on the Nightingale is very good, but we do not perceive it to be more conversational than Cowper's Task which is the best poem in that style that our language possesses' (B&J, p. 325). But it was Harper who made the generic title stick by lumping the piece with five other Coleridge poems, a 'genre'

characterised by Gérard as 'personal effusion, a smooth outpouring of sensations, feelings and thoughts, an informal releasing of
the poetic energies in Coleridge's capacious mind and soul'
(Coburn, 1967, p. 78). Technically the poem *is* a conversation in
its digressiveness and its sense of audience (William and
Dorothy are tangible presences), but the images well up from an
essentially contemplative state of mind – a poet communing, like
the Wordsworth of 'Lines Written in Early Spring', with himself
and his 'green earth'. As G. G. Watson observes, 'The Nightingale' moves 'between two poles – the particular occasion and the
general reflections to which that occasion gives rise' (1966,
p. 71). Indeed, the parallels with Keats's later ode to the same
bird are strikingly apparent. None the less the speaker manages
to avoid the excesses of solipsism – the mute presence of friends
gives a 'confiding familiar and often colloquial' air to what is, in
essential respects, a 'dramatic monologue' (Hill, 1983, p. 19).

The poem opens with a series of negative impressions –
external images imperfectly descried or remarkable by their
absence, sensations barely experienced. The sky contains 'No
cloud, no relique of the sunken day', 'no obscure trembling
hues'. There is 'no murmuring' from a stream that merely
glimmers in the late dusk, no breath of wind on a 'balmy
night' when the stars are yet 'dim' and 'all is still'. The
assonance and soft vowels of 'murmuring' and 'verdure' reinforce this mood of peace; it is as though nature is making a *tabula
rasa* of the poet's mind and emptying it of all irrelevant
associations.

The absence of distracting influences has a twofold effect. It
nudges the poet back to a contemplation of the simple mysteries
of nature ('the vernal showers / That gladden the green earth' –
ll. 9–10); it also gives the nightingale's refulgent song, when it
suddenly pierces the gloom, an immediacy and potency that
might otherwise be compromised in competition with other
sights and sounds of the night. None the less the poet's first
response reveals just how full of literary resonances his mind still
is as, in the first of a sequence of literary allusions, he apostro-
phises this 'most musical, most melancholy Bird'. Whether or
not we feel that Coleridge's irony here 'slips into a vein of
patronising satire' (Hill, 1983, p. 58), the effects are calculated
ones. 'Melancholy' (the word is used four times in emphatic
succession) is not only the stock-in-trade of derivative emotion

('many a poet echoes the conceit') but a traditional symbol whereby the bird – itself the stuff of romantic cliché – is associated with unrequited love, or a mood of self-pity. Such epithets are transferred. The 'melancholy', after all, is an emotion felt by the listener – 'some night-wandering Man, whose heart was pierc'd / With the remembrance of a grievous wrong' (ll. 16–17). And that is at odds with the perceived reality of a bird that sings to communicate its joyous sense of well-being. It is in fact another example of what Ruskin, later associating its practice with Romantic poetry, would dub the 'pathetic fallacy'.

The poet too is alert to the dangers of stale repetition and derivative emotion – the annexation of tired metaphor to pad out the poem ('building up the rhyme'). There is, he affirms, no substitute for felt experience, for the kind of total immersion in nature that his friend Wordsworth freely advocates elsewhere in the volume, in 'Tintern Abbey' and the credal lyrics, and that Coleridge is partaking of here.

The process is two-way. By surrendering his whole spirit to the influxes of 'shapes and sounds', the poet, now 'forgetful' of fame, will, paradoxically, create a more sincere and profound 'song' that will benefit nature in its turn. This symbiotic process recalls Coleridge's letter to Sotheby of 1802 where he affirms that 'everything has a Life of its own . . . we are all *One Life*. A Poet's *Heart and Intellect* should be *combined, intimately* combined and *unified* with the great appearances in Nature' (*CL*, ii, 459).

But the note of regret, as pervasive in Coleridge as his moonscapes, is not far away. Literally preached to the converted, or the proselytisers ('My Friend and my Friend's Sister! we have learnt / A different lore' – ll. 40–1), the poem insists that dilettantes who frequent 'ballrooms and hot theatres' can be no part of the 'deep'ning twilights of the spring'. They can only modishly 'heave their sighs / O'er Philomela's pity-pleading strains' (ll. 38–9) – in the misguided exercise of the fancy. The use of the literary name for the nightingale is parodic. It bespeaks an 'arty' and second-hand response – as well as a misplaced one – to an outpouring that is essentially joyous: 'a love chant', which 'disburthen(s) his full soul / Of all its music' (ll. 48–9). Perhaps Coleridge himself here sails too close to the reefs of personification – a device Wordsworth abhorred – but there is no denying his attentive ear for a melody that 'crowds

and hurries and precipitates / With fast thick warble' (ll. 44–5).
No one has better captured the nightingale's song in words.

By now the poet's associative processes are in full flow as a
single sequence of notes prompts memories of a chorus of
birdsong pouring from a thicket near an abandoned Gothic pile
(Enmore Castle near Stowey). There a profusion of nightingales
create such harmonious music that the senses are almost
deceived into thinking it day. What proclaims this active,
diurnal principle is their eyes, so 'bright and full' that they rival
the luminosity of the glow-worm's 'love-torch'. No food for
nightingales, insects here coexist with birds in a radiant harmony, as both send forth their messages of joy.

Such sentiments lead naturally to the second section, where 'A
most gentle Maid' (sister probably of Coleridge's friend John
Cruikshank) becomes the human figure in this pullulating
Gothic gloom. So immersed in nature that she bird-like 'glides
thro' the pathways' and knows all their notes, she watches as the
nightingales, in yet another image of unison, 'tune their wanton
song' to the rhythms of the wind-tossed branches. This breeze –
as in 'The Eolian Harp', 'The Ancient Mariner' and Wordsworth's 'The Thorn' – is an animating force, yet another
manifestation of cosmic harmony. So too is the moon. Deprived
of moonlight the birds become silent. 'Emerging', the moon
awakens 'earth and sky with one sensation' so that the nightingales erupt into a sudden 'Gale' (note the metaphor) of 'choral
minstrelsy'.

The final movement – the 'tail' that, according to Coleridge,
generated 'inglorious harmony' and thus compromised that
organic unity that should ideally have been a feature both of the
poem's matter *and* of its manner – bids farewell to friends in an
effusive apostrophe. But thoughts of home recall memories of
another natural being, 'my dear Babe'. Too young to articulate
his feelings, Hartley Coleridge has already revealed an intuitive
kinship with the cosmos that parallels that of his father's friends.
Whether listening to nightingales or watching the evening star,
he is, as 'nature's playmate', partaking of an education in the
senses. And its therapeutic powers (the anecdote recalls Coleridge's own horrendous nightmares) are demonstrated when
father takes son, victim of a bad dream, into the moonlit
orchard. Sobs turn spontaneously to laughter. The message is
clear. Man, woman and child – to all these in turn Nature

dispenses joy, the joy of being part of the 'one life', so long as we attend to her harmonies. The poem, both its external observations and its inner reflections, celebrates a cosmic unity that exists not just between environment and bird but between *natura naturans* and the whole range of responsive humanity.

Yet the poem, true to the spirit of *Lyrical Ballads*, is not without its paradoxes and problems. Less than straightforward, 'The Nightingale' has been generally regarded as more disjointed than its author would have wished. J. S. Hill finds it perplexing; G. G. Watson complains of its 'scattered air as if it had been written with an altogether exceptional indifference to design and scale' (1966, p. 71). Coleridge, as we know, apologised for the 'inglorious harmony' of its 'Tail'. Personally I find it hard to share these critical misgivings about formlessness. Nor do I think that critics have always posed the right questions. Hill, for example, wonders whether the poem's tripartite structure produces 'a unified poetic construction, or a digressive series of heterogeneous incidents and anecdotes'. He concludes, a shade ominously, that 'the answers . . . are by no means easy' (1983, p. 54). One could retort that the poem's logic is an associative one, that, as in Keats' great ode, its very digressions are a manifestation of the creative mind in process.

In any case there *are* formal patterns within the poem. It has a circular structure, for example, whereby the particular occasion becomes a springboard for a reflective reverie only terminated by the poet's awareness of his duty to bid farewell to his friends. Moreover, the poem's positively charged leitmotivs derived from the natural world – moonlight, breeze and above all birdsong – and their interaction both with each other (the bird's song beneath the moon is a 'Gale') and with human consciousness give the poem a structural coherence which reinforces its theme of the 'one life'. And human responsiveness to that 'one life' can exist, as the poem demonstrates, no less in the child than in the adult.

Nor is it difficult to argue the relevance of Coleridge's gesture against modish sentimentalists. In satirising 'Philomela's pity-pleading strains', the poet deliberately devalues experience that is not only artificial (in both senses of the word) but also at odds with 'Nature's joyance'. Coleridge knew only too well – as his verse letter states – just how hackneyed this 'subject stale' was. And, in attributing mournful human feelings to the bird, he is parodying the Gothic and quasi-Miltonic mannerisms of late Augustan melancholic verse. 'The Nightingale' does, however, posit a viable alternative, an alternative grounded in a natural world which must be personally observed and explored if the imaginative response is to be truthful. If you want to write about nightingales, then you must listen to them in *their* habitat – and in the right frame of mind.

What is, however, a cause for worry is the knowledge that Coleridge's inspiration was, despite his conscious endeavours to make it otherwise, generally bookish. Even here, with Wordsworth as companion, he cannot resist the temptation that his fellow poet always found resistible in *Lyrical Ballads*: the lure of literary showmanship. That these allusions and Miltonisms provide an effective antidote to the poem's real message in undeniable. But it is odd that they should proliferate in a piece that exhorts its readers – Wordsworth-style – to leave books and theatres for a 'different lore'. Since 'The Nightingale' pays homage to Wordsworthian values – as indeed it must, in view of his presence both as listener in the poem and collaborator in the enterprise – it also reveals other Coleridgean obsessions. It is a pity that 'some night-wandering Man' should feel the irrepressible need to parade his erudition, and thereby forfeit some of that earthy power that characterises Wordsworth's contribution to *Lyrical Ballads*.

7

From Advertisement to Albatross: Unity or Diversity?

Any attempts to consider matters of contextual coherence – the 'unifying' rationale behind the joint enterprise and the success of *Lyrical Ballads* in demonstrating this authorial 'intention' – are bound to be dogged by difficulties. Indeed, a growing chorus of critics view with suspicion 'traditional Anglo-American practice, where the quest is for the unity of the work, its coherence', and interpret this search as a procedure for 'repairing any deficiencies in consistency by reference to the author's philosophy or the contemporary world picture'. The effect, maintains Catherine Belsey (1980, p. 109), is to 'close the text and make criticism the accomplice of ideology'.

Yet such an approach, suspect though it may be in certain quarters, has its saving graces. After all, *Lyrical Ballads* started life as a collaborative venture with stated aims. It arrived in households complete with its own brief manifesto (the Advertisement) and went on to generate a fuller declaration of intent (the Preface). Precept and practice may sometimes be out of kilter, but the theory is intended to illuminate the poetry. And, though Wordsworth's unease about 'The Ancient Mariner' is well known, it was given pride of place in a deliberately arranged sequence which has the poems which bulk most impressively at the beginning and end of the volume. John Beer in fact goes further in proposing the existence of a sequential pattern in the 1798 volume, first exhibited in 'The Ancient Mariner' and bearing the discernible imprint of Coleridge's mind. Moreover,

there *are* strategies and features common to many of the poems –
for example Wordsworth's conscious attempt in the rustic
ballads to share a redemptive experience with his audience in
what Sheats defines as a mutual 'act of charity': 'If their music
rises towards planes of feeling and thought more appropriate to
the ode, the hymn or the tragedy than the ballad, it nevertheless
remains a music of humanity, which is sung in unison' (1973a; in
Abrams, 1975, p. 147).

One remembers too the thrust of the Advertisement, which
attempts to discredit stock subjects or stilted diction by privileging the '*natural* delineation of human passions, human characters and human incidents' (emphasis added) using 'the language
of conversation in the middle and lower classes'. And in the
Preface emphases on 'rustic life' and 'essential passions' are
allied to an endeavour to capture humanity's behaviour at
moments of intense feeling and to explore 'the manner in which
we associate ideas in a state of excitement' (B&J, p. 245).
Unconvincing as argument and inconsistently maintained in
practice – according to the Coleridge of *Biographia Literaria* –
such pronouncements at least reveal Wordsworth *trying* to
pinpoint unifying principles in *Lyrical Ballads*.

Personal and public circumstances add fuel to the argument
that there are pervasive elements in these poems. Often about
people who are profoundly affected by the situation in which
they are involved but who only intermittently find solace or
deliverance, the poems can be construed as presenting projec-
tions of those crises – with their attendant feelings of strain and
relief – experienced by the poet. Wordsworth was, after all,
newly restored to health after the nervous prostration induced by
his disillusion with the French Revolution and his remorse-laden
rejection of Annette Vallon. Only two years earlier he had found
himself at the age of twenty-eight penniless, a reluctant father
and an object of governmental suspicion. Now, through human
friendship and his contact with the Alfoxden countryside, he had
fought his way through to the peace of mind given palpable
expression in 'Tintern Abbey': 'Nature never did betray / the
heart that loved her' (ll. 123–4). But even here, in the volume's
final and most mystical utterance, Wordsworth's brooding
anguish – successfully erased from most of the poem – surfaces
in his outburst against 'evil tongues', 'rash judgements' and 'the
sneers of selfish men' (ll. 129–30). The memory of events in

France, both personal and political, plus his still-powerful sense of the continuing oppression of the unlettered poor in enclosed and industrial England, provide a continuing stimulus and subject matter for the poetry. Both in terms of what *Lyrical Ballads* actually confronts *and* in terms of its evasions and omissions, those worlds still dominate a consciousness which gives poetic life to 'a mixed rabble of idle apprentices and Botany Bay convicts, female vagrants, gypsies, meek daughters in the family of Christ, of idiot boys and mad mothers, and after them "owls and night-ravens flew" ' (Hazlitt, 1818, 1944 edn, p. 249).

Coleridge also felt the need to emphasise the volume's cohesive virtues. Writing to Cottle in May 1798, he stressed his point with a literary analogy: 'We deem that the volumes offered to you are to a certain degree *one work in kind tho' not in degree*, as an Ode is one work – and that our different poems are as stanzas, good relatively rather than absolutely: – Mark you I say *in kind* tho' not in degree' (*CL*, I, 250). What strikes one about this pronouncement – aside from Coleridge's implied and predictable assumption of the inferiority of his own efforts – is his insistence on *context*: the parts must be judged not in isolation but in relation to each other, as episodes in an on-going poetic narrative. 'Tintern Abbey', an ode whose fluctuations of perspective and mood are fused by the 'esemplastic' power of the imagination, offers in minuscule an approach that characterises the whole enterprise. To elaborate on Coleridge's ode-inspired parallel 'The Ancient Mariner' is the 'strophe' or introductory section, the poems that follow are stanzas ('anti-strophe' and 'epode' in the Pindaric Ode) that stand – however tenuously – in some sort of relation to each other.

In order to ascertain whether this notion of unity in diversity carries much weight, we ought to begin our quest with the Advertisement. It alerts the reader both to specific features of *Lyrical Ballads* and to some general issues raised by the enterprise in ways that the individual poems cannot. In this sense it clearly *is* an authorial attempt to repair any overall 'deficiencies in consistency' and has usually be so regarded by commentators. In compiling evidence to confirm the unity of *Lyrical Ballads* one would expect to start here.

The Advertisement was of course strategically positioned – the first item that readers would encounter on opening the slim volume – and as much intended to encourage them to read on as to disarm potential critics and forestall punitive reviews. Yet in crucial ways the Advertisement fails to deliver. While the notion of a grand design *is* first mooted here, the prose statement, too preoccupied with matters of style, makes an unconvincing case. It is my contention that there is a sense of relationship and unity in *Lyrical Ballads* that stems naturally from the still-shared opinions of the poets in 1798 and that this is frequently reflected in the recurrent themes and motifs of the poems themselves. Perhaps more by accident than design, this consanguinity often appears where least expected – in 'maverick' poems such as 'The Ancient Mariner' or 'The Nightingale'. But the prose Advertisement is disappointing as a rationale.

For a start, its tone is inconsistent. There is, for example, more than a hint of apology in that blanket word 'experiments'; even perhaps a hint of obsequiousness in the Wordsworthian confession that his readers 'will look round for poetry and will be induced to enquire by what species of courtesy these attempts can be permitted to assume that title'. Yet in the same paragraph where readers are invited to take stock of their response to the modish poetry currently flooding the magazines, there is clearly *no* pulling of punches. Our 'advertiser' warns of mindless habituation to 'the gaudiness and inane phraseology of many modern writers'; such a habituation will result in a 'struggle with feelings of strangeness and aukwardness' when they encounter everyday words ('the language of conversation in the middle and lower classes of society') in which some poems are couched.

The Advertisement betrays other than *tonal* inconsistencies. True, such a democratic view of the language available to the poet (Hamilton goes further in suggesting a 'subversive note in the otherwise innocuous introduction of a lower class of diction' – 1986, p. 43) is reinforced by his opening statement about subject matter. We are told that there are no special subjects for poetry any more than there should be a rarefied diction for describing them, for 'its materials are to be found in every subject which can interest the human mind'. An admirable and surprisingly modern sentiment, this determination to wring feeling from the apparent trivial events of ordinary life incurred the predictable displeasure of Jeffrey and Southey. 'Our poet', complained the *New London Review*, 'seems to want nothing but more fortunate topics.'

But even in this endeavour the document is not entirely convincing as an attempt to adumbrate the pervasive features of the collection. Wordsworth's poetic practice is less inclusive and consistent than he would have readers of the Advertisement believe. There are, after all, significant areas of 'common' experience that the poet chooses not to tackle, including the plight of the urban poor – he was to announce in the 1800 Preface that their craving for extraordinary incident' had already rendered them unsuitable material for poetry – and the taboo areas of sex and violence were clearly part of that 'outrageous stimulation' that Wordsworth deplored.

Moreover Wordsworth was representing his *own* views and not those of his collaborator, Coleridge. While there is a passing reference to the 'Ancyent Marinere, professedly written in imitation, of the style as well as the spirit of the elder poets', the gloss privileged Wordsworth's and not his friend's contributions. Indeed, as Griggs has pointed out, it was not until the appearance of the *Biographia Literaria* in 1817 that an adequate explanation of the contrast between the aims of the authors was revealed' (1963, p. 49). Though Coleridge there 'revealed' that his 'endeavours should be directed to persons and characters supernatural, or at least romantic', the Advertisement eschewed any mention of 'supernatural' or 'romantic' subject matter at all. One is tempted to conclude that the omission consciously reflected Wordsworth's already firm conviction – to be recorded later – that 'the imagination . . . may be called forth as imperiously . . . by incidents within the compass of poetic probability, in the humblest departments of daily life' (Dedication to 'Peter Bell' 1798, published 1819, *PW*, ii, 331).

More significant, Wordsworth's language in *Lyrical Ballads*, if never intended to *mirror* the 'language of conversation in the middle and lower classes' – he talks, ambiguously, of 'how far it *is adapted* to the purposes of poetic pleasure' (emphasis added) – does resort to mannered effects in a number of poems and not just in the jejune 'Female Vagrant' or the grandiloquent blank verse of 'Tintern Abbey'. Consider, for example, the arch tone and stilted inversions of 'The Idiot Boy':

> Poor Betty! in this sad distemper,
> The doctor's self would hardly spare,
> Unworthy things she talked and wild,

> Even he, of cattle the most mild,
> The pony had his share.
>
> (ll. 247–51)

Or the artificial attitudinising of

> Poor victim! no idle intruder has stood
> With o'erconcerning complacence our state to compare . . . .
>
> ('The Convict', ll. 45–6)

Such passages lend some substance to Walter Raleigh's assertion that in the 'simpler numbers' Wordsworth

> offends consistently and continually against prose standards of speech. The prose choice of words is, in the main, observed. But the prose order is broken, not for the sake of emphasis or melody, but from the constraint imposed by metre and rhyme. Now, for the presentation of that simplicity and sincerity which he valued so highly, the prose *order* or words is much more important than the prose *choice* of words.   (1939, p. 91)

Raleigh cites an example of 'absurd' dislocation from 'Simon Lee' to prove his point:

> Of years he has upon his back
> No doubt, a burthen weighty.

Since 'weighty' is first 'needed for the rhyme', 'then every word in the sentence must take up a forced artificial posture for the rhythm' (p. 92). Raleigh has a point (one could in fact make a similar case for 'The Idiot Boy' stanza already quoted). But the judgement is a bit harsh. Rhyming poetry will always to some extent involve syntactic rearrangement. And, anyway, Wordsworth's pronouncements about language have vocabulary and diction centrally in view. The strictures about 'inane *phraseology*' in the Advertisement offer clear confirmation of this.

One could also attempt to defend Wordsworth by pointing to the unassertive and mitigatory tone when he talks about language elsewhere in the document. But that, in a sense, compounds the problem. When Wordsworth does own up to experimenting with the 'language of conversation', he so qualifies his remarks – 'it will *perhaps* appear . . . that he has *sometimes* descended too low and that *many* of his expressions are too familiar, and not of sufficient dignity' (emphasis added) – that much of the propagandist and unifying potential of the document evaporates.

It is also worth reminding ourselves that such lenitive statements are intended to excuse the verbal banalities of *Lyrical Ballads* and not the 'lapses' into poetic diction. It is a mystery that Wordsworth of all people should not have aimed for a greater degree of linguistic ordinariness than he in fact achieves. Admittedly he states that only 'the *majority* of the following poems are to be considered as experiments' (emphasis added). But, since he then dismisses 'the gaudiness and inane phraseology of many modern writers', it is surprising that certain poems in *Lyrical Ballads* should seem so impervious to his charge. Why, for example, include 'Lines Written Near Richmond, Upon the Thames, at Evening'? That it is part pastiche and composed with Collins' 1749 'Ode Occasioned by the Death of Mr Thomson' in mind seems scant justification for its jarring presence. Nor is it, as 'The Female Vagrant' is, an obvious relic of an earlier manner. The poem was written in 1798. Yet it achieves precisely that effect which Wordsworth was to accuse Gray of in the Preface, that of widening 'the space of separation betwixt Prose and Metrical Composition (B&J, p. 252). Consider, for example, the extended personification in the opening stanza, where a 'so smiling' river is 'beguiling' the 'loiterer' with 'faithless gleam', the stilted rhetoric of 'How bright, how solemn, how serene!' or the periphrasis of the opening description.

True, the poem does sound a characteristic Wordsworthian chord in linking the natural and human worlds in 'Till all our minds for ever flow, / As thy deep waters now are flowing' (ll. 23–4). But the poetical *manner* is late Augustan, a manner for which Wordsworth, despite his bold 'experiments', still had a sneaking respect – if we are to believe the Advertisement. Indeed, there is a distinctly Augustan feel to its penultimate paragraph: 'An accurate taste in poetry, and in all the other arts, Sir Joshua Reynolds has observed, is an acquired talent, which can only be produced by severe thought, and a long continued intercourse with the best models of composition.'

Taken out of its context, how many of us would recognise in this passage the author of *Lyrical Ballads*? With its citing of the 'authority' of Reynolds, the doyen of neoclassical art critics, and its reverence for the canon, for 'severe' cerebration as an essential concomitant to the development of accurate taste, the statement could pass muster as a piece of Augustan criticism apparently in conflict with the 'levelling' instincts of the rest of the Advertisement – or, indeed, of the rustic ballads themselves.

By no stretch of the imagination was Wordsworth defending the Popes or even the Collinses of this world – consider the chasm, temperamental and artistic, that separated him from them; rather he was inveighing against the current inanities of magazine scribblers or the worst excesses of Bürger or Darwin – or their imitators. As Mayo observes, 'it was a period witnessing widespread dislocations in literary taste' (*WC*, p. 97). But this passage serves to remind us that the Advertisement was hardly all of a piece. Admittedly it fulfilled some useful functions. It warned Wordsworth's public to expect something very different and to guard against the stock response. It anticipated reader resistance to expressions 'too low' and 'too familiar'; it grounded the majority of the poems in 'the language of conversation' and eschewed anything that was not 'a natural delineation of human passions, human characters, and human incidents'. It provided a note of explanation about two poems ('The Thorn' and 'The Ancient Mariner') where Wordsworth – rightly – expected criticism. But it stressed the thematic links in the volume only in the most general terms, and offered a comment on the sources of the poems ('facts' or 'observations' or 'inventions') so wide-ranging as to be quite unhelpful. If the Advertisement were intended to valorise the coherence of *Lyrical Ballads*, it fell short of its objective – in part as a consequence of its own inconsisten-cies and its failure to address the issue of themes, but also because the volume's *stylistic* diversity defeats the most strenuous authorial attempts at unification.

None the less the shortcomings of the Advertisement – probably hastily cobbled together anyway – do not undermine my contention that recurrent elements weave in and out of the fabric of *Lyrical Ballads*. Significantly, it is possible, I believe, to show this process at work even in those poems whose right to a place in the collection has been most open to question. To that end, I intend to consider Coleridge's two main contributions, 'The Ancient Mariner' and 'The Nightingale'. It looks a risky enterprise. Both have been consistently treated in isolation from their 1798 context, and, though Wordsworth's opinion of 'The Nightingale' is not recorded, he was convinced that 'The Rime' was already proving 'an injury to the volume' since 'the old words and the strangeness of it have deterred readers from going on' (letter to Cottle, 24 June 1799, *EL*, p. 226).

On the face of it, the 'maverick' 'Mariner' certainly sticks out like a sore thumb. After all, it was written to a different formula; it was one of only four poems by Coleridge in the volume and sufficiently bizarre to contemporary taste to be rounded on by the magazines. Even today, despite its unassailable place in the canon, it is normally treated as an autonomous text, a unique poem closely conjoined to Coleridge's psyche, experience and reading, but only arbitrarily annexed to the rest of *Lyrical Ballads*. Yet in a number of ways 'The Ancient Mariner' does display a kinship with other ballads in the collection, containing elements which reappear, in various guises, elsewhere in the book. Here, as in so many other ways, readers of *Lyrical Ballads* may find their stock expectations defeated.

This consanguinity is less surprising when we recall that, on a purely collaborative level, Wordsworth supplied the subject and some of the central incidents – the shooting of the albatross, the spectral persecution, and the return of the 'ghastly crew' to work the ropes of the stricken vessel. Even the figure of the Mariner – and sailors put in supporting appearances in 'The Female Vagrant', 'The Thorn' and 'Old Man Travelling' – derives from Wordsworth's old salt in 'Guilt and Sorrow' (1793–4), who, afflicted by remorse, finds no relief in sleep:

> All night from time to time under him shook
> The floor as he lay shuddering on his bed;
> And oft he groaned aloud, 'O God, that I were dead!'
>
> (ll. 637–9)

Moreover, the poem displays a number of features common to other pieces in the collection. Like 'The Thorn' and to a lesser extent 'The Mad Mother' and 'The Female Vagrant', it bears some hallmarks of the dramatic monologue. The gullible speaker, bewildered by events beyond his control, is in the tradition, if not the landscape, of Wordsworth's simple peasants. More sinned against than sinning, he suffers, like the subjects of 'Old Man Travelling' or 'The Complaint of the Forsaken Indian Woman',

even the 'statesman' of 'The Last of the Flock', a punishment
that bears no just relation to personal conduct.

The whole movement of the poem seems to prefigure the
direction of many of the ensuing poems. While the Mariner's
return to a world of everyday appearances hints at Coleridge's
shared sense of relief after the pulsating events of the French
Revolution, it also anticipates the tales of 'common life' illustrat-
ing the 'primary laws of our nature' which are the staple of
Wordsworth's contributions. There the 'excitement' will be
generated not by surreal incident or the imagery of nightmare,
but by crisis situations in which his characters' feelings – and
with them *our* sympathies – are exposed and thrown into relief.
Wordsworth's world *is* the 'firm land' of Coleridge's 'mine own
Countree' rather than the disordered seascape of the mind that
earlier confronts the guilty sailor. That Coleridge longed to
inhabit and draw sustenance from that serene natural world is
clear from 'The Nightingale', his next most significant contribution to the 1798 volume.

None the less the 'crime' and its concomitant curse do crop up
elsewhere in *Lyrical Ballads*. Here the curse of the dead men
('Seven days, seven nights I saw that curse / And yet I could not
die' – ll. 253–4) is the malediction that society imposes on that
individual who creates problems for its members. 'Goody Blake
and Harry Gill' offers a homely variation on Coleridge's Gothic
treatment of the theme. Harry, also seemingly in control of his
destiny, abuses his position by cruelly denying sticks to poor,
shivering Goody Blake. Like the 'criminal' Mariner, he then
becomes the recipient of a curse delivered by his victim. His
punishment is to endure the torment not of thirst, abject terror,
or a 'bloody sun at noon' (l. 108) but of perpetual cold (That,
live as long as live he may / He never will be warm again' –
ll. 119–20).

We know, of course, that the theme of crime, punishment,
remorse and atonement was a current obsession with both
friends. After all, it issued in their simultaneous attempts to give
the fashionable crime motif a genuinely literary expression – in
verse drama. But this joint preoccupation is also manifested
within the pages of *Lyrical Ballads*, in the obvious parallels
between 'The Ancient Mariner' and 'The Thorn'. As we have
already seen, the compulsively garrulous Mariner shows up
again in Wordsworth's ballad as a retired sea captain recounting

a landlocked experience. More voyeur than participant, he is obsessed by a motiveless crime: the hinted-at infanticide for which the 'criminal', Martha Ray, endures a twenty-one-year vigil of remorse. Her feelings drive her, compulsively and recurrently, to a 'dreary mountain top'; the unrelenting elements of 'mist and rain, and storm and rain' (l. 188) recall the sublime backdrop to Coleridge's poem, as well as echoing the internal rhyme, syntax and rhythms of 'In mist or cloud on mast or shroud' (l. 73). Like the Mariner with his inexhaustible and guilt-laden rituals, Martha is one of the obsessional figures of the volume. Even the supernaturalism is there, though it is a magic only believed in by superstitious villagers. For it is their belief that the threat to exhume the infant bones from the 'burial mound' has provoked a miraculous response from Mother Nature:

> And for full fifty yards around,
> The grass it shook upon the ground. . . .
>   (ll. 238–9)

It is tempting to conclude that, like 'Peter Bell', this poem is a demonstration of Wordsworth's conviction that the supernatural can be incorporated into a natural setting. The credulous country-folk, half-believed by the sea-captain narrator, only *imagine* that they are in the presence of the paranormal. Such events have acceptable psychological explanations. In the same way 'Good Blake and Harry Gill' treats of superstition or at least psychosomatic illness masquerading as supernaturalism. Harry's punishment, to suffer as Goody has, from hypothermia, was explained by Wordsworth's contemporary Erasmus Darwin as *mania mutabilis*, in which the patient substitutes 'imaginations for realities'. It is worth mentioning that several modern critics of 'The Ancient Mariner' offer a similarly 'clinical' reading of that poem.

The centrality of the fecundating bond between man and nature, temporarily severed by the Mariner, is a pervasive motif in *Lyrical Ballads*. Though it reaches its most eloquent and transcendental expression in 'Tintern Abbey', where 'these forms of beauty' have induced both 'sensations sweet' and a state of reverie where selfhood is suspended, it is a nexus explored in the credal and expository lyrics (for instance, in 'The Tables

Turned': 'Sweet is the lore which nature brings'; or in 'Lines Written . . . My House': 'There is a blessing in the air'). At the lowest level of human awareness the 'Mad Mother' trusts the benevolent ministrations of nature ('And underneath the spreading tree / We two will live in honesty' – ll. 73–4); and Coleridge's incarcerated criminal's one hope of salvation lies in his exposure to the 'soft influences' of nature's 'general dance and minstrelsy' ('The Dungeon' – ll. 22, 27). Wordsworth's companion piece, 'The Convict', similarly proposes a pastoral solution where the transplanted victim 'might blossom again'. The Mariner's good fortune is to be constantly in contact with nature: though near-fatally impervious to its beneficent ministrations for so long, he can finally arrive at the intuitive conviction that it is fundamental that we both love one another and make every effort to relate to the whole world of living things. Unfortunately those incarcerated in dungeons are denied these opportunities for personal salvation.

But both friends were all too aware that even the natural world could become a prison if man *deliberately* insulated himself from humankind and took refuge in a solitary, self-regarding contemplation of nature. The protagonist of 'Lines Left Upon a Seat in a Yew-tree' is just such a person. A 'man of sensibility', but embittered by worldly experience and defeated by 'neglect', he reacts by retreating to a fastness where the rocks are an objective correlative of his own barren and reclusive existence. This withdrawal provokes a homiletic retort which has overtones of 'The Ancient Mariner' in its insistence that

> he who feels contempt
> For any living thing, hath faculties
> Which he has never used.
>
> (ll. 48–50)

In a conclusion that appears to deliver a personal reminder to the poet – a procedure employed elsewhere in the anecdotal pieces – Wordsworth valorises an 'art for life's sake' philosophy and appeals to readers of his ballads to approach 'knowledge' in the right spirit:

> O, be wiser thou!
> Instructed that true knowledge leads to love,
> True dignity abides with him alone

Who, in the silent hour of inward thought,
Can still suspect, and still revere himself,
In lowliness of heart.

(ll. 55–60)

Coleridge's fragment 'The Foster-Mother's Tale' adopts a similar but less compelling narrative strategy. A 'strange man', like the Mariner, has told a 'perilous tale' which has troubled the minds of the youthful listeners with 'wilder fancies'. This prompts the Foster Mother to unfold her own cautionary tale – a story which has points of contact both with 'Lines Left . . . in a Yew-tree' and with 'The Ancient Mariner'. About 'a pretty boy, but most unteachable', who is fed first on a diet of nature, this orphan of her tale is subsequently taught to read by a friar. But, instructed too late and too narrowly, the youth becomes deranged by an exclusively bookish diet, is seized as a heretic and incarcerated in a 'hole'. However, unlike the victims of 'The Dungeon' and 'The Convict' he contrives to escape and discovers anew his primitive roots in America, where "'tis supposed / He lived and died among the savage men' (ll. 83–4). Like the sardonic protagonist of 'Lines Left . . . in a Yew-tree', he has achieved a sort of Rousseauesque *retour à la Nature*. But, devoid of a sense of balance and a mature feeling for human community, his future is, to say the least, unpromising. He has been deprived, from birth, of that gentle loving care that the Foster Mother has given her Maria and Albert. As listeners, the moral is *not* lost on them.

On this evidence, nature *alone* (or the printed word for that matter) is not sufficient. As the Foster Mother and her orphans already know, as the Mariner discovers and the 'man of sensibility' fails to realise, *human* nature too is an essential ingredient in the equation. It is that humanising contact which the 'poor mad youth' has been denied in his formative years. While the Mariner's sense of empathy with nature is painfully and haltingly acquired, the orphan's is achieved too hectically and soon – and at the expense of a balanced education in the feelings.

The lesson in all three poems is clear: love of nature must coexist with love of man. As the Preface forcefully reminds us, it is a lesson that Wordsworth's figures in a landscape – intuitively in touch both with nature's primal sympathies and with man's better nature – scarcely need to be taught. That the Mariner does need to be is good reason for placing his education at the beginning of the enterprise. And, as with the Wedding Guest, the lesson is transferable. The reader in his turn – like the listener – is divested of spurious feeling, the better to respond honestly to the human dramas about to be enacted in the succeeding poems.

It would be equally easy, granted the circumstances of composition and the poem's literary ancestry in Cowper and Milton, to forget that Coleridge's nightingale is just as much a part of the fauna of *Lyrical Ballads* as his other bird, the albatross. We recall, for example, that its appearance in the volume at all constituted a last-minute reprieve – as a replacement for the already published 'Lewti'. 'The Nightingale' can thus hardly be regarded as part of a preconceived design. As a consequence, critics have usually considered it – like 'The Ancient Mariner' – in isolation from the main currents of *Lyrical Ballads*, one of five 'conversation pieces' by Coleridge that generate their own independent sense of unity. That 'The Nightingale' has clear affinities with these other 'poems' is undeniable, but it also has an unmistakable right, despite its provenance and formal characteristics, to be a part of *Lyrical Ballads*.

Its filiation with 'Tintern Abbey' for example is obvious enough: both celebrate the spirit of a particular place; both avoid solipsistic excess by assuming the presence of friends; both employ blank-verse sections and a highly wrought language and meditative manner. But it would be a mistake to over-emphasise the connections. 'Tintern Abbey' was itself a late addition and is, in many ways, an atypical contribution to the volume. More important for our present purposes, 'The Nightingale' yields up resonances that link it to *Lyrical Ballads* in more pervasive ways: it shows a poet, after the recent supernaturalism of 'The Ancient Mariner', foregrounding the Wordsworthian values of the familiar and the pastoral – that world of 'man and bird and beast' which the Mariner craves and to which he eventually returns. The poem is about the outgoing and joyous relationship that must needs exist between the world of man and nature, the feeling of unity in 'multeity'. This theme, a feature of 'Frost at Midnight', is also a leitmotiv in Wordsworth's credal lyrics. Indeed, in 'The Nightingale' Coleridge is actually 'conversing' with William and Dorothy – on a mossy bridge as night closes in – and absorbing with his co-celebrants those 'impulse[s] from a vernal wood', here in the music of birdsong, that Wordsworth pays homage to in 'The Tables Turned'. Once again the theme, as in all Wordsworth's expository pieces, is 'Let Nature be your teacher.' The 'lore which Nature brings' is here metamorphosed, as Coleridge addresses his companions, into 'we have learnt a different lore'. As in 'The Tables Turned', natural 'lore' is ironically juxtaposed to the literary lore of books, the experience of urban aesthetes. While Coleridge is often keen to admit a kinship with the literati, here he is anxious to convince his listeners that he is truly a child of nature, a devotee of Wordsworthian values.

The sound of birdsong is a pervasive and positive presence in *Lyrical Ballads*; here it once more uplifts and gladdens. Wordsworth's 'woodland linnet' and 'blithe . . . throstle', daytime denizens of a sun-drenched landscape, become the nightingale of an April scene now lit by moonshine. But for Coleridge the *time* is irrelevant: by sun- or moonlight what counts is the receptive mood of the worshipper. The whole poem, observation and reflection alike, celebrates the 'one life', the potent reciprocity that exists not just between environment and bird but between *natura naturans* and the whole range of humankind — man, woman and child. And the message of *Lyrical Ballads* is that the child is a guiding spirit in this cosmic harmony. Coleridge reinforces this idea when his son 'Suspends his sobs, and laughs most silently' (l. 103) at the sight of the moon. We are reminded of the Idiot Boy's immersion in the joyful sounds of night or the unassailable spirituality of the 'little cottage girl' in 'We Are Seven'. Like Wordsworth, Coleridge believed in the heightened awareness and intention of the child, in the special capacity of youth to respond spontaneously to natural phenomena. 'To that extent the child experiences naturally (like the nightingale) what the adult poet can only experience in a state of heightened awareness' (Brett, 1971, p. 106).

A poem about organic unity, 'The Nightingale' celebrates the harmony of the human and natural worlds. Less explicitly it signalises another: that between the individual poems of *Lyrical Ballads*. When Wordsworth assured us that 'we murder to dissect', he meant dissection in any and every context — be it life or art. For at the heart of 'The Nightingale' — as of 'The Ancient Mariner' — are beliefs that the two friends shared passionately in 1798 and which surface persistently in *Lyrical Ballads*. That they coexist with other, particularly Coleridgean notions is not to devalue these poems' potential for shoring up the volume's sense of thematic unity. It would have been relatively easy to show how the summational statement that is 'Tintern Abbey' contributes massively to this process: other critics have done just that in pointing out how it 'shows us the vision of Nature that lies behind "Expostulation and Reply" ' or offers 'an answer and a reassurance to the metaphysical terror of "The Ancient Mariner" ' (Prickett, 1974, p. 50). But that would be to diminish the sense of paradox and surprise that informs *Lyrical Ballads*, whereby our anticipations need constantly to be revised and modified. *Lyrical Ballads* defies reductionism at each and every turn. Nearly two centuries on, it continues to question 'our own pre-established codes of decision'.

Bibliography

This bibliography lists all the works cited in this book by author or editor and date, but excludes the primary texts and collections of criticism identified by an abbreviation. For these see the List of Abbreviations.

Abercrombie, Lascelles (1952): *The Art of Wordsworth* (London: Oxford University Press).

Abrams, M. H. (ed.) (1972): *Wordsworth*, Twentieth Century Views (Englewood Cliffs, NJ: Prentice-Hall).

—— (ed.) (1975): *English Romantic Poets: Modern Essays in Criticism* (London: Oxford University Press).

—— (1984): *The Correspondent Breeze: Essays on English Romanticism* (New York: Norton).

Aers, D., Cook, J., and Punter, D. (1981): *Romanticism and Ideology* (London: Routledge and Kegan Paul).

Arnold, Matthew (1879): Preface to *The Poems of Wordsworth*, repr. in *Essays in Criticism*, 2nd ser. (London). Extracts repr. in *WC*.

Averill, J. H. (1980): *Wordsworth and the Poetry of Human Suffering* (Ithaca, NY: Cornell University Press).

Babbitt, Irving (1919): *Rousseau and Romanticism* (Boston, Mass.: Houghton Mifflin).

Bald, R. C. (1940): 'Coleridge and *The Ancient Mariner*', in H. Davies, W. Vane and R. Bald (eds), *Nineteenth Century Studies* (Ithaca, NY: Cornell University Press).

Barrell, John (1988): *Poetry, Politics and Language* (Manchester: Manchester University Press).

Bateson, F. W. (1956): *Wordsworth, a Reinterpretation*, rev. edn (London: Longmans, Green). (1st edn 1954.)

Beardsley, M. C. (1958): *Aesthetics* (New York: Harcourt, Brace).

Beardsley, M. C., and Wimsatt, W. K. (1954): *The Verbal Icon* (Lexington, Ky: University of Kentucky Press).

Beatty, Arthur (1927): *William Wordsworth: His Doctrine and Art in their Historical Relations*, 2dn edn (Madison: University of Wisconsin Press). (1st edn 1922.)

Beer, John (1959): *Coleridge the Visionary* (London: Chatto and Windus).

—— (1971): 'Coleridge', in Dyson (1971).

——— (1977): *Coleridge's Poetic Intelligence* (London: Macmillan).

——— (1978): *Wordsworth and the Human Heart* (London: Macmillan).

Belsey, Catherine (1980): *Critical Practice* (London: Methuen).

Benziger, James (1950): ' "Tintern Abbey" Revisited', *PMLA*, LXV. Repr. in *WC*.

Beres, D. (1951): 'A Psychoanalytic Study of the Origins of *The Rime of the Ancient Mariner*', *International Journal of Psycho-Analysis*, XXXII.

Blair, Hugh (1763): *Lectures on Rhetoric and Belles Lettres* (London: Strahan and Cadell).

Bloom, Harold (1962): *The Visionary Company* (London: Faber and Faber).

——— (1976): *Poetry and Repression* (New Haven, Conn.: Yale University Press).

——— (ed.) (1986): *S. T. Coleridge's 'The Rime of the Ancient Mariner'*, Modern Critical Interpretations (New York: Chelsea House).

Bloom, Harold, and Trilling, Lionel (eds) (1973): *Romantic Poetry and Prose* (New York: Oxford University Press).

Bodkin, Maud (1934): *Archetypal Patterns in Poetry: Psychological Studies of Imagination* (London: Oxford University Press).

Bostetter, E. E. (1963): *The Romantic Ventriloquists* (Seattle: University of Washington Press).

Boulger, James (ed.) (1969): *The Rime of the Ancient Mariner*, Twentieth Century Interpretations (Englewood Cliffs, NJ: Prentice-Hall).

Bowra, M. (1950): *The Romantic Imagination* (Cambridge, Mass.: Harvard University Press).

Bradley, A. C. (1965): 'Wordsworth', in *Oxford Lectures on Poetry* (London: Macmillan). (First published 1909.)

Brett, R. L. (ed.) (1971): *S. T. Coleridge*, Writers and their Background (London: Bell).

Brooks, Cleanth (1947): 'Wordsworth and the Paradox of the Imagination', in *The Well-Wrought Urn* (New York: Harcourt Brace).

Buchan, A. M. (1963): 'The Influence of Wordsworth on Coleridge, 1795–1800', *University of Toronto Quarterly*, XXXII. Repr. in *WC*.

Burke, Kenneth (1967): *The Philosophy of Literary Form*, 2nd edn (Baton Rouge: Louisiana State University Press, 1967). (1st edn 1941.)

Bush, D. (1951): 'Wordsworth: A Minority Report', in G. R. Dunklin, (ed.), *Wordsworth: Centenary Studies* (Princeton, NJ: Princeton University Press).

Butler, Marilyn (1981): *Romantics, Rebels and Reactionaries* (Oxford: Oxford University Press).

Campbell, O. J., and Mueschke, P. (1933): 'Wordsworth's Aesthetic Development, 1795–1802', *Essays and Studies* (University of Michigan), X.

Caudwell, Christopher (1937): *Illusion and Reality* (London: Macmillan).

Clarke, Colin (1962): *Romantic Paradox* (London: Routledge and Kegan Paul).

Coburn, Kathleen (ed.) (1967): *Coleridge*, Twentieth Century Views (Englewood Cliffs, NJ: Prentice-Hall).

Coleridge, S. T. (1919 edn): *The Table Talk and Omniana* (Oxford: Clarendon Press).

Cowell, Raymond (ed.) (1973): *Critics on Wordsworth* (London: Allen and Unwin).

Danby, John F. (1960): *The Simple Wordsworth* (London: Routledge and Kegan Paul).

Darbishire, Helen (1950): *The Poet Wordsworth* (Oxford: Clarendon Press).
Darwin, Erasmus (1796): *Zoönomia, or the Laws of Organic Life* (London: J. Johnson).
Davie, Donald (1952): *Purity of Diction in English Verse* (London: Chatto and Windus).
De Man, Paul (1960): 'Intentional Structure of the Romantic Image', rev. and tr. in Harold Bloom (ed.), *Romanticism and Consciousness: Essays in Criticism* (New York: W. W. Norton, 1970) and in Abrams (1972).
Drabble, Margaret, (1966a): *The Garrick Year* (Harmondsworth, Middx.: Penguin).
——— (1966b): *Wordsworth* (London: Evans).
Dyson, A. E. (ed.) (1971): *English Poetry: Select Bibliographical Guides* (London: Oxford University Press).
Eagleton, Terry (1976): *Marxism and Literary Criticism* (London: Methuen).
Easson, Angus (1980): ' "The Idiot Boy": Wordsworth Serves out his Poetic Indentures', *Critical Quarterly*, XXII, no. 3.
Easthope, Anthony (1983): *Poetry as Discourse* (London: Methuen).
——— (1988): *British Post-Structuralism* (London: Routledge and Kegan Paul).
Eaves, M. and Fischer, M. (eds), (1986): *Romanticism and Contemporary Criticism* (Ithaca, NY: Cornell University Press).
Ebbatson, J. R. (1972): 'Coleridge's Mariner and the Rights of Man', *Studies in Romanticism*, II, no. 3.
Empson, William (1964): 'The Ancient Mariner', *Critical Quarterly*, VI, no. 4.
Ferry, David (1959): *The Limits of Mortality* (Middleton, Conn.: Wesleyan University Press).
Fruman, Norman (1972): *Coleridge, the Damaged Archangel* (London: Allen and Unwin).
Frye, Northrop (1957): *The Anatomy of Criticism* (Princeton, NJ: Princeton University Press).
——— (1976): *The Critical Path* (Bloomington: Indiana University Press).
——— (1983): *A Study of English Romanticism* (Brighton: Harvester).
——— (1986): 'The Survival of Eros in Poetry', in Eaves and Fischer (1986).
Gérard, A. (1963): 'Dark Passages: Exploring Tintern Abbey', *Studies in Romanticism*, III. Also in *English Romantic Poetry* (Berkeley, Calif.: University of Californian Press, 1968).
——— (1964): 'Of Trees and Men: The Unity of Wordsworth's "The Thorn" ', *Essays in Criticism*, XIV. Repr. in *WC*.
Gill, Stephen (1989): *William Wordsworth: A Life* (Oxford: Clarendon Press).
Glen, Heather (1983): *Vision and Disenchantment: Blake's Songs and Wordsworth's 'Lyrical Ballads'* (Cambridge: Cambridge University Press).
Godwin, William (1798): *An Enquiry Concerning Political Justice* (Dublin: Luke White).
Gose, Elliott (1960): 'Coleridge and the Luminous Gloom', *PMLA*, LXXV. Repr. in Bloom (1986).
Grant, Allan (1972): *A Preface to Coleridge* (London: Longman).
Gravil, Richard (1982): '*Lyrical Ballads* (1798): Wordsworth as Ironist', *Critical Quarterly*, XXIV, no. 4.
Gravil, R., Newlyn, L., and Roe, N. (eds) (1985): *Coleridge's Imagination* (Cambridge: Cambridge University Press).

Griffin, Andrew (1977): 'Wordsworth and the Problem of Imaginative Story: The Case of "Simon Lee" ', *PMLA*, XCII.

Griggs, E. L. (ed.) (1939): *Wordsworth and Coleridge* (Princeton, NJ: Princeton University Press).

—— (1963): 'Wordsworth through Coleridge's Eyes', in G. T. Dunklin (ed.), *Wordsworth Centenary Studies* (Hamden, Conn.: Archon Books). (First published 1951.)

Grob, Alan (1973): *The Philosophic Mind: A Study of Wordsworth's Poetry and Thought* (Columbus: Ohio State University Press).

Hamilton, Paul (1986): *Wordsworth* (Brighton: Harvester).

Harding, D. W. (1941): 'The Theme of *The Ancient Mariner*', *Scrutiny*, IX. Repr. in Coburn (1967).

—— (1976): *From Blake to Byron*, Part II (Harmondsworth, Middx: Penguin).

Harper, G. M. (1916): *William Wordsworth: His Life, Works and Influence* (London: John Marray).

Hartman, Geoffrey (1954): *The Unmediated Vision* (New Haven, Conn.: Yale University Press).

—— (1964): *Wordsworth's Poetry 1787–1814* (New Haven, Conn.: Yale University Press).

—— (1987): *The Unremarkable Wordsworth* (London: Methuen).

Haven, R. (1972): '*The Ancient Mariner* in the Nineteenth Century', *Studies in Romanticism*, XI.

Hayden, J. L. (1978): *Romantic Bards and British Reviewers* (London: Routledge and Kegan Paul).

Hayter, Alethea (1968): *Opium and the Romantic Imagination* (Berkeley, Calif.: University of California Press).

Hazlitt, William (1944): *Lectures on the English Poets*, World's Classics (London: Oxford University Press). (First published 1818.)

—— (1954): *The Spirit of the Age*, World's Classics (London: Oxford University Press). (First published 1825.)

Hearne, Samuel (1795): *Journey from Hudson's Bay to the Northern Ocean* (London: Strahan and Cadell).

Hill, J. S. (1983): *A Coleridge Companion* (London: Macmillan).

Hilles, F. W. and Bloom, H. (eds) (1965): *From Sensibility to Romanticism* (New York: Oxford University Press).

Hirsch, E. D. (1960): *Wordsworth and Schelling* (New Haven, Conn.: Yale University Press).

Hodgart, M. P., and Redpath, R. T. H. (eds) (1964): *Romantic Perspectives* (London: Harrap).

Holmes, Richard (1989): *Coleridge: Early Visions* (London: Hodder and Stoughton).

Hough, Graham (1953): *The Romantic Poets* (London: Hutchinson).

House, Humphry (1953): *Coleridge* (London: Rupert Hart-Davis).

—— (1955): *All in Due Time* (London: Rupert Hart-Davis).

Jacobus, Mary (1976): *Tradition and Experiment in Wordsworth's 'Lyrical Ballads' (1798)* (London: Oxford University Press).

Jakobson, Roman (1975): *Fundamentals of Language* (The Hague and Paris: Mouton).

Johnson, Samuel (1905): *Lives of the English Poets* (Oxford: Clarendon Press). (First published 1783.)

Jones, Mark, and Kroeber, Karl (eds) (1985): *Wordsworth Scholarship and Criticism, 1973–1984* (New York and London: Garland).

Jordan, John E. (1976): *Why the Lyrical Ballads?* (Berkeley, Calif.: University of California Press).

Keats, John (1960): *Letters*, ed. H. L'Anson Fausset (London: Nelson).

Knight, G. Wilson (1960): *The Starlit Dome* (1941), 2nd edn (London: Methuen).

Kroeber, Karl (1957): '*The Rime of the Ancient Mariner* as Stylised Epic', *Transactions of Wisconsin Academy*, XLVI (1957) 179–87.

Land, Stephen (1973): 'The Silent Poet: An Aspect of Wordsworth's Semantic Theory', *University of Toronto Quarterly*, 52.

Leavis, F. R. (1964): *Revaluation* (Harmondsworth, Middx: Penguin). (First published 1936).

Legouis, E. (1897): *The Early Life of William Wordsworth* (London: J. M. Dent).

—— (1922): *William Wordsworth and Annette Vallon* (London: J. M. Dent).

Levinson, Marjorie (1986): *Wordsworth's Great Period Poems* (Cambridge: Cambridge University Press).

Lodge, David (1986): *Modern Criticism and Theory: A Reader* (London: Longman).

Lowes, J. L. (1927): *The Road to Xanadu* (Boston, Mass.: Houghton Mifflin).

Maclean, Kenneth (1950): *Agrarian Age: A Background for Wordsworth*, Yale Studies in English, vol. 115 (New Haven, Conn.: Yale University Press).

Margoliouth, H. M. (1953): *Wordsworth and Coleridge, 1795–1834* (London: Oxford University Press).

Maxwell, J. C., and Gill, S. C. (1971): 'Wordsworth', in Dyson (1971).

Mayo, Robert (1954): 'The Contemporaneity of the *Lyrical Ballads*', *PMLA*, LXIX. Repr. in *WC*.

McEahern, P. A. (1987): *A Complete Concordance to 'Lyrical Ballads'* (New York: Garland).

McFarland, T. (1972): 'The Symbiosis of Coleridge and Wordsworth', *Studies in Romanticism*, II, no. 4.

—— (1981): *Romanticism and the Forms of Ruin* (Princeton, NJ: Princeton University Press).

McGann, Jerome (1983): *The Romantic Ideology: A Critical Investigation* (Chicago: University of Chicago Press).

McMaster, Graham (ed.) (1972): *William Wordsworth*, Penguin Critical Anthologies (Harmondsworth, Middx: Penguin).

Miller, J. Hillis (1985): *The Linguistic Moment: From Wordsworth to Stevens* (Princeton, NJ: Princeton University Press).

Montefiore, Jan (1987): *Feminism and Poetry* (London: Routledge and Kegan Paul).

Moorman, Mary (1957): *William Wordsworth: A Biography*, I: *The Early Years, 1770–1803* (London: Oxford University Press).

Olson, Elder (1948): 'A Symbolic Reading of "The Ancient Mariner" ', *Modern*

Philology, 45. Repr. in R. S. Crane (ed.), *Critics and Criticism* (Chicago: University of Chicago Press, 1952).

Onorato, Richard (1971): *The Character of the Poet: Wordsworth in 'The Prelude'* (Princeton, NJ: Princeton University Press).

Owen, W. J. B. (1969): *Wordsworth as Critic* (Toronto: University of Toronto Press).

—— (1974): *Wordsworth's Literary Criticism* (London: Routledge and Kegan Paul).

Page, Judith (1983): 'Style and Intention in Wordsworth's *Lyrical Ballads*', *Philological Quarterly*, Summer.

Paglia, Camille (1985): 'Sexual Personae', in Bloom (1986).

Parrish, Stephen M. (1957): ' "The Thorn": Wordsworth's Dramatic Monologue', *Journal of English Literary History*, XXIV.

—— (1958): 'The Wordsworth–Coleridge Controversy', *PMLA*, LXXIII.

—— (1973): *The Art of the 'Lyrical Ballads'* (Cambridge, Mass.: Harvard University Press).

—— (1985): 'Leaping and Lingering: Coleridge's Lyrical Ballads', in Gravil, Newlyn and Roe (1985).

Perkins, David (1959): *The Quest for Permanence* (Cambridge, Mass.: Harvard University Press).

Pinch, Adela (1988): 'Female Chatter: Meter, Masochism and the *Lyrical Ballads*', *Journal of English Literary History*, Winter.

Piper, H. W. (1962): *The Active Universe: Pantheism and the Concept of the Imagination in the English Romantic Poets* (London: Athlone Press).

Pirie, D. B. (1982): *William Wordsworth: The Poetry of Grandeur and of Tenderness* (London: Methuen).

Pottle, F. A. (1960): 'Modern Criticism of "The Ancient Mariner" ', in E. J. Gordon and E. S. Noyes (ed.), *Essays on the Teaching of English* (New York).

Prickett, Stephen (1975): *Wordsworth and Coleridge: The Lyrical Ballads* (London: Edward Arnold).

Purkis, John (1986): *A Preface to Wordsworth* (London: Longman).

Rader, Melvin (1967): *Wordsworth: A Philosophical Approach* (Oxford: Clarendon Press).

Raleigh, Walter (1939): *Wordsworth* (London: Edward Arnold).

Reed, M. L. (1965): 'Wordsworth, Coleridge and the "Plan" of the *Lyrical Ballads*', *University of Toronto Quarterly*, XXXXIV, no. 3. Repr. in *CC*.

—— (1967): *Wordsworth: The Chronology of the Early Years, 1770–1799* (Cambridge, Mass.: Harvard University Press).

Reiman, Donald, (ed.) (1972): *The Romantics Reviewed: Contemporary Reviews of British Romantic Writers*, I–II (New York and London: Garland).

Richards, I. A. (1935): *Coleridge on Imagination* (New York: Harcourt, Brace).

Roe, Nicholas (1988): *Wordsworth and Coleridge: The Radical Years* (Oxford: Clarendon Press).

Ryskamp, C. A. (1965): 'Wordsworth's Lyrical Ballads in their Time', in Hilles and Bloom (1965).

Salusinszky, Imre (ed.) (1987): *Criticism in Society* (London: Methuen).

Schneider, Elizabeth (1953): *Coleridge, Opium and Kubla Khan* (Chicago: University of Chicago Press).

Shapiro, B. A. (1983): *The Romantic Mother* (Baltimore: Johns Hopkins University Press).

Sharrock, Roger (1953): 'Wordsworth's Revolt against Literature', *Essays in Criticism*, III. Repr. in *WC*.

Sheats, Paul D. (1973a): 'The *Lyrical Ballads*', in Sheats (1973b). Repr. in Abrams (1975).

––––– (1973b): *The Making of Wordsworth's Poetry 1789–1798* (Cambridge, Mass.: Harvard University Press).

Simpson, David (1987): *Wordsworth's Historical Imagination: The Poetry of Displacement* (London: Methuen).

Siskin, Clifford (1988): *The Historicity of Romantic Discourse* (Oxford: Oxford University Press).

Smith, E. (1932): *An Estimate of William Wordsworth by his Contemporaries 1793–1822* (Oxford: Basil Blackwell).

Smith, C. J. (1957): 'Wordsworth and Coleridge: The Growth of a Theme', *Studies in Philology*, LIV.

Spencer, J. S. (1983): *A Coleridge Companion* (London: Macmillan).

Stallnecht, N. P. (1958): *Strange Seas of Thought*, 2nd edn (Bloomington: University of Indiana Press).

Stephen, Leslie (1892): *Hours in a Library*, 3rd ser. (London: Smith, Elder).

Stevens, Wallace (1951): 'Two or Three Ideas', *Chap Book*, supplement to the *CEA Critic*, XIII, no. 7.

Stevenson, Lionel (1949): ' "The Ancient Mariner" as a Dramatic Monologue', *The Personalist*, XXX.

Stevenson, Warren (1983): *Nimbus of Glory* (Salzburg: University of Salzburg).

Stoll, E. E. (1948): 'Symbolism in Coleridge', *PMLA*, LXIII.

Storch, R. F. (1971): 'Wordsworth's Experimental Ballads: The Radical Uses of Intelligence and Comedy', *Studies in English Literature* (Rice University), II.

Tate, Allen (1941): *Reason in Madness* (New York: Putnam).

Thompson, E. P. (1969): 'Disenchantment or Default: A Lay Sermon', in C. C. O'Brien and W. D. Vanech (eds), *Power and Consciousness* (London: Athlone Press).

Tillyard, E. M. W. (1948): *Five Poems 1470–1870* (London: Chatto and Windus).

Venis, Linda (1984): 'The Problem of Broadside Balladry's Influence on the *Lyrical Ballads*', *Studies in English Literature 1500–1900*, 24, no. 4.

Ward, J. P. (1984): *Wordsworth's Language of Men* (Brighton: Harvester).

Warren, Robert Penn (1946): 'A Poem of Pure Imagination: An Experiment in Reading', *Kenyon Review*, VIII. Repr. in R. P. Warren, *Selected Essays* (New York: Random House, 1958).

Watson, G. G. (1966): *Coleridge the Poet* (London: Routledge and Kegan Paul).

Watson, J. R. (1982): *Wordsworth's Vital Soul* (London: Macmillan).

Whalley, George, 'The Mariner and the Albatross', *University of Toronto Quarterly*, XVI (1946–7). Repr. in Coburn (1967).

White, R. J. (1938): *The Political Thought of S. T. Coleridge: A Selection* (London: Jonathan Cape).

Williams, Raymond (1987): *Culture and Society* (London: Hogarth Press). (First published 1958.)

Woodring, Carl (1961): *Politics in the Poetry of Coleridge* (Madison: University of Wisconsin Press).

Wordsworth, Jonathan (ed.) (1970): *Bicentenary Wordsworth Studies* (Ithaca, NY: Cornell University Press).

Wright, Elizabeth (1984): *Psycho-Analytic Criticism* (London: Methuen).

Yarlott, G. (1967): *Coleridge and the Abyssinian Maid* (London: Methuen).

Index

174

Index